W9-AAN-576

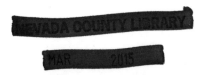

1963
THE YEAR OF THE REVOLUTION

ALSO BY ARIEL LEVE

It Could Be Worse, You Could Be Me

ALSO BY ROBIN MORGAN

All About Bond

The Eltonography

Sinatra: Frank & Friendly

The Book of Movie Biographies

Rainbow Warrior: The French Attempt to Sink Greenpeace

The Falklands War

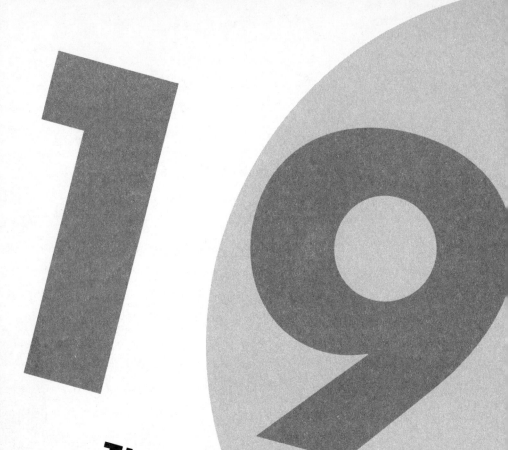

19

THE YEAR OF THE REVOLUTION

HOW YOUTH CHANGED THE WORLD WITH MUSIC, ART, AND FASHION

ROBIN MORGAN AND ARIEL LEVE

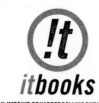

itbooks

AN IMPRINT OF HARPERCOLLINS*PUBLISHERS*

*it*books

HarperCollins books may be purchased for educational, business, or sales promotional use. For information please e-mail the Special Markets Department at SPsales@harpercollins.com.

FIRST EDITION

Designed by Sunil Manchikanti

Library of Congress Cataloging-in-Publication Data is available upon request.

ISBN 978-0-06-212044-1

13 14 15 16 17   OV/RRD   10 9 8 7 6 5 4 3 2 1

CONTENTS

INTRODUCTION

It remains a unique and prophetic coincidence—one that has gone unnoticed for more than fifty years. On January 13, 1963, in Birmingham, England, an attractive young boy band recorded its first appearance on British national television, dazzling viewers with an exuberant tune called "Please Please Me." That same night, viewers found a more cerebral experience on the BBC, then the only other TV channel in Britain, when an unknown, tousle-haired American musician made *his* broadcast debut by intoning a hymn entitled "Blowin' in the Wind."

Neither the Beatles nor Bob Dylan could have known it, but within the year their voices would enthrall millions of ears around the world. The Beatles would become the poster boys for a revolution, and Dylan would become its prophet.

In 1963, the world was undergoing extraordinary social upheaval triggered by postwar prosperity and adolescent defiance; the tectonic plates of class, money, and power were colliding, and socioreligious rules were crumbling.

It was the year that the Cold War protagonists sought a truce, the race into space shifted up a gear, feminists and civil rights activists flexed their political muscles, a bimbo/spy scandal engulfed the British government, and President John F. Kennedy's assassination stunned the world. But as the front pages of history were being printed, there was one scoop slipping by virtually unnoticed: the world was witnessing a youthquake.

In January 1963, teenagers were picking up musical instruments, cameras, paintbrushes, pens, and scissors to challenge conformity. A band calling itself the Rolling Stones auditioned a new bass guitarist and drummer. Eric Clapton, Stevie Nicks, David Bowie, and Elton John were picking at strings and fiddling with keys. On the West Coast, a band aptly named the Beach Boys gained notoriety on Los Angeles radio stations, while in Detroit a girl group changed its name to the Supremes and reached toward the limelight.

In London, an anarchic Irishman pursued a piratical approach to breaking the music industry's middle-of-the-road stranglehold on the airwaves; after buying a fishing trawler, he anchored it in international waters so he could broadcast the kind of music he liked without license or interference. A designer called Mary Quant cut six inches—or more—off a hem, and an ambitious hairdresser named Vidal Sassoon adapted the principles of architecture to a look that complemented her miniskirted models.

In just one year, the landscape of our lives, loves, and looks changed forever. Musicians, fashion designers, writers, journalists, and artists challenged the established order, forcing cultural elders not only to share political and commercial power with a new elite but to seek its endorsement as well. The social, cultural, political, and technological blueprint for a new world was being drawn and updated daily. And for the first time in history, young people were directing the redesign.

It had been half a century in the making. A generation born of one devastating war at the century's outset had handed the world over to a generation shaped by a different war. By halftime in the twentieth century, the world was ready for a game changer. Returning servicemen both traumatized and empowered by war, and women who had gone from doing domestic chores to machining bombs, wanted something better for themselves and for their children. People demanded that their appetites, expectations, and rights receive consideration. Many formerly compliant or corralled individuals once respectful of authority and a regular wage began rejecting rigid cultural, social, and political divides.

The baby boomers were growing up in a time of postwar prosperity: rebuilding the world had fueled economic expansion. Wealth rained down in paychecks that bought automobiles, televisions, frocks, and fridges. And plate-size pieces of vinyl called records could produce music on affordable home-based boxes that soon replaced pianos and radios as the primary source of domestic entertainment.

At the threshold of the sixties, the baby boomers were waiting in the wings of history. Their stage had been built; 1963 was the opening night.

Television broadcast a world in flux to their homes, democratizing knowledge and public opinion; it both chronicled and accelerated the shift. In 1963, the baby boomers witnessed Martin Luther King have a dream and the civil rights movement gather speed at the march on Washington while Mississippi burned. They watched the handsome young president, John F. Kennedy, declare *"Ich bin ein Berliner,"* double NASA's budget to send men to the moon, and bring the world back from the brink of nuclear war—only to die in an open-top car in Dallas.

They watched the birth of nations as the flag of imperialism was lowered and European empires disintegrated. The first TV program was broadcast by satellite, the first polio vaccine was made freely available. Betty Friedan published *The Feminine Mystique*, and something called simply "the pill" was made widely available by prescription to married women. But young single girls needed only to wear a gold ring on their ring finger and lie to a doctor to obtain a packet of contraceptive pills that gave them the power to experiment with their bodies free from the fear of unwanted pregnancy.

And youth had its own history to make. In the fifties, Elvis, Buddy Holly, Little Richard, Howlin' Wolf, Muddy Waters, and Chuck Berry had founded the religion, but it was Dylan and the Beatles who became its messiahs in 1963.

In just one year, the sixties were conceived and carried to term. A sixteen-year-old piano student called Reginald Kenneth Dwight was a pupil at London's esteemed Royal College of Music, practicing Chopin during the day and belting out his own songs in London pubs and clubs at night; he would soon be known as Elton John. And a boy called Eric Clapton got kicked out of art school and joined a band.

Riding their coattails were an American soldier called Jimi Hendrix, who had just been discharged—dishonorably—from the 101st Airborne, and a UCLA film student named Jim Morrison who had begun writing songs. Carly Simon started singing in 1963. Mick Jagger and Keith Richards cut their first record. After his performances in New York clubs received mediocre reviews, Paul Simon traveled to England to rethink his music. Nineteen sixty-three was the university, the apprenticeship, the breakout year of the immortal icons who have occupied the universe of fame ever since.

In 1963, young men and women swelled the ranks of aspiring musicians. A young girl named Barbara Hulanicki couldn't find anything to wear, so she borrowed her sister's nickname to brand a shop called Biba. Women stopped wearing garter belts and stockings because Mary Quant miniskirts were so revealing, thereby creating a market for pantyhose. Young guns like David Hockney, Andy Warhol, Allen Jones, and R. B. Kitaj experimented beyond their art school nature classes.

This amorphous new aristocracy rose mainly from the working- and lower-middle classes to represent the baby boomers' ideals and aspirations—and their heroes were duly anointed. Music, fashion, and the arts challenged, defied and even transcended class, politics, and religion, and in doing so began to redefine humanity.

No longer were family, formal education, an old school tie, or the long climb up a career ladder the only routes to success. Horizons expanded as fast as vinyl could be pressed and airtime filled. Hot on the heels of music and fashion came film, books, and art. Young people shed convention to express themselves in a subversive riot; they stormed the barricades of a bemused, reactionary old order that thought laws, conventions, and cops could be deployed to corral the counterculture.

In that first wave, in 1963, a young Andy Warhol moved into a fire-house on New York's East Eighty-seventh Street to stretch the bound-aries of the art world, and a young David Hockney invented his own palette. Coca-Cola unveiled the first diet drink, Tab, to cash in on the changing shape of women, now more Jackie Kennedy and Jean Shrimpton than Marilyn Monroe. A clothing company called Levi's recognized a trend and launched its preshrunk jeans, Timothy Leary was fired by Harvard and began his Millbrook experiment; the Mon-terey and Newport folk festivals created a new template for the mass celebration of youth.

In film and publishing, the barnacles of suppression were being scraped from the hull of free expression. The Hays Code, which mon-itored the content of movies with buckets of cold water, began to un-ravel under the pressure of filmmakers prepared to fight for their art. Jean-Luc Goddard's *Contempt* and Billy Wilder's *Irma la Douce* ignored the poised red pen of censorship, and the overtly sexual British romp *Tom Jones* won four Oscars. Most important, an actress bared her breasts for the first time in the mainstream cinema and dared the censors to stop her or Sidney Lumet's *The Pawnbroker*. Thus the fate of the prim and proper Hays Code was sealed.

Publishing had recognized the time was ripe to confront authority and assert its own. *Fanny Hill*, the "pornographic" novel written in a debtor's prison when George Washington was still a seventeen-year-old frontier surveyor, was published in the United States and the UK for the first time, breaching obscenity laws and directly challenging lawmakers.

All this happened in 1963, facts in a timeline that this book draws together for an indisputable declaration—this one year changed our world.

Our contributors are the people who lived it. We learned that the Beatles were refused entry to a northern England nightclub in the winter of 1963 because they wore leather jackets. One year later they were headlining for an audience of seventy-three million in America. We discovered that a bunch of kids who'd formed a band called the Dave Clark Five to sing at bar mitzvahs and raise money for a soccer game had begun 1963 belting out songs in a north London dance hall for twenty-five pounds a week. Little more than two years later, they were invited aboard Air Force One to shake hands with President Lyndon B. Johnson: the most powerful man in the world wanted *their* autographs.

We interviewed the remarkable woman, who, in 1963, equipped with little more than looks and a libido, found herself partying with aristocrats and politicians and at the center of a sex scandal—the Profumo Affair—that brought down the British government. She found herself hounded by Scotland Yard and dragged before Britain's High Court. Confronted by the loftiest powers in the realm, this seventeen-year-old arrived at the courthouse decked out in her finest, hair coiffed, and waved to the rubbernecking crowds with chutzpah that only the youth of the day could conjure.

Lord Astor, one of the most senior peers of the realm, denied that he'd slept with her. But when confronted with his denial in court, she slapped down one of the most preeminent trial lawyers of the day with a simple, disdainful response: "Well, he would, wouldn't he?"

The phrase soon passed into popular culture. And hers was just one voice among a multitude that would prompt *Vogue*'s editor in chief, Diana Vreeland, to label 1963 "the year of the youthquake."

Scores of household names who have achieved global recognition gave us their time and support. The inspirational Vidal Sassoon, knowing he had only days left to live, entertained us at lunch in his home high up on Mulholland Drive. Looking out over the citadel of fame that is Hollywood, he shared his own memories of 1963 in what was to be his last interview. Eric Clapton, Keith Richards, Jeff Lynne, and Carly Simon, towering talents who shy from publicity, recognized the need for a book that put their youth into perspective and generously contributed their time to this project.

It's said that if you can remember the sixties, you weren't there. Our contributors' stories expose this received wisdom as no more than a trite reference to the drug culture that emerged as a consequence of 1963 and the youthquake.

This is the oral history of that year, told by the men and women who, with guitars, cameras, pens, brushes, scissors—and even mere notoriety—endowed youth with universal and democratic membership in a new meritocracy. In 1963, youth no longer waited, cap in hand, for an invite to the best tables—they simply built their own banquet hall.

PART ONE

Your sons and your daughters

Are beyond your command

Your old road is

Rapidly agin'

Please get out of the new one

If you can't lend your hand

For the times they are a-changin'.

Bob Dylan

In November 1960, John F. Kennedy, aged forty-three, became the young-est president in American history. The sixties, he announced, were a new frontier. That same month, compulsory conscription for all healthy males between eighteen and twenty-one was abolished in Britain. Earlier that year, Britain's prime minister, Harold Macmillan, had declared that "a wind of change" was ending centuries of empire and thus the need to send young men to fight colonial uprisings in Africa and Asia. Meanwhile, Ser-geant Elvis Presley, benefiting from the rollback of the American draft, cele-brated his demobilization with a string of hits.

In 1960, another civil rights act was inscribed in the U.S. statute books, the Supreme Court ruled Louisiana's segregation laws unconstitutional, and Harper Lee published To Kill a Mockingbird. *Penguin Books was cleared of obscenity charges by UK courts for publishing* Lady Chatterley's Lover. *Cassius Clay won an Olympic gold medal, Chubby Checker sang "The Twist," and Roy Lichtenstein, Robert Rauschenberg, Andy Warhol, and Jasper Johns laid the foundations of pop art.*

But even as television and radio pursued a conservative, apple pie agenda that prolonged the chart-topping success of Elvis and Sinatra—and a crew of fifties crooners, balladeers, songbirds, folksters, and instrumentalists—a new generation of singers was emerging in dive bars, coffeehouses, and smoky cellars from California to Detroit, from East Coast campuses and Greenwich Village basements to the industrial heartland cities of Britain.

A band called the Beatles embarked on a forty-eight-night run in a seedy Hamburg club. Robert Zimmerman prepared to drop out of his freshman year at the University of Minnesota and travel to New York City to play in folk music clubs as Bob Dylan. Two boys called Mick Jagger and Keith Richards met on a railway platform in East London and discussed a shared passion for Chicago R&B epitomized by Chuck Berry and Muddy Waters. And three brothers practiced harmonies that would form the foundation of the Beach Boys. A new frontier beckoned its pioneers.

1

AWAKENINGS

"People were coming back from the U.S. with
78s of Fats Waller and Little Richard and
Chuck Berry. That's when it happened for me.
I was thirteen when I first picked up a guitar."

ERIC CLAPTON

At the end of World War II, Britain recoiled from war—and its war hero prime minister, Winston Churchill. In 1945, the British elected a Labour government on a progressive agenda of radical social reform. By 1960, for teenagers all over Britain, the threat of the draft—and three years in khaki fighting colonial insurgencies or protecting Cold War frontiers—had vanished. They needed new uniforms and the beat of a new drum. Foods such as meat, cheese, and sugar had been rationed during the war and well into the fifties, along with "luxuries" like materials for clothing. Now prosperity, and the free time that came with it, permitted a new generation to explore its own agenda through music, fashion, and art.

Keith Richards [guitarist and founding member, the Rolling Stones]: Growing up in a postwar England era spurred us on. We'd heard enough about the war, which was all grown-ups ever seemed to talk about. We wanted to get out of this war mind-set. We'd all grown up facing the draft. I was thinking, "I just wanna get out the god-damned house. I don't want to go in the army."

It was dopey. But conscription had ended a couple of years before in 1960. We were all facing this new space and suddenly we didn't have to do that. Your whole life you'd heard, "When you're eighteen you'll be in the army and that will sort you out."

Suddenly this miracle happened and we didn't have to do the draft. And you are seventeen or eighteen and you have all that testosterone and this amazing spare free time. Woo-hoo! Just go with what I feel like. They lied to me. I don't have to go into the army. I dread to think how my life would have been if I'd been in the army. We wouldn't be talking right now, I can tell you that. No. Discipline doesn't agree with me.

Eric Clapton [guitarist, Cream; the Yardbirds; Derek & the Dominos]: Postwar England was a very dull place. And that's what the sixties is all about—an explosion, a reaction to rationing, the hardship, and the tremendous suffering that the nation went through with the Second World War.

I was born at the end of it, and actually I probably recall the sound of doodlebugs [*Nazi V-1 "flying bombs"*] going over and stuff like that. But I was very aware of all the constraints that the war had placed on everyone, and how it affected everything.

Vidal Sassoon [pioneering British hairstylist]: We'd lost the Empire. But the socialists [*Labour Party*] were great. The National Health Service, education, the rebuilding that was done. It was extraordinary. We were broke, Britain was broke. But the kids were brought up in that mood of rebuilding. We were given council flats [*government-built housing projects*] and cheap rents. It was the first flat that I ever lived in that had a bathroom. I used to wallow in it.

Georgie Fame [jazz and blues musician, virtuoso keyboard player]: I remember rationing. In the fifties there was no television and no entertainment, and everyone in our street [in Leigh, near Manchester], even in the poorest houses, had a piano. Dad played, everyone played. You heard Rosemary Clooney and Frankie Vaughan on the radio and someone would try and play it.

Our saving grace was if you tuned in to the short wave—everyone had a radio—you could get American Forces Radio, and you'd hear Duke Ellington and all the latest American stuff and it was the only way you'd get it—rock and roll. We didn't realize it was all about sex. We thought it was about dancing. Dancing was what got our mothers interested.

I was playing in pubs in my hometown when I was fifteen. On my own. People were queuing up. I'd play Jerry Lee Lewis and everyone would be singing along and having a great time. I didn't get paid. I didn't get tips. I was given half a pint of mild beer.

Bill Wyman [guitarist and founding member, the Rolling Stones]: When I was seventeen, I went to my grandma's house in South London—I lived there some of the time. She had a six-inch black-and-white TV. I used to watch the sports. And one night watching the *Saturday Night at the London Palladium* variety show I saw someone on the stage, tears running down his face—Johnnie Ray—the most soulful singer before rock and roll. Girls ran to the stage and tore his trousers off him. They mobbed him.

Eric Stewart [guitarist, songwriter, and vocalist, the Mindbenders; 10cc]: I was supposed to go into architecture at Salford Tech. I went there for about four weeks. I was sixteen, a working-class boy living right in the center of Manchester in a two-up-two-down with an outside loo. [*Small, two-bedroom homes with only a living room and a kitchen on the ground floor and a toilet in the backyard were the standard post-Victorian housing built for British blue-collar factory workers.*]

We had a piano—a front-room piano. Most families had one. My father played piano fantastically: classic, blues, jazz—there was always music in the house from him and from the radio, and about that time I was getting into Jerry Lee Lewis. I was buying records, but the main influence was a family across the road called Allen.

One of the three sons was a merchant seaman. He was probably eighteen and he was doing the Atlantic route, and he'd come back to Liverpool and Manchester with these 45s—little discs of American rock and roll from Presley and Buddy Holly—and we used to play them. I had a little record player, a Dancette [*a portable suitcase-size record player*], and I'd play these records that weren't on sale anywhere. Not a lot of this music was being played on TV or radio. It was only available through foreign radio. None was being played on the BBC. You couldn't put a Buddy Holly record on the BBC. You had to be Frank Sinatra, Matt Monro, or Helen Shapiro—someone presentable. "How Much Is That Doggie in the Window" and "I Saw a Mouse." People were buying that stuff.

Justin de Villeneuve [British sixties entrepreneur]: I'd spent the war as an evacuee in J.B. Priestley's house, a grand manor house north of London, but it had full staff, cooks, and nannies in uniforms. [*Children were sent to the country for safety when Hitler's Luftwaffe began blitzing civilian London*]. Priestley [*an author and broadcaster*] wrote Churchill's speeches. I was born Nigel Jonathan Davies. Near Hackney. I am a genuine Cockney [*only those born within hearing of the St. Mary-le-Bow church bells in the old City of London are regarded as "genuine" Cockneys*]. So when I got back to London after the war, in 1945, it was, "Oh my god, little two-up and two-down houses." The lavatory was in the garden. And the houses were gas lit. No electricity and always the smell of leaking gas. That was what hit me when I first went back—after having silver and bone china on the table. I knew things were going to be different. I *wanted* something different. We all did.

Sir Frank Lowe [advertising agency pioneer and owner]: I feel that our parents emerged from the war exhausted. It was impossible for us, the children, to know what it was like—a whole nation at war. My father came back and hardly talked about the war at all. They were totally exhausted. Britain went through a miserable time after the war. I think my whole generation said, "Fuck it! There must be something better."

I was brought up in a pub in Manchester not far from Old Trafford [*Manchester United's soccer stadium*]. I was brought up by my grandmother. My mother had gone off when I was two to be an opera singer at the Sadler's Wells [*a theater in London*] in the chorus and my dad was in the RAF [*Royal Air Force*], so I was left with Granny. I left school at seventeen and I decided I can't live with Granny in Manchester for the rest of my life, so I wrote off for a number of jobs and I was offered two—one was called a "junior reporter" but it was really being the tea boy, and it was up in Scotland, and the other was an errand boy at J. Walter Thompson advertising agency in Berkeley Square in London.

On balance I thought that Berkeley Square was more acceptable than Aberdeen. So in 1958 [or] '9, I took the job as errand boy at four pounds fifteen shillings a week plus luncheon vouchers [*a subsidized meal plan*], which we all got in those days. I delivered the post [*mail*] to everybody, and in those days advertising was a bit like *Mad Men*. The ads weren't any good but the people were having a whale of a time with the models coming in, and the receptionists all had Gucci handbags with scarves tied 'round them. The account executives were all officers out of the army and it seemed like most of them came into the office in the morning in their dinner jackets having just left Annabelle's nightclub [*an elitist private members' club in Berkeley Square*] at five or six a.m. It was a curious world.

Mary Quant [British fashion designer]: I grew up knowing what I wanted to do. I used to wear the clothes handed down to me from my cousin. I was always focused on fashion. I used to go to dancing classes as a little girl. I was in one of those classes and I heard the music next door and there was this girl tap dancing, and she was everything I wanted to be.

This girl was all in black. She wore black opaque tights and ten inches of pleated skirt, with white ankle socks over the black tights and tap dancing shoes with an ankle strap with a buckle on top. I wanted to look like that. She was about two years older than me. I must have been seven. She also had a bucket hair cut—a rudimentary Vidal Sassoon. That was always the image in my head. I used to cut up the bedspread—I used to cut up everything—and so I started to design clothes. I never wanted to do anything else.

Jackie Collins [British author]: I was brought up in a showbiz family. [*Collins was the youngest daughter of Joseph Collins, a theatrical agent whose clients included the Beatles, Shirley Bassey, and Tom Jones*]. My father was a chauvinist and my mother was a stay-at-home mom. I was a school dropout. I was always a rebel, older than my age, and thought I knew a lot more about everything than anyone else.

I had to be independent. My parents didn't wrap me in cotton wool [*weren't overprotective*]—they kind of ignored me. My sister Joan was already in Hollywood, and I was acting and I'd traveled a lot. There were no boundaries, so if I didn't get caught I could do whatever I wanted—I was the original wild child.

Justin de Villeneuve: I left school at fourteen and worked for a wine merchant. Why did I do that?—I was friends with Reggie and Ronnie Kray, the East End villains [*London's most notorious gangsters*]. I spent my youth in Tottenham Royal, a dance hall, and the big influence was clothing. All my friends were gangsters. They were the smart guys. The gangsters would always bring out a big roll of money. They had bespoke suits and handmade shirts and I aspired to that. When I worked at the wine merchant the first thing I did was to knock off [*steal*] a load of wine.

Eric Clapton: One of the things people could do was to join the merchant navy and sail around the world and live like a bum, really, but you got paid and you'd be on the boat. People were coming back from the U.S. with 78s of Fats Waller and Little Richard and Chuck Berry, so that's when it happened for me. I was thirteen when I first picked up a guitar [in 1960].

My father was a Canadian airman. I never met him. My father apparently was a jazz pianist and he played in a band. I may have inherited his gene in that respect. But I imagine he had a musician's philosophy, which is pretty much an existential one—live for the day. Try and live in the moment. And that somehow affected my responses to authority and convention very early on.

I really think my love of music is genetic. It's almost like dyslexia—it's a slant, how you look at things, and it means when you pick up an instrument you play it without knowledge. I can't read music. I learned by ear. I was thrown out of Kingston Art School. At the time I was working on a building site with my grandfather, playing gigs sometimes in the evening and listening to the radio, and I didn't have that many friends—two or three maybe, and they were geeks. They were obsessive about music or about clothes. Conscription had ended. I missed it by a year. Terry O'Neill and Bill Wyman did national service. That was a normal thing then in your late teens. I dreaded it. I already had a hippie mentality. Don't ask me where I got it from but I was like a dropout.

Terry O'Neill [British photographer famous for chronicling the sixties]: I don't remember much other than growing up loving jazz music and wanting to play drums. I was conceived in Ireland, born in the East End and brought up in West London under the flight path of Heathrow Airport. I did my national service in the army and when I got out all I could think of was getting to New York and trying to play in the clubs there. That's where the greats were. I was playing the clubs in London and I wanted to be better and bigger.

I was a working-class lad with no money so I got this idea that if I could get a job as a flight attendant with British Airways—they were called British Overseas Airways then—I could go to New York regularly for free and play drums in the clubs in the Village during the layover. Crews got three or four days rest in those days.

There were no jobs for flight attendants at BA. Instead they offered me a job in the technical department. Basically, they wanted me to photograph people getting off the planes, pictures they could use for publicity, of couples hugging and greeting and stuff. I thought I'd get a shot at being an attendant later and then I could get to New York to play jazz.

They gave me a camera and sent me to art school two nights a week to learn about the darkroom and stuff. I didn't know what the hell I was doing really, but one day I took this photo of an old English gent asleep in the departures lounge in a bowler hat. He was surrounded by all these colorful African chiefs in tribal dress, a delegation or something. It was just an amusing, candid shot, and then this bloke tapped me on the shoulder.

"Do you know who that is?" he asked. Apparently it was Rab Butler, the British home secretary, a really important politician on the world stage in those days. The guy was a newspaper reporter, and he bought my film off me. The picture editor of the newspaper must have liked it because they asked me to do more work at the airport and then they offered me a job.

Justin de Villeneuve: I was totally convinced I could do anything I wanted. I think it was the vibe in the air or something. Teenagers saw how servile our parents were and how they seemed to accept their fate, and we knew we could do more. My big influence was B movies. Black-and-white films. They were always full of rascals, working-class boys who never had the silver spoon and conspired their way to it. You had to have a street-smart attitude.

Mary Quant: I was at art school and I wanted to design clothes, and I made them and sold them to other people—including hats. At art school I met Alexander [Plunkett-Greene], who was to become my husband. We decided we'd like to start a shop in Chelsea. It was the first boutique. [*Before Mary Quant, women purchased their clothes in department stores or from dressmakers working with standard patterns.*]

I designed my first miniskirt at art school, and the first image for the mini came from that ballet class. Other art students liked it and they bought the things I designed and made. I thought, "This is terrific," and people liked it. We started in '56.

Before we opened the shop I was making hats. I was walking down Bond Street looking for things to go on the hats, and suddenly there was a sign, "Vidal Sassoon," and a picture of a haircut that knocked me sideways. I went up in a tiny, rickety lift and at the top was Vidal in one room cutting hair.

I knew I wanted my own hair cut like that. I had a ponytail all tied up. I watched Vidal cutting. I knew I'd have to save money to have a haircut like that. I was one of the first to have it done.

Justin de Villeneuve: When Vidal got married I supplied all the wine. His salon was in Mayfair at the time. In the sixties, [that neighborhood] was the posh one. He was jack the lad [*a carefree, self-assured, brash young man*] and wore beautiful suits. He had lots of villain [*gangster*] friends. He was boy, a Cockney like me. All the wine I had knocked off was garbage, paint stripper, so I had a problem. I had to do a bit of ducking and diving. The night before the wedding I put all the wine in the bath and took off the labels and put on new posh labels.

At the wedding I thought, "Stay near the exit in case you have to do a runner [*leave in a hurry*]." But Vidal knew what I'd done and he must have been impressed because he came over to me and said, "I like the cut of your jib [*style*]. Would you like to be my personal assistant?" I handed hairpins to Vidal Sassoon. I became posher the more I worked with Vidal. He had great style. So we changed my name then to Mr. Christian San Forget—so I wouldn't *forget* my name. One thing I learnt very quickly. You had very posh clients come in—Lord Tittybates's daughter or whatever. They were such mugs. You could tell them anything and they would believe you.

One day Vidal lost his temper with me and threw his scissors in the air; they landed in the ceiling and they stayed there for a month. During my years of skullduggery Vidal sacked me three times.

Vidal Sassoon: Justin spent a lot of time in the elevator making out with some of our lady clients when he should have been working.

Justin de Villeneuve: I would often go back because he had a soft spot for me, and if he wouldn't take me back I'd speak to his wife, Elaine. She'd get me my job back.

By then I was a hairdresser—I'd moved on from handing him pins and rollers and scissors. I was terrible. But Vidal's shop was full of everybody who was anybody. Everyone was talking about him and everyone wanted his look. Not just the aristocrats' wives and posh people but people you just knew were on the way up, like Michael Caine or Mary Quant. They were still unknown then but they were creative and finding their own way of making a name for themselves.

Mary Quant: I used to buy fabric from Harrods. Alexander's mother lived around the corner and she had an account at Harrods, and she said, "You can use my card because Harrods are very amenable and you can run up an account for a year until you have to pay." So that's how we did it.

So I'd go to Harrods and find what I wanted—men's suiting, Prince of Wales check, and City stripe suiting, and I liked to use them with very, very feminine things. Flounces underneath and very short tunic dresses. I liked to exaggerate the femininity with the masculine. They had the best haberdashery. The best buttons and bits. Then I'd walk it back to our bed-sit flat [*a one-room apartment*] where

I worked with two machinists [*seamstresses*]. I would cut it and they'd make it up and then I'd walk it down to the shop.

Grace Coddington [*today the creative director of* Vogue] modeled my dresses when we put on shows in the shop. The models had to have great legs and had to move well. Grace was a fantastic model. She had the same Vidal haircut as me.

Vidal Sassoon: I got more help from Mary Quant than anyone else from the point of view of people in the clothing industry or the craft. She came in once and—I've never done it before or since—I nipped her ear. Blood was flowing. "Do you charge extra for that?" asked her husband, Alexander, who was sitting in the salon waiting for her.

It felt like London—well Chelsea and Mayfair, really—was suddenly the center of the universe. It was a melting pot of creative young people and then suddenly all these working-class boys from the provincial cities were converging on our scene with their own ideas. There was a sudden marriage of their music and our look.

Graham Nash [musician, the Hollies; Crosby, Stills & Nash]: I lived in Salford near Manchester, near where Eric Stewart comes from, too. It was the biggest slum in Britain, but what the fuck, I didn't know that. We had a ball to kick around and we never went hungry.

When I was thirteen or fourteen a friend of mine cycled all the way to Germany to see Elvis. I was so impressed. I wanted a bike, too. This would have been in the fifties. I had a choice, a bicycle or a guitar, but we couldn't afford a bike so I got the guitar. Then when I was sixteen or so I made my own out of plywood, a copy of a Fender. By then I was really into the music.

Allan Clarke [*fellow founding member of the Hollies*] and I had been singing together for years, in school choirs, and we had a music teacher at school and through that I absorbed what music was.

Me and Allan Clarke wrote our first song on a bench outside Regent

Road Public Baths, with our two little cheap guitars. We wrote a song called, "Hey, Just What's Wrong with Me?"

In November 1959, at the Ardwick Hippodrome in Manchester, we entered a talent show—you know, where you get a bunch of local musicians from a local town and put on your show and do your act, then you'd all come on the stage together and whoever got the loudest applause won. On this show was me and Allan with two acoustic guitars, and we won.

There was me and Allan who became the Hollies, there was Freddie Garrity who became Freddie & the Dreamers, Ron Wycherley who became Billy Fury, and Johnny & the Moondogs, who were John Lennon, Paul McCartney, and George Harrison, all on the same fucking show!

Bill Wyman: I had a homemade bass guitar. I made that in 1961. I didn't have money to buy one, so I made it. Then I made an amplifier.

I was working for a diesel engineer in Streatham, London, after doing my national service in the Royal Air Force. I was married with an eight-month-old son and living in a shitty flat costing me three or four pounds a week in Beckenham, in Kent, and playing in a band called the Cliftons. We had to readjust from peeling potatoes, "left-right, left-right, yes sir, no sir," and suddenly that went out the window.

Sir Alan Parker [advertising copywriter; film director, *Bugsy Malone, Fame, Evita, Mississippi Burning*]: National service—the draft—didn't affect me, as it ended in 1960, so we were the first to dodge it by the skin of our teeth. We didn't realize how lucky we were and how close we had been to having years of our lives squandered away.

Allen Jones [internationally exhibited sculptor, pop artist, and Royal Academician who studied with Hockney and Kitaj]: I didn't do national service because I was exempted by full-time study, otherwise I would have been in the Korean War. They abandoned conscription in 1960. I had a letter saying that I could go straight to college. That year out of twenty people in my class half of the guys had been in Korea. They'd been shooting people and surviving trench warfare. They were very obviously men and had a very different attitude to authority. They'd blow their grant straightaway buying Lambrettas and picking up girls. I remember thinking, "Where will they get the money for their supplies?"

I wasn't living in digs like many of the students. My folks lived in West London, so I lived at home when I was an art student and I had money to travel and buy supplies, and in a way I was slightly sheltered from having to make ends meet, so the whole thing for me was very exciting. The campus [of Hornsey College of Art] was very spread out. The fashion school was in one place and the sculpture school was somewhere else. Jazz was very active. And that cross-fertilization was very energizing.

Mary Quant: Up to then there was nothing for young people. Clothes weren't designed for young people. We were the first to do it. Then it spread and affected everyone. People felt happy and emancipated. The war had settled a gloom on everyone. It took ages for the world to realize it was over. I used bright yellow and purple combined with stripe suit stuff. The combination was the point. I think I live through my eyes and I always collect things in my pockets—textures or colors I like, all sorts of things.

People seemed to start to enjoy life because of what they were wearing. They could dance more freely. And the clubs! We'd go to all the jazz places at night. It gave us that feeling of freedom and liberation. We could run our own lives.

Johnny Gold [renowned nightclub owner, Tramp London; Tramp Los Angeles]: I'd come out of the army after three years of national service and I was living in Brighton, and there was a bookmaker who used to go to the dog races in London and he asked me if I'd drive him there and back as a job and carry the money and pay it out. He had a beautiful Jaguar. So we'd come to London, go to the dogs, and go to a club in Berkeley Square called the Nightingale—this is before discotheques. They all had cabaret and hostesses and we'd go and we'd mingle with all sorts, from all walks of life, people like Jack Warner of Warner Bros.

We'd gone through the drab 1950s and suddenly there were people like Vidal and Mary Quant. I used to come up to London just to feel the buzz; it was tangible, a bit like Moscow today. In the clubs you'd bump into all sorts. I remember meeting Lulu, the singer. She was only fifteen then, and Mandy Rice-Davies just sixteen or seventeen, before [Rice-Davies] became notorious as one of the two girls whose partying with aristocrats and government ministers and Russian spies brought down the government. It was called the Profumo Affair after John Profumo, the war minister. He had to resign because one of the girls, Christine Keeler, not Mandy, was also sleeping with a Soviet naval attaché in London. It was a huge scandal, as you can imagine. At the height of the Cold War our minister for war was sharing a girl with a Russian spy. Who knew what pillow talk might have passed between them?

Mandy Rice-Davies [model, actress, and author]: I was Miss Austin Mini at the Earls Court Motor Show in 1960. That's how I went to London. I arrived there on the train from my home in Birmingham— "Cor! This is the place." Then I had to go back home. But I had earned eighty pounds for four days' work, which was a lot of money. I went home and said, "Dad, I really think I can make it in London as a model."

My father said, "No way, not until you are eighteen." He'd been a policeman in London so he knew what London was like for a young girl. But I was determined.

I sold the sewing machine I got for Christmas and packed a suitcase [and] hid it in the hedge, and I slunk out at night and got the train back to London. I was sixteen. My dad knew where I had gone. I got on the train with the logical thought [that] if I don't find a job before the money runs out I'll get the train back. I got a job the same day. I bought the London newspapers, *The Evening Standard* and *The Evening News*; there was thousands of jobs. I saw this ad for Murray's. They was looking for dancers. It was a cabaret club. I got the job that very same day.

Terry O'Neill: The big thing for a lot of young lads was that they could leave school at fifteen with no educational or technical qualifications. They lived from week to week but they never went without. It was the same for girls. There were lots of jobs, and flats were cheap and plentiful.

Cilla Black [singer and television presenter]: I was working in an office in Liverpool, and back then the clubs would have lunchtime dances so on my lunch break I'd work as a hatcheck girl at the Cavern, although nobody wore hats except on a Sunday to go to church. I hung the coats up in my lunch hour and I got to see all the bands as well and sing with a few of them. I was singing from the age of fourteen in and around Liverpool.

A lot of our families in Liverpool would be working on the boats going to New York and bringing us back American records. I always sang to my school friends, and one day we were in a club called the Iron Door. I don't quite know why the Cavern was ever so famous because there was lots of these coffee clubs. The girls always used to ask me to sing, and whatever band was playing they said, "Ooh, give Cilla a go."

There were all-night sessions, too. We'd go to a club, especially the Iron Door, at eight o'clock in the evening and finish at eight o'clock the following morning. Back in those days the dairies used to deliver milk and leave it on your doorstep, and after playing all night in the club we'd pinch a bottle of milk from someone's stoop on the way home.

Peter Brown [music industry entrepreneur]: I was in Liverpool working in a department store. I was twenty-one. And on the management course with me was this guy who was Jewish who I became best friends with. Alistair his name was. He then introduced me to some friends, all Jewish boys, and I sort of became part of the group.

One of this group, who was a law student, was having a twenty-first birthday party and Brian [Epstein, who would become the Beatles' manager] came to it. We became instant friends. I mean, we were really close friends, but we were never boyfriends. We were attracted to each other but we liked different types—he wasn't my type, I wasn't his type. There was an underground group of us in Liverpool, gay men who knew each other, but it wasn't public, you know.

I was very unhappy at the department store so they said to me, "Is there anything you want to do?" I loved music and I said, "Well, you have a record department which is very badly run." So they gave it to me and it was very successful—it wasn't difficult to turn it around.

Brian used to come over to the department store and have coffee with me in the canteen in the mornings. Brian at that time was running his family's record shop across the road, literally across the road.

In the evening the department store closed at five-thirty. Bryan kept his shop open until six so I would often go across to wait for him if we were going out. I would look around at what he was doing, and what happened was, his shop was very successful and the family decided to open another shop, and Bryan asked me if I would come and run the one that he'd been running.

Hilton Valentine [guitarist, the Animals]: My father, after getting out of the army, was a bus conductor, and my mother raised the family. A job in the coal mines was the cream. Terrible jobs, but well paid.

My brother, who was two years older than me, was buying records like the Comets, Gene Vincent, and Chuck Berry, and that was my introduction to rock and roll. I was putting on shows in the backyard.

This was before TV did rock and roll. We didn't have one. I went to watch TV at my friend's house.

We were putting on shows in the backyard and we'd get local lads involved and charge a penny. We didn't make much but we were on our way. The band was originally called the Headers. At first I was playing a friend's guitar. He was the only one who had a guitar—it was a left-handed guitar—but it didn't matter because we didn't play any chords. We didn't even have a pick—we strummed using a penny We had a saxophone with one note working, and a biscuit tin for a drum—a proper skiffle band. I got my first guitar from my mother.

By 1962, I was in the Wildcats; it was a cult band around Newcastle. I was playing guitar and we were earning. One place in Whitley Bay outside Newcastle was called the Hop, and on a Saturday night we got five pounds and on a Tuesday two pounds for gigs. And that was between all of us. What we did was pool the money to buy new equipment on the never-never [*installment plan*]. We bought guitars, and as the leader of the band, once something was paid off I'd get a new guitar, and my guitar would get passed down to the green player. I got a new amp and the old one got passed down.

Even when I was going to school all I could think of was getting back home and standing in front of the mirror with my guitar and practicing. I had a leather jacket, which was actually plastic, and I'd stand in front of the mirror and sing. I was into Chuck Berry, Bo Diddley.

I just wanted to perform and play the guitar and make a living playing music. I went to the City Hall to see the big bands, and I'd see the bus come up and I'd see the band go in the stage door, and I used to dream that the guitarist would be ill and they'd come out and say they needed a guitarist.

Peter Frampton [British musician, songwriter, and singer, the Herd; Humble Pie]: Ours was the first generation that was growing up in peace and had the potential for prosperity. My father was in college and then he volunteered for the war and didn't see my mother for six years. My mother survived the Blitz and my father was in every major battle, and now we were at this point and they were so thrilled to be together and alive. That had a lot to do with their psyche, and they allowed me to do what I wanted to do.

By the time I was eight I had a guitar. It had no name on it. It was probably Japanese. You had to bleed to play a C chord. It wasn't until later you realized that it was so bad. I was mainly self-taught. I became addicted to playing music. I would come straight home from school and [run] up the stairs. My mother would bang on the ceiling with the broom: "Turn it off!"

I turned my acoustic into an electric as soon as possible. My father worked out that we could plug it into the radio in the living room. I was about ten years of age. I was into the Shadows. I saw Eddie Cochrane, Gene Vincent, and Buddy Holly around '58 and '59. I was not really into Elvis.

Jeff Lynne [British musician and producer]: It feels like a lifetime between fifteen and eighteen, not just three years. I was a working-class boy living in a council house in Birmingham, England. It was pretty bleak and a job on the production line of the car factory was looming. I picked up a guitar at fifteen from a friend's closet. It was a tiny plastic guitar with Elvis's face on it and one string. That was it. I got him to lend it to me. It was worthless. I'd learn all the tunes of the day and I'd have to work it out on one string. It gave me a certain unique style for later on. I took it home and learnt everything on it. My sister gave me a set of strings. I was trying to make an electric guitar in the woodwork shop after school. I never did finish the school guitar. I got this set of strings and put the E string on this plastic guitar.

Pattie Boyd [British model and photographer]: I was sharing a flat with five girls in South Kensington, London, not far from the Kings

Road. None of us had much money; we slept on mattresses on the floor. I was seventeen and I hadn't started modeling yet. It was a really crazy flat—there was never any milk for tea in the morning, we never knew what was in the fridge. It just seemed chaotic and everybody borrowed each other's clothes. I mean, it was fun.

There was no sense of ambition; everybody was just having a great time. Money was never an issue. I only needed money to pay my rent and buy shoes and clothes. Those were the things that were important

There was this sense of lots of things going on, and [in] the Kings Road on a Saturday there was nothing better than to just cruise up and down. You would see all sorts of people that you knew and would like to know and there was just a kind of sizzle in the air.

Peter Frampton: It started for me with the Cub Scouts when I was eight. By the time I was nine I got my music proficiency badge by playing two songs in front of the local troop. It would have been Peggy Sue/Buddy Holly numbers. The gang shows [*talent shows*]—we had a local one. They didn't have a piano, and yours truly was asked to be the accompanist to the lost-and-found lady at school. I said yes, yes, yes, but I want my own spot in the show.

It was just one show. St. Mary's Church scouts. I was scheduled for two numbers, and I go out finally and I accompany the lost-and-found lady on "There's a Hole in My Bucket," and I go down really well. I say, "Thank you, and since you like me so much I'd like to do one of my own compositions." The place fell about in hysterics—this precocious nine-year-old is taking over. And the head scout master is telling me to get off [the stage].

Right there and then, when you have the stage, no one can tell you what to do once you are out there and communicating with the audience. You've got the stage, that's it. I learnt very early on that's where I am most happy. No one comes on and no one tells you what to do. It's the music and the audience. By now I am realizing that I can enjoy playing in front of other people.

I was not self-confident. I was introverted and shy, but I knew I could do one thing really well. I think a lot of performers are insecure and shy and it's like they choose the worst possible profession, where you put yourself out there to be reviewed by the crowd. They can love or hate you. It's the fear as well—the fear of the unknown. But I do have courage. That's what the guitar did for me. It was like my sword.

Jeff Lynne: The greatest thing ever happened. I put the E string on this plastic guitar and started playing Duane Eddy, but the neck snapped. Since I'd borrowed it from this guy down the road, I had to fake an accident by the garbage can at his back door so he would think that was how it got broken and that I'd hurt myself when it was busted. I thought it would be better that way rather than just giving it back broken in a plastic bag, even though he was never going to play it anyway.

Soon after we were out in the street playing football and this mate of mine said, "I've just seen a bloke cycling down the road with a guitar on his back." He couldn't see who it was because it was dark. And I went home and my dad said, "Look over there in the corner," and there was this Spanish guitar with six strings. I nearly died. It was the most thrilling thing. I was fifteen and still at school. I had swapped this plastic thing for a real one and now I had to learn to do it properly and read music. My dad recognized I had a passion. I never got anything more or anything else for free. That was it. That guitar cost two pounds and I still have it, and it's beautiful.

Graham Nash: The music of the time was important, but if a lot of musicians were more truthful they'd have to say it was women, too. It made us less lonely, it made us have friends. The girls loved it when you played guitar and that was the big thing for me—it was women.

Eric Clapton: The stuff I really homed in on and identified with was music being made by individuals in an untutored and noncommercial way—so the deeper I dug, the more I valued music that was made in this adversity and didn't follow any rules. I was very shy. So that was another identification. I identified with the isolation and solitude, and that kind of thing reflected in the music. Musicians would travel on their own, and the great blues players were happy to go from one place to the next. But they didn't go looking for contracts or fame or fortune. You could get it but it didn't seem that that was their appetite.

Eric Stewart: I wanted to be the guitarist. I loved the sound. I would open the front door of our house in Prince Street, Manchester, put on a record, and say, "Listen to this," and my mates would say, "What the fuck's the matter with him?"

"Listen to this guitar. Don't you hear what this guy is doing?" I'd protest. I wanted to do that. I didn't want to be the lead singer; I was happy to be the sideman like Eric [Clapton]. I wanted to be the guitarist—it excited me so much.

A lady two doors away from me, Mrs. Roland, bought my first guitar on hire purchase [*an installment plan*]. My mother couldn't afford it, and Father had gone by then. It took me about three weeks to learn how to tune it up. And then I had to learn the chords. I knew how to play bits on the piano. I had an ear already. I could sing. I had a voice.

The thrill of listening to Scotty Moore with Presley, James Burton with Ricky Nelson, Cliff Gallup with Gene Vincent. I never thought, like Keith [Richards], that I could earn some money. I just wanted to play guitar and get up and do it.

It wasn't going to be a day job. There was this mate of mine, he had an amplifier and an electric guitar, and we used to swap the guitar and we used to do little gigs in working-class clubs on a Sunday afternoon, and they'd pay us about a fiver—but it wasn't the money—to get up onstage and do it; playing through [an] amp was a thrill. I couldn't explain it to you. It sends shivers still. I was already there playing but had no money for an electric guitar.

One day someone knocked on my door and they said, "We hear you can play guitar," and I said, "Yeah, I know a few chords." So they said, "Do you want to join this band—Jerry Lee & the Stagger Lees? We've lost our guitarist. He got married." And so I said, "Yeah, I'd love to, but I haven't got a guitar." "Oh, we have a guitar for you, an electric guitar." And I went and did a rehearsal and got the gig. I was sixteen.

Graham Nash: Allan Clarke and I were singing together; Everly Brothers, skiffle, playing in a coffee bar in the center of Manchester in 1959. This guy comes up to me and Allan, and we had just done this little set of three or four songs—blues. This guy comes up to me and says, "You need Bocking." I said, "I'd love that but . . ." and he said, "No! Not fucking, Pete Bocking."

Pete could play every fucking solo we loved, every Buddy Holly song, every Gene Vincent song. He was unbelievable, and he looked like a total fucking nerd, he was not a rock-and-roll guy, he was like a fucking accountant, but man he could play. So with Pete came Joey Abrahams, who was the drummer, and Butch Mepham [*who was in a band called the Jets*]. So we went from me and Allan singing together to me and Allan with a bass player, lead guitarist, and a drummer that knew what the fuck they were doing. We became the Fourtones, even though there were five of us.

We were just doing coffeehouses and bar mitzvahs. Being paid peanuts. Nothing! Some of our contracts were ten pounds for the entire night, and that was a good night. But we didn't care as long as we had money for gas and other basic things. We loved what we were doing, so we didn't care.

I realized this could be a career when I started making more money than my dad, around 1961/1962. That was kind of shocking to me. You were supposed to do what your dad did and what your granddad did, but my mother and father would never let me go for that.

Chrissie Most [British record producer and record label owner]:
My parents had emigrated from London to South Africa after the war.
My mum had made a lot of money selling secondhand furniture—
there were a lot of bombed out houses and a lot of soldiers coming
home who needed something to sit on. My father was a musician.

When I was sixteen we came back to England on a long holiday. It
was 1959, and I'd been told to go to one of the coffee bars, which was
where all the young people hung out. Kids drank coffee and played
guitar. My parents dropped me off at the 2i's in Soho, and Mickie Most
was there with his guitar. [*The 2i's was the venue where many of today's
biggest names in music first performed.*] Guitarists went everywhere in
those days with their guitars. I think it was because they never knew
when the opportunity would arise to play and earn money. Anyway,
we hit it off—it was love at first sight. I was sixteen, he was nineteen,
and a couple of hours later my parents came back in a taxi to pick me
up and Mickie ran out of the coffee bar and leaned into the car and
said to my mum, "I'm going to marry your daughter"!

Jeff Lynne: Growing up we'd always had a piano in the front room.
But the piano seemed to have too much baggage, like learning how
to read music and formal lessons, whereas the guitar you could teach
yourself and learn at your own pace. As soon as I picked up that plastic guitar I was in love. And all the music I loved featured electric
guitars. People like Roy Orbison, Del Shannon, Duane Eddy, the
Shadows, Jet Harris, Chuck Berry.

Hilton Valentine: I was nineteen in '62 and I had been in the Wildcats
since the age of fifteen. I'd got my first guitar at thirteen and I was
mostly self-taught, with just three or four lessons from a guy down
the street. I didn't read music ever and still don't read music today.

We ended up getting a van. We never saw this as a career. I was
working in a factory as a machinist. I was playing nearly every night

plus Saturday and Sunday lunchtimes, and I'd even creep out to do lunchtime gigs. On a Saturday in Newcastle there was a lunchtime thing for kids called the Embassy Ballroom, and there was a club in South Shields on Sunday.

I was working so hard and rushing around. After one of the gigs, I suddenly got this pain in my chest and passed out. My brother told my mother and father and they said I had to get checked out. The doctor said you have to do one job or the other.

Terry O'Neill: It wasn't just kids who were really into their music, like Keith Richards or Eric Clapton, but kids who saw it as a means to an end, like the Dave Clark Five. They became as big as the Beatles in America. Their vocalist and keyboard player, Mike Smith, was a serious talent, a great rock-and-roll voice, but none of the others were really serious musicians. They just banged out a fairly repetitive foot-stamping kind of pop, like "Glad All Over," in the dance halls.

The story goes that they only started the band to raise money for their football club, picking up some instruments and playing around with sounds. Their only ambition was to make some dough, and they played the dance halls in North London, which weren't really cutting-edge musically like the rhythm-and-blues clubs where you'd find the Stones or the Yardbirds, but more middle-of-the-road, sing-along stuff.

Sir Frank Lowe: We were all looking to make our mark somehow, any how, rather than follow in our parents' footsteps and get a boring, pensionable job. We wanted excitement. In London, in advertising, I was just in the mailroom delivering the post. I went in 1960 to see the head of personnel, who of course had a double-barreled name [*hyphenated names denoted upper-class origins*], and I told her I wanted to be an executive. "Oh, no," she said, "you haven't been in the army, and besides, you couldn't be an executive till you were thirty."

I wasn't even twenty yet. Britain at that time was really dull. It was *so-o-o* dull. So I talked to Granny and said I wanted to emigrate to America because there's no future here. I saved up a bit of money and she gave me the rest. And I got on Pan Am and went to New York with two hundred and fifty pounds and a book called *How to Live in New York on Ten Dollars a Day.* I got a room at twenty dollars a week on Fifty-third, just off Broadway. It was not posh, I can assure you. It was opposite the Peppermint Lounge and the neon [sign] was interminably flashing through the bedroom window, so sleeping wasn't easy. I remember that first night I was walking out onto Times Square and I thought, "Oh my god, I'm in Times Square and this is going to be wonderful."

Allen Jones: By chance, in our class at the Royal College of Art was a group of artists who dominated the art of the 1960s, which became known later as pop art. Most famously were Hockney, Peter Phillips, and Derek Boshier, and myself. But at that time there was no sense of a group, and when we left three years later—[that] was the difference between 1961 and early 1964. By 1964 the pop movement had been codified and was making a noise.

Peter and Hockney were from Yorkshire—without exception we were all from working-class families. Ron Kitaj's presence was quite a catalyst. I wasn't influenced stylistically by him but by his very presence, as a real live American. To have this kind of free agent in amongst us, who was quietly painting cowboys and Indians, was from another planet and really energizing. No one had yet found their signature or language.

Pattie Boyd: When I left school we never discussed the idea of having a career. Girls were meant to go to school, do something, and then get married, and that was it. But once I was away from home I was able to wear jeans—my stepfather wouldn't allow me to wear them at home because he thought they represented anarchy.

Jeffrey Kruger [nightclub owner and show business impresario]: I was a frustrated jazz pianist, pretty good I thought, until I heard people like Tommy Pollard and I knew I couldn't compete. But I loved jazz, and every time I took a girl out and wanted to take her to a jazz club we would go to Studio 51 in London, and you'd have to breathe in the beer and the smell and the taste of it—and you couldn't take a nice girl there.

So I decided to try and open a club where the atmosphere would be non-drinking, purely for the music, and to give the people I was speaking to and [who I] wanted to become members the opportunity to get dressed up and meet others of their kind—people who were viewed as antisocial and antiestablishment just because of their taste in music or clothes, [although] many of them went on to be big names in politics and other things of stature.

One night, after taking a girl to the Prince of Wales Theatre we went into the Mapleton on Coventry Street near Leicester Square to have a meal, and when I went downstairs to the men's room there was this huge empty room, and I said to the manager, Tony Harris, a very charming man, "What's the room used for?" and he said, "It's shut except for Masonic functions."

"I tell you what," I said, "I'd like to hire it. You take the soft drink bar"—the police wouldn't give you a liquor license in those days for an all-night club—"and let me run a club for jazz." That's how the Flamingo was born—at midnight on that Saturday night.

We went from two nights to seven and we sold out no matter who I put on.

Mandy Rice-Davies: I was only dancing at Murray's cabaret club for a short period. That's when I met Christine [Keeler]. I moved into an apartment with her and met everybody. Stephen Ward, et cetera. [*It was Ward who introduced the girls to the politician and aristocrats who became the cast of characters in the Profumo Affair.*] I had already had a proposal from the Earl of Dudley—Eric was sixty and I was sixteen. He was dead serious and chased me around for ages. No sex. That was the weird thing. He sent me champagne. And then came 'round to drink it. I didn't drink and I didn't smoke. But I wasn't a virgin. I'd lost that in Birmingham to a nice boy.

One night [the Earl of Dudley] rings me up and, of course, he wants me to meet some close friends of his. He said, "Don't spike your eyelashes." I took it to mean don't wear mascara. I go over to his flat and I meet this woman. "I'd like you to meet Wallis Simpson, the Duchess of Windsor." She was awfully nice.

Pattie Boyd: We felt we were walking into something incredibly new and different, something that had never happened before. We were in the middle of it and it was surrounding us, this newness. London was a big melting pot, everybody was excited by everybody else, nobody felt threatened. What was happening was people from lower-class backgrounds were making money and so they didn't feel inferior, and they had something to offer with photography or painting or making films or whatever they decided they were going to do.

Jackie Collins: I always had a sense I could do anything—I know that's rare—I kind of tore up the town before I was married. I practically lived at the Flamingo.

Chrissie Most: My parents were very protective and wouldn't have let me go to nightclubs. They thought it was just a holiday romance with Mickie, and when it came time to sail back to South Africa, he had hatched this plot. He would come down to Southampton to wave us off, and just before they lowered the gangway, I'd run down it to the dockside, leaving my parents onboard, and we'd run off together.

But when he came down we had time to kill and he played his guitar for my mum, and something must have plucked her heartstrings because she said if Mickie was serious about me he'd come to South Africa and get a job, and if we still felt the same after a few years we could get married.

Mickie's dad was military, a sergeant major, very strict, and I don't think Mickie had a great childhood in North London, and he'd left home very young, so he had no roots or family.

A few months later he just turned up in South Africa with his guitar. He'd borrowed the airfare from Lionel Bart. [*Bart was a British songwriter best known for early pop song hits, the musical* Oliver, *and the* 1963 James Bond *theme song, "From Russia With Love."*] But there was no work, so I suggested he give guitar lessons. There was no rock and roll in South Africa, but there were loads of kids bursting for somewhere to go, looking for a scene, so I said, "Why don't you form a band?"

"Who with?" he said.

"You're teaching them," I told him.

We rented out town halls in places with populations of more than ten thousand, and I had posters printed, "Mickie Most & the Playboys," and plastered them in Springs [outside Johannesburg]. We had to go in the middle of the night—pasting them up on trees, shop windows. We took a diabolical liberty but we didn't give it a thought.

Jeffrey Kruger: The key thing [about the Flamingo] was the all-nighters, and it was through them that I attracted the major names— Billie Holiday and Ella Fitzgerald. They'd come to the club to relax after their own shows had finished.

It was the off-duty GI's [from U.S. air bases in the UK] who came over to me and said, "Open up all night."

"If we do that we will have trouble,' I told them.

"No," they said, "we will guarantee it. We will provide protection for the club and underwrite any damage if any of our boys do it."

Regular GI's found it a home away from home because they could mix with anybody. They were black and they could dance with white girls and no one bothered them. And they were getting music sent to them from their parents and friends from home but they had nowhere to play it. And this was the one place they could be safe and enjoy all night, and it developed from there.

Georgie Fame: I got offered a job as a professional musician at sixteen in London, and toured with Eddie Cochrane and Gene Vincent. I played piano with Billy Fury & the Blue Flames, but the backing group split from Billy and we renamed it Georgie Fame & the Blue Flames.

In March 1962 I started working in the Flamingo Club in London. We started doing all-nighters, from midnight to six a.m. We would play all night. No one was playing our stuff in the clubs or giving it any airplay at all. I was packing the place out with GI's. Fantastic atmosphere.

Jeffrey Kruger: Later [on] famous people would come into the Flamingo. The first was John Lee Hooker. He was here touring American bases and they had nowhere to go. He said, "If you like I will get Jerry Lewis, Chuck Berry—can we play down here?" I didn't think I could afford people like that, but it wasn't the money they wanted, it was the atmosphere and the music, and that was most important.

Georgie Fame: The Flamingo was completely different to the rest of the scene. It was frequented by American GI's who would come down from the bases—they'd come in loaded with bourbon, these black guys. The Flamingo was their home in London on the weekends. We were all in it together because they didn't have a bed—they would come back home with us. They'd sleep in a chair or on the floor. There was a black American GI called Carl Smith from Michigan who I haven't seen since. He came from an airbase at Newbury. He'd sleep on a chair or on a floor and play a new album—Mose Allison—and then he'd come back a month later with another album.

Jeff Lynne: In Birmingham I had to go to work every week. There was no choice. I'd take my guitar to work and practice and hide behind things and try not to get caught while I was learning.

My influences were Del Shannon and Roy Orbison. I didn't study music and didn't read music and still don't read music. No one I know can read music. I learned from Bert Weedon's *Play in a Day* book [a classic tutorial guide that influenced many great guitarists in the 1960s].

I'd put on my sister's records and try the first few bars. I didn't buy any records—I didn't have the money. I borrowed other people's. I was too busy trying to learn it. I had the opportunity to go down to the community center where this band, Mike Sheridan & the Nightriders, used to play. They were my favorite group; I loved them. They had great suits and looked really cool. Though they were very popular, I got to talk to the lead guitarist. I pushed myself at him, Big Al Johnson.

I asked him, "Any chance of having a go on your guitar after you've finished?" He'd leave the amp on. I thought, "Fuck." It was "Oh my god, I'm holding this thing." It was so amazing to hold it. It was like a piece of art or a bar of gold, a professional musician's instrument.

I used to practice anywhere on my own guitar that my father bought me: in the car, in the street, on the street corner. Sometimes the girls would sing along with it. I was living on a council estate. It was cool, just hanging out playing guitar.

Girls weren't that important, though—just the guitar. I got up thinking about the guitar and went to bed thinking about the guitar. That's all I would do—think about what I could do and how I could learn to write songs. I get in the zone—a lot—and I really get the music exactly as I want it. To produce a record is always different. It's different each time you play a song back. You can't always do exactly what you want to do with it. The music answers back sometimes.

I couldn't make up my mind if I wanted to be a drummer or a guitarist. I loved playing the drums to records I was listening to. I had a piano stool and some brushes and I'd play all these hits that my sister had got—whenever she was out, of course. Ultimately, I realized that my greatest pleasure was the guitar and great chord changes.

Jeffrey Kruger: It was the most original music you ever heard. I had been persuaded by some of our black GI clients to go for more noise, and when we first heard the drums of Ginger Baker it bounced off the wall. Georgie Fame, Chris Farlowe, and this young guy Eric Clapton. They were the only ones who cared about the music, not the money. We had an audience who were ready to listen to new music they had never heard before.

Terry O'Neill: You had your serious musicians, young kids turned on by the great blues and jazz players who just wanted to get better and better, and then you had these bands like the Dave Clark Five. Dave is a serious entrepreneur—always was. He's very reclusive these days, but for him, from day one, it was always about the money. He was a born businessman, not a drummer.

There was a great story about him having some business cards printed to get gigs. The Stones would never have printed business cards. They made it through word of mouth and talent. Apparently one of those business cards Dave Clark had printed ended up at Buckingham Palace and they got invited to play at the palace's staff ball.

Chrissie Most: In South Africa, my mum and dad said, "You aren't going on the road without us. We'll do the tickets and the doors."

We all got in one car. We had a station wagon with all the kit [equipment]. My dad had a walking stick with a sword inside, so he was head of security. Three hundred teenagers were there for our first gig. The first night we made a profit. We paid the band a couple of quid each and Mickie and me made three pounds on the first show. We got the kids there through the posters. They had nowhere else to go. I could see it was working, so I booked more halls. I didn't care where it was, and I'd phone the halls and make up tours, and suddenly it starts to take off.

Then we went to Kimberley, the diamond town. And a lot of blacks and coloreds [indigenous Africans and Asian immigrants] turned up. We weren't allowed to let them in but we did anyway, and because of that Mickie was served with deportation papers.

I made an appointment to see the prime minister, Hendrik Verwoerd—you could do that then. I was seventeen. I went with my dad and said to the prime minister, "Look, these papers have been served on my husband, but don't you realize the good we are doing for young people? They have nothing. We keep them off the streets." It worked because he said, "Tear up those papers," and we walked out.

In England up until then there was the class system. If you didn't go to university you went to work in the factory. But we didn't think there were any rules. You didn't need certificates and education—you could just do it. One thing we knew was we wouldn't ever work for anyone else. When we got married Mickie said we'll be fifty-fifty partners. From the day we were married we were partners in the business [*Rak Records, a legendary British record label*].

Peter Frampton: My father was head of the art department at Bromley Technical School in South London and was a big cheese. He was producing an end-of-term variety concert, "Sunday Night at the Bromley Technical High School," and I had a band, the Little Ravens: a piano player, who was a classical player, and a bass player—a classical double bass player—and we had no drummer. We did one show for the kids and a second show for the parents.

The headliners were George & the Dragons, George Underwood [*a musician, artist, and album illustrator*] and Davy Jones [David Bowie]. David would sing. They were my best buddies. They were thirteen or fourteen and I was eleven or twelve. We didn't see ourselves as competitors. In the morning my father would leave his door ajar and we'd bring our guitars to school and put them in the office, and in the lunch break three of us would sit on the stairs and play.

Keith Richards: I had only just left home and had moved out from Mum and Dad's and actually gone to live with these mates in London.

It was an incredible sense of freedom—if we could make enough money to pay the rent.

In England in those days if you went to enough parties you could pick up beer bottles—empty ones—and you could take them back to the pub and get a couple of pennies for each one. So we used to hit all these parties just to gather the beer bottles. We'd take the empty bottles away and count them up and say that's the rent for the week—fine—everything else is groovy. It was an absolutely nuts existence.

Food? Oh, we stole that. I would check out the bacon, Brian the potatoes. Yeah, we were professional thieves—shoplifters. We never got caught—never. The statute of limitations must be over by now.

Bill Wyman: The Stones had a rough band in 1962 with people changing all the time. It was Brian Jones's band. He created it. He brought various people into it. Mick and then Keith. Didn't have a drummer. Then they had a drummer from my band, the Cliftons, July to December '62. They were doing about two or three gigs a month, and they were the Rolling Stones.

My drummer said to me, "Come up and give it a try and see what you think." They play slow, small-bar blues. We were doing Fats Domino and Larry Williams, all the black R&B at that time. So the blues, I knew very little about. I went up for the audition on 8 December—they didn't really talk to me much. Mick said hello. I met Ian Stewart, the keyboard player. Brian and Keith were up at the bar and didn't really want to talk to me.

I brought in all my equipment. I had a homemade bass guitar. I made that in '61. Then I made an amplifier and then a cabinet. I brought it all to the rehearsal. That's what first inspired them. I had all this equipment. And I had cigarettes and they didn't have any. Then they talked to Charlie Watts and fired my drummer.

2

AMBITION

"We went up to Motown and we auditioned, and at the end
Berry Gordy said to us, "You girls really sound good, but
come back when you have graduated from high school."

MARY WILSON, THE SUPREMES

*Americans had enjoyed a decade of unparalleled economic growth when
John F. Kennedy was elected in 1960. And the baby boom had fueled a
twenty percent growth in population during the 1950s. On East Coast campuses and in Greenwich Village coffee bars, white, middle-class college kids
sang songs inspired by traditional British, Irish, and Scottish folk laments
in their quest for social reform. In the housing projects, song had always
been integral to the African American struggle for equality, but now a new
kind of music helped define blacks' increasingly assertive crusade for civil
rights.*

Mary Wilson [vocalist and founding member, the Supremes]: From
the time when I was born my mother says I was always singing. I was
always humming and listening to all the musicals. I was always involved in music, but never did anything about it. Then, just barely
thirteen, I signed up for this talent show. I borrowed my brother's
boots and black leather jacket. I did it because I was into Frankie

Lymon & the Teenagers, who were the Jackson 5 of the day. I fell in love with their song "I'm Not a Juvenile Delinquent." I was gyrating to "Juvenile Delinquent" and the crowd went crazy.

Me, Florence Ballard, and Diana Ross, we all lived in the Brewster-Douglass projects in Detroit. Florence sang "Ave Maria" in the talent contest. We migrated towards each other. I said, "Your voice is so big and beautiful," and she said, "You had everyone in the gymnasium saying 'Go Mary! Go Mary!' " This was '56 or '57. And we walked home from school and we became friends right there.

Al Kooper [American musician and producer]: I was born in Brooklyn in 1944, and I was fascinated by Manhattan. I started going there as soon as I could. I was very into music at an early age. At six I could play the piano and I was just hooked. Fortunately, my mom played music on the radio and there was always music in the house.

I discovered rock and roll from my babysitter—she lived down the hall. And I was ten or about that and she was fourteen or fifteen. So about ten minutes after my parents left, her friends came over to play music and dance. She listened to the Channels and the Penguins—all this doo-wop stuff. I went nuts. [I thought], "I really like this."

Some days my father would take me to the diner and I would start playing this music on the jukebox. Then he knew I was listening to the "voodoo music." Elvis came along and it was more fashionable to play the guitar in the midfifties, so I started playing, and I was a quick starter. God put music in me but it took a little while to realize it.

Carolyn Hester [American folksinger]: Many of us were seventeen and eighteen years old [and] coming up for the draft in '54, '55— it just radicalized us. My father was a lawyer—he graduated from Texas State University with LBJ at the same time—and he got accepted to Georgetown Law School, and we went East. We lived in Washington, DC.

When I got to New York having graduated from high school, I aimed to be part of the folk scene. My mother wanted me to go see this man she knew called Norman Petty [*Buddy Holly's producer*], so she wrote him a penny postcard and he called her.

He said, "I don't know much about folk, but she can audition." Norman Petty said, "Do you have enough for an album?' I was twenty. I recorded my first album and it came out in 1958. My dad played harmonica on it. He wanted me to be a folk musician.

Buddy Holly was in the studio when I was recording. He came to see me and he asked if I would go to see Chuck Berry and Fats Domino with him. In the meantime I found out that he was singing one of my songs.

Henry Diltz [American musician and photographer]: My mother was a stewardess for TWA. We lived a nomadic life, stationed different places. My father died in WW2. He was in the air corps. Then my mother remarried—he was in the state department—and we moved to Tokyo in 1947. I grew up there for five years. Then my stepfather was stationed in Germany in 1958 or 1957. I got into classical music and jazz. My family were very musical. I had played piano, my father played the cello, and my mother played the piano. I liked music. And then I had a friend who played the guitar and I got into country music.

Al Kooper: It was a great period for jazz. Jazz just reached me. That was what I liked. It touched me in some way. The doo-wop music you could dance to and it was the sort of punk music of its time. It was a distillation of blues and gospel music. Originally it was all black acts, then white people embraced this music and then slowly participated in it.

I had a friend in a band with a record deal and I'd spend the weekend at his house. One time we went into Manhattan and I auditioned for the record company—I was fourteen and I actually passed.

This band at the time, 1958, had the number one record in U.S.— "Short Shorts." They were called the Royal Teens. I would sneak away—my parents would have killed me if I quit school. The other guys were sixteen or more. I would go allegedly to my friend's in Brooklyn for the weekend, but I would be in Pennsylvania or Chicago or Boston and playing rock-and-roll shows with them—it went on for about two-and-a-half years. And then I was writing songs by this time and I got hooked up with a publisher, with these two guys who wrote lyrics, and we became a writing team. I was finishing high school now and had to go to college. This was now 1959.

I wanted to study music but there was no rock and roll, and the music they taught was music I wasn't interested in. After a year I told my parents I was quitting, and that was a bad thing. If you didn't go to college you were considered a bum. But I just didn't fit in and I couldn't do it. So I said, "Give me a couple of years, and if I can't make a living I'll go back to school."

Mary Wilson: Florence [Ballard] and I became really close, and someone came up to me in the playground—"There's someone who wants to put together a girl group." We go home and we meet with Diane [Diana Ross]—we were living in the same complex. We walked down to these guys' apartment—there's Paul Williams, Eddie Kendricks, and another guy, their manager. They were a group called the Primes and would later form the Temptations.

"Oh my god, I'm in this apartment with these guys and they are all older than we are and my mother is going to kill me," I thought.

One of the guys said, "Can you guys sing?" and we had never sung together before but Diane started singing Ray Charles and we chimed in on the harmony, and it really sounded beautiful. She was a very easy singer. This is before we had any ideas about what we were doing: we were only thirteen. It was just a natural thing that we did.

The guy says, "Fine. Okay. You are the Primettes and I am going to manage you girls." We went by their apartment every day. Diane sang one of the Drifters' songs, "There Goes My Baby," and we jumped in and did the harmonies, and then I sang a ballad—it was one of those things that felt natural and it fit so naturally. We had a girl group, and

I realized I was happier than I had ever been. It made me feel complete. We would meet after school, we would rehearse, we were the three of us. We directed our own songs.

Henry Diltz: I took another left turn. All my friends in this American College in Munich—there were a hundred girls and boys—were all studying for West Point and Annapolis. And then I read that sons of deceased veterans can automatically take the exam. So I wrote a letter and they said yes. I had to fly to London in 1958 to take the medical. I stayed in a little hotel in Hyde Park, and I went into a club one night. And they were playing skiffle music. I had no freaking idea what it was, but it hooked me.

I got accepted to the Military Academy at West Point—the dean of the school was saying, "Congratulations, my boy. What a rare opportunity." The first three months were physical training and exercises that put me in great shape. So while I was out there I joined the Columbia Record club. And I would get these mail-order records. I heard these banjos. A banjo has a fifth string. I had to play that. I contrived to leave West Point. It was the army. Oh, man! Four years in there. It's an engineering school. Math six days a week. Analysis and calculus. I bought a banjo and went to Hawaii.

Al Kooper: When I was in the Royal Teens they had record hops—they were things radio stations sponsored. They had them at schools and gyms primarily, and they had the artists who made the record come to the schools and lip-sync their songs for the school kids, and this helped sell records, and it helped the radio station.

The Royal Teens did a record hop somewhere in Queens and I met this group Tom & Jerry, who had a hit record called "Hey Schoolgirl" in the top ten. This had to be 1959. We realized that the three of us all lived in Queens, and we became friends. They were my age.

I didn't know they were destined to be anything. They were Simon & Garfunkel! Paul [Simon's] father was a bandleader, but a band-

leader that played events—weddings and bar mitzvahs and debu-
tante balls. Paul called me once and said, "Every forty minutes I
stand up and sing a Twist song and I wonder if you would play lead
guitar behind me. It's good money: fifty dollars." And so we would
both sit onstage with electric guitars. Paul switched to folk music,
but when he started he was playing rock and roll. We were friends,
and we played together.

Mary Wilson: There were weekend dances in Detroit and we would do
union dances. We wouldn't do nightclubs or that sort of thing because
we were too young. I don't think we were paid. We had this manager;
he would buy us clothes and his girlfriend would take us shopping.
Our beginning was different from others who were singing on the
streets.

Our parents were happy because they knew where we were at all
times and they knew we were doing something that we enjoyed and it
was keeping us out of trouble. We did that till 1961, until we decided
we wanted to go further.

We sang the popular music. We loved harmony. We rehearsed a lot,
always. In school they had special classes like home economics for
girls and shop for boys. So we used those special classes to do our own
thing, to sing. It was a different age then.

We entered a contest, an international contest—it was in Canada—
and we won. We were singing the Drifters, Ray Charles.

Al Kooper: What was the first record I ever bought? There was a big
white record at the time in 1955/'56—"Autumn Leaves" by Roger Williams on Kapp Records. And then there was this doo-wop song, "The
Closer You Are," by the Channels. I wanted both records, but I only
had a dollar. I was probably thirteen or fourteen, or even younger. I
went to the store and I had to make a decision, so I bought the black
record. That was my first record—a 45. The black music was getting to
me and changing me. And I still love that record.

Neil Sedaka [American singer/songwriter]: I had a scholarship, and I had the intention of becoming a classical pianist. I won a competition when I was sixteen as one of the top high school pianists. I was at Lincoln High School in Brooklyn. Songwriting was natural—my heroes were Gershwin and Irving Berlin, Rogers & Hammerstein, Rogers & Hart.

Then at Lincoln High School I heard rock and roll, and I was fascinated. I was not a star in high school. I was the nerd, not a jock. I played Chopin and Bach and wasn't invited to the parties. I wanted from a very early age to be recognized and famous. I was teased and I wanted to show I was somebody special. I started a group called the Tokens that went on to do "The Lion Sleeps Tonight." I became, from the little pipsqueak to a big shot in high school because I had a group and we did rock and roll.

I was thirteen, started studying at Juilliard on Saturdays to be a concert pianist, and [*lyricist and Grammy-nominated songwriter*] Howard Greenfield's mother heard me play Chopin. Howard lived just across the hall and he asked me if I wanted to write songs, and I said I didn't know how to write songs. We wound up writing more than three hundred songs together.

Robert Christgau [American rock critic]: By June of 1962 I was twenty. I wanted to be a writer and lived in Manhattan. I joined a brokerage house—it overreached and went bankrupt, but not while I was there. My boss, by complete luck, was a painter. Bob was ten years older than me and became my best friend till the day he died. He was an extremely smart and aesthetically open person.

I had no money. Sometimes I would sit by the Village Gate [*a nightclub on the corner of Thompson and Bleecker streets in Greenwich Village, New York*] and listen to Coltrane and Monk—it was a jazz thing and I was a jazz fan. But at the same time I was very into art. The radio was playing top 40, and it was always on in my apartment. I had a little record player and about a dozen albums—mostly jazz, Ray Charles—

[but] basically my music was through the radio. The biggest thing that happened to me from '62 was all pop art. In the course of that period there was Lichtenstein and then Warhol.

In October/November '62 I walked into the Green Gallery on Fifty-Seventh Street—it was something I did frequently; it didn't cost anything. In this gallery I heard Connie Francis sing "Vacation." "Where is this coming from? I can't figure it out—it's an art gallery!"

I saw that one of these paintings had a radio in it and it was plugged in and it was playing. This was an epiphany. I went to see John Coltrane—Aretha Franklin was opening and she was terrible—but Coltrane did an encore, and it was one of these moments that happens in jazz and if you are in the right mood they really come off. I was ecstatic. I had these two epiphanies close by each other about music and art. A musical epiphany and the epiphany in the art gallery; it changed the way my boss Bob and I thought about music and art.

Neil Sedaka: I'd moved into the Brill Building [*America's "song factory," it housed many songwriters and publishers*] on Broadway. Everyone was there writing every day for the record companies and artists: "You Lost That Loving Feeling" [*by the Righteous Brothers*], "One Fine Day" [*by the Chiffons*], and the Dixie Cups got "Going to the Chapel." "Will You Still Love Me Tomorrow" was Carole King's for the Shirelles. It was the time of the small publishing firms. Basically across the street from the original Brill Building, which was 1619 [Broadway] was 1650, and it catered to younger listeners and writers.

In the Brill Building each one of us had a room with a piano and a desk. And at the end of the day we would all come into the big office to play our songs, and we were all in competition with each other. But good competition. The best song won out and someone like the Chiffons would record it. We were there ten to five, five days a week. At the end of the day sometimes your song was unfinished and you'd finish it the following day.

I was the first to sing and record my own songs. That was in '58.

I was auditioned for RCA Records. They had just signed Elvis with "Heartbreak Hotel."

Carole King and I dated at the time but we didn't write together. I did write "Oh! Carol," which was dedicated to her. And she wrote an answer called "Oh! Neil." That wasn't a hit but it was a very nice gesture. Her mother didn't like me because I took her away from school and her academic work.

Sir Frank Lowe: New York wasn't paved with gold or anything like that. It was dirty and grubby, but I can remember walking by a music shop, and coming out of it [was] something that made me feel quite at home—I could hear them playing Acker Bilk [*an English clarinetist*] with "Stranger on the Shore" [*a song for solo clarinet that reached number one in the United States and the UK*].

I couldn't get a job and went to see a bloke who my mother had known, Jock Elliott. He was running the Shell account at Ogilvy & Mather. Big businessman. Big guy. I got an appointment, and I was so impressed by him. He said, "Come back to the house and have a drink." I remember his license plate on the car in the garage—it was just *J*—and his phone number was *BUtterfield 8*, which was the film that had come out with Liz Taylor—a fabulous film with Laurence Harvey.

I got a job selling carpets at a shop on Fifth Avenue. I was very successful. The English were rather curious to the New Yorkers. Then I got a flat on Eighty-fifth Street—a basement flat in a brownstone. I shared that with several thousand cockroaches. Curiously, Jock Elliott called me and asked me, "How are you getting on with a job?' And I said, "I am selling carpets."

"Well," he said, "There is a job going at Benton & Bowles." So I went to the ad agency—big agency founded by an American congressman. I got a job as a very junior executive. I was twenty-one or twenty-two. This is '61. I worked there and I was quite enjoying my life in New York. I made ten thousand dollars a year. I could afford to do what I wanted and I could afford to go to a steakhouse, and you could get a good meal for $1.99. It was fun. You'd go out to the Hamptons and sleep on the beach on weekends.

Carolyn Hester: I was moving into the New York scene, playing in the Village. The Village was very much like a lot of places: kids hung out in coffee bars where music was played [if they couldn't get into clubs where liquor was served]. We attracted a fantastic audience, such a variety, and there was no generation gap. There were people from uptown and downtown. Suddenly I was playing the Ivy League colleges. The Greenwich Village scene was transferring to the Eastern Seaboard and, as in the Village, you would have musicians and comics touring together. (I was twenty-three going into the 1960s.)

There were a cast of characters that were part of this renaissance. Tom Paxton, Eric Anderson, Buffy Sainte-Marie. Through gigs I'd bump into Carly, her and her sister, the Simon Sisters. So I knew them from when they started out together. She was fun to be around. A real New Yorker. Fun was being able to talk about the music business and hang out, and we'd go to the coffee shop just like you do now. We'd somewhat talk about politics but we all knew we were on the same wavelength [politically], so we shared notes and stories about being on the road.

I had met Bob Dylan in the Village in 1961 because he came to the club and I was playing one night and he heard me sing a song—Buddy had taught me to sing this song. And Bob was all over that. He loved Buddy Holly, and that is how it started. I crossed paths a lot with Dylan in clubs and on the street. Dylan wanted to get to know me. I didn't know that at the time. I told him, "I've got a guitar player, but if you want to play harmonica [on my next album] would you mind?" He said, "Here's my phone number, and don't lose it."

The first time I heard him play I just remember him and his guitar. Not a band. I was in the audience. The crowd was young, happy, and a very mixed crowd like all our crowds. The political mind was the same. Some older people brought their children. I called him the next day. He played harmonica on my album and it was his first recording, and then he did a session for Harry Belafonte.

He was confident. He wasn't nervous. He was like an old soloist. He said I was his link to Buddy Holly. We'd talk about Buddy. I didn't see him for quite a while, and then one day he came to my apartment and stayed and wrote songs all night while I did a gig. When I got back he'd left me a message, "Thanks Carol. Me, Bob."

I was playing England, too. Tons of folk clubs. Folk music was more of a way of life in England at that time. All the pubs had folk music. There was a huge following for it. Five hundred people came to hear me play in Surbiton. Donovan would come—he was a kid. There were so many English artists. There was a national folk festival at Cambridge, and I had my own half hour on the BBC.

Mary Wilson: We won [a] competition in Canada [when] we were sixteen. That was when we started. We did so many shows in Detroit with the local DJs—there were loads of radio stations, and we said, "Wow, we can do this, and they need to find us a place to record. Let's look around and find a record company."

Motown was the company, and it had Smokey Robinson & the Miracles and we knew these people. We get the audition with Smokey & the Miracles through Claudette, who was Smokey's wife—she was one of the Miracles. And we let them listen to us and we said, "What do you think of us? Because we want to go to Motown." He said, "I can get you an audition."

So we went up to Motown and we auditioned and at the end Berry Gordy said to us, "You girls really sound good, but come back when you have graduated from high school." This was '61. We wore our own uniforms. We were making our own clothes. We had skirts and tennis shoes and socks. We got so disappointed that he didn't take us—he just didn't want young girls running around the company with all these guys and he'd be responsible. That's why he turned us down. But we thought he didn't like us.

Al Kooper: I wanted to do music for [the rest of] my life. I just didn't know what was going to keep me going. So I attempted to educate myself in every aspect I could. And in retrospect I am really glad I did that. As time went by I thought, "So, this is a good thing I am doing—if they didn't want to hire me as a songwriter, I can work as a studio guitarist, and if they don't want to hire me as a studio guitarist, I could play in a band." I just wanted to stay in the music business and earn a living.

Mary Wilson: You had all these people at Motown. Marvin Gaye had just come in. It was the atmosphere—and so much creativity going. We hitchhiked every day after school and hung around Motown and pretty soon we were inside: "Hey, Smokey!" "Hey, Mary!" We got to know everyone. It was a big house with a receptionist. And we'd just sit there. One day someone said, "Our background vocals aren't here," and we said, "We'll do it." That was our way into Motown.

Then Berry Gordy said, "You've got to change your name." He didn't like "the Primettes." We wanted it so much we said okay. We asked everyone for ideas. We didn't really want to change our name. We thought no one would know who were are, but then no one knew who we were anyway. And pretty soon we had a contract and a name. Names were scribbled on little bits of paper and one was "the Supremes." Me and Diana, we didn't like the name, but they wouldn't sign us without a new name. We didn't know why, then. It was only much later that we realized that it was so the name would belong to Motown. We didn't read the fine print, and at the bottom it said any name you come up will be owned by Motown Records. We didn't even realize that till years later. It was a brand. It belongs to *who*? Hey, that's our name!

Henry Diltz: When I got to Hawaii I had a name to look up whom I knew from New York, called Cyrus, so I asked around. "Yes, he is in the drama class and he's opened up this beatnik coffeehouse."

I put my banjo on my Vespa, drove down there, and they said, "Oh, a banjo!" He became my very best friend of my whole life. He got up on a big stepladder with a guitar, I'd sit at the bottom, and we would sing. Then we worked up songs together and built a stage in the corner, and so I began going down there every night and singing. It was great. It was all bare feet and shorts and T-shirts and lots of girls. Hundreds of them—wonderful college girls.

I smoked my first marijuana cigarette. Many folksingers were coming through. The Kingston Trio—they popularized folk music. And the Everly Brothers. Finally one guy says, "Let's learn some songs together and form a trio. We were called the Lexington Three, and when Cyrus joined us we were the Lexington Four. We were earning a few bucks a week. But we'd play there every single night. If you have a place to play every night, you get better and better. We had some pretty damned good songs ready to go, and finally we made our way to California to make our fortune. I remember the first few nights we slept on the apartment floor of a hooker—late '62. December '62. Then we stayed in Hollywood in a little apartment near Capitol Records.

Al Kooper: I was working very hard in New York to make a living; I was being subsidized by my parents. I was trying to break out and figure out how I was going to make money in the music business. At the same time, I was playing guitar on recording sessions. Most of it was nothing, I mean, obscure records that no one ever heard.

My first studio gig! That was exciting—it's bizarre I did so many things. I worked in a recording studio at 1615 Broadway doing odd jobs because the engineers would teach you stuff, and so I engineered a session.

The first session I engineered was Dionne Warwick doing radio spots. I engineered it and I was nineteen and it was only radio spots. I just *did* that. Then also I would cut acetates—when people would work in the studio they would have discs covered and personalized. And someone had to do the discs, so they taught me.

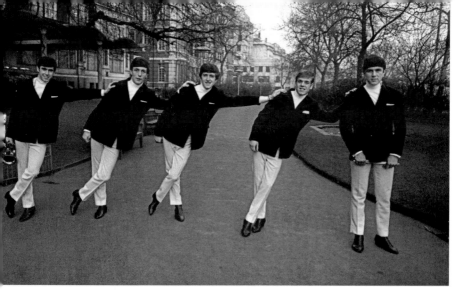

In the search for publicity, the Dave Clark Five aped the fresh and emerging face of pop inspired by the Beatles throughout 1963.   BOTH PHOTOGRAPHS BY TERRY O'NEILL

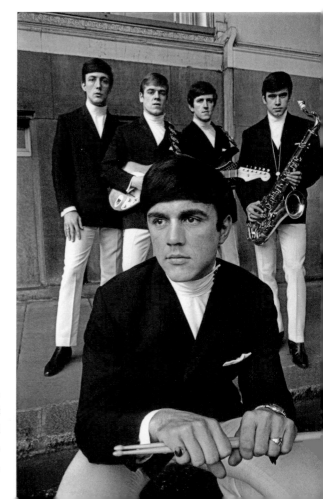

The Dave Clark Five, summer 1963. The band was named after its front man, but it was keyboard player and vocalist Mike Smith (rear left) who gave the band credibility.

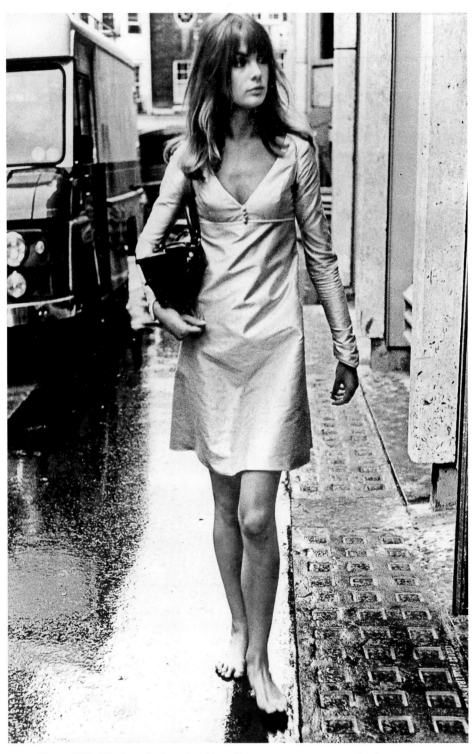

Terry O'Neill's shot of a barefoot Jean Shrimpton on a rain-soaked street on her way to a fashion shoot typified the unconventional and informal attitudes of young women in 1963.

Vogue photographer David Bailey and his muse Jean Shrimpton were the couple that exemplified London's emergence as the fashion capital of the world in 1963.

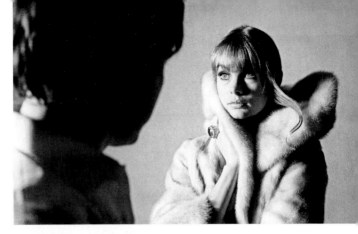

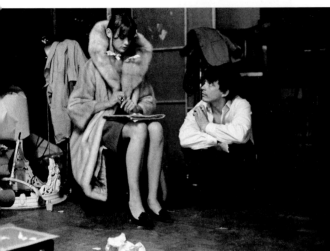

Convent-educated Jean Shrimpton was the highest-paid supermodel of the 1960s and Cockney rebel Bailey the most in-demand photographer in the world.

David Bailey was the enfant terrible of fashion photography whose working class charm and chutzpah delighted American *Vogue* editor Diana Vreeland.

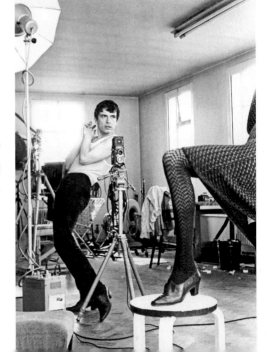

ALL PHOTOGRAPHS BY TERRY O'NEILL

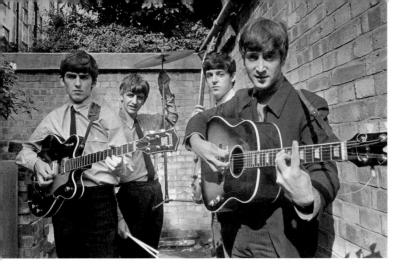

The Beatles take a break in the backyard of the Abbey Road studios in London in January, 1963, while recording their first hit single, "Please Please Me."

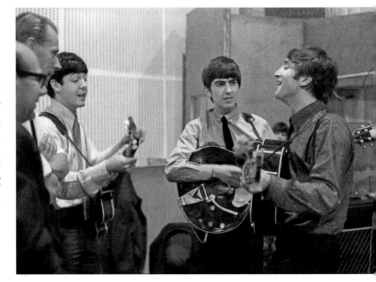

The Beatles share a joke with legendary producer Sir George Martin (*second left*) during the "Please Please Me" recording session.

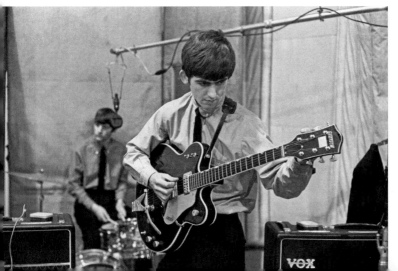

George Harrison tunes his guitar.

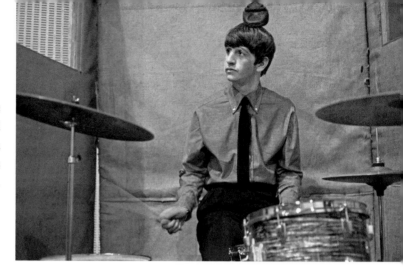

Ringo Starr gave the Beatles and Sir George Martin new vigor with his drumming.

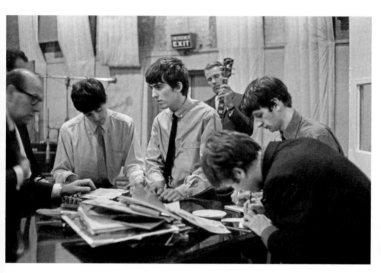

The Beatles, with Sir George Martin *(background)*, do the paperwork. The "Please Please Me" album took three three-hour sessions and cost £400 to record.

(below) Listening to the playback.

ALL PHOTOGRAPHS BY TERRY O'NEILL

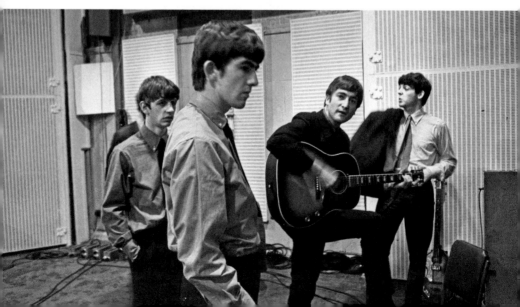

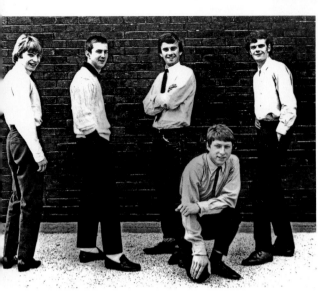

"I was just seventeen playing gigs. There was a club mentality, a very strong underground like the Stones or Brian Augur. We were all club musicians. I liked it. I identified with it."

Eric Clapton

"The Stones told us 'when you get paid,' you went straight to Mr. Fish and bought clothes. We had fire in us and we had money. I was earning more than my father."

Eric Stewart

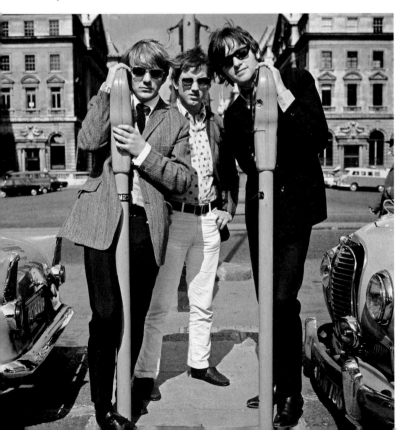

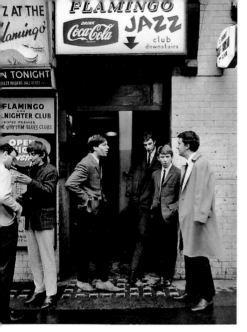

"The Flamingo Club was different, frequented by black American GIs from the airbases. It was their home in London. They'd come down loaded with Bourbon and play an album, Mose Allison, then come back a month later with a new album."

Georgie Fame

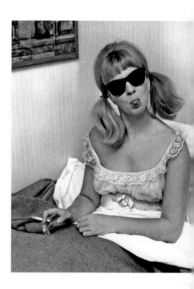

"We were the first generation of girls who could leave home before getting married. We were a power to be reckoned with because it was easy to get a job. There were two million of us with buying power. Teenagers were having a ball everywhere."

Mandy Rice Davies

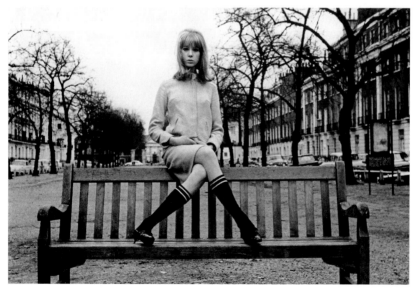

"We all wanted to be thin, to look great in the new clothes. The doctors gave us slimming pills, speed, if we wanted them, and there were biscuits you could buy that made you feel full. I would eat them so I didn't have to eat all day."

Pattie Boyd

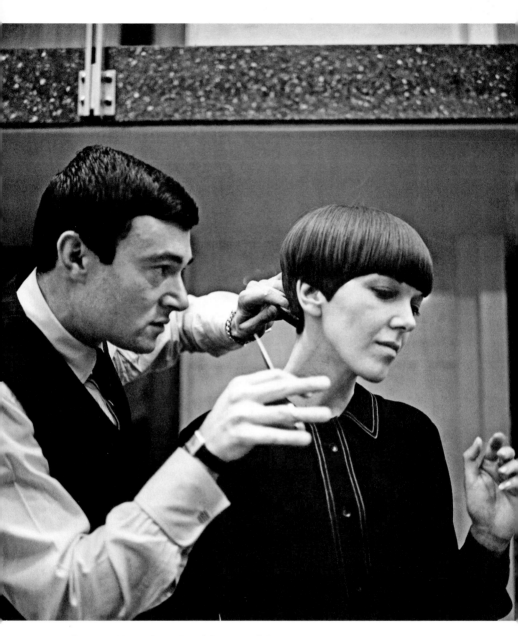

"I was walking down Bond Street and there was a sign, VIDAL SASSOON, and a picture of a haircut that knocked me sideways. I knew I wanted *my* hair cut like that." **Mary Quant**   CREDIT: GETTY IMAGES

Nineteen sixty to sixty-four was a blur for me because I was working really hard and doing so many different things. I think it was
1963, I found this unbelievable nightclub run by the mafia. Forty-
seventh Street between Eighth and Ninth—the Sweet Chariot—and
they only had gospel music there. And I really like gospel music.
So that became my hangout at night. It was so strange—one of the
strangest places I have ever been in my life.

Mary Wilson: I don't know how British houses are structured. In
America, we usually have basements. At the Motown house you had
the basement area that ended up being the recording studio. You
walked in off the street onto the reception area and there were little
rooms which were probably bedrooms, and they were offices, and
you had the financial office, and Berry Gordy's sisters—he had a
couple of sisters—they all had positions. It was a family business.
What was unique was the mother and father were working there.
You could always see the father repairing something. He was a
grand old guy.

It wasn't a factory, but everything was in-house. They even had
someone cook lunches, and everyone from the singers, musicians,
and workmen would eat there. It was a real family business. Then
they started purchasing other homes around the area, and then we'd
have other buildings down the street or across the street.

We hung out, and you'd want to live there if you could. You'd want
to be there because there were so many exciting people coming in. It
was exciting. The guys were handsome, and we were just teenagers.
You were right there, and you had the opportunity to grow there.

Motown was very progressive in artist development. And we'd go
there and record a couple of songs, and then we'd work out the choreography, and then Mrs. Powell . . . did motivation [*stage presence and
movement*]. It was probably the only place in the world which had this.
You walk in the door and there are all these talented people to help
you develop and grow.

Bob Gruen [American rock-and-roll photographer]: I was into the music on the radio. I had a few albums. I was shaped in the sense that I was drawn to it from the late fifties when rock and roll started and it was called "delinquent music" and "the music of the devil." I didn't feel like a criminal. I liked the music, and I was a teenager and it shaped me because it made me feel like an outcast.

Neil Sedaka: England, strangely enough, had a great respect for the original American rock and rollers, and I was one of them, like Roy Orbison, Buddy Holly, Gene Pitney—even though he was finished in America—and Little Richard.

Years later—1972, 1973—we were shopping in Savile Row, London, and I met Mick Jagger, and he said that mine was the first record he ever bought. I was very flattered. He'd bought the record as a kid.

Mary Wilson: The Supremes were always glamorous. We were show-stoppers. We would buy plastic pearls from Woolworth's. We were always elegant looking. Our parents were elegant. Diane had a beautiful, glorious mother. My mother was a tall and handsome woman. We had a presence onstage. We had attitude but we were refined.

We had the choreography teacher, Mrs. Powell, she taught you how to turn your body, and poise, and moderation, and all that kind of stuff. She taught the guys as well. Those of us who learnt from her tell her all the time what she did for us. We had a certain amount of innate stuff. She was a woman probably in her thirties and she had a modeling school. We looked up to her. The guys, too. It was all about you as a human being and how you carried yourself, and that was what she taught us. Whenever a Motown artist came onstage you could immediately tell they were from Motown. Even some of the bad guys learnt to have carriage.

Mrs. Powell said at Motown, "One day you will be singing in front of kings and queens. You are diamonds in the rough, and we just need to polish it."

Neil Sedaka: I had been listening to local radio in Los Angeles and heard something by an unknown group called the Showmen. It was a local hit. There was something about the recording—the tune, the production, and the lyrics—that inspired me to write "Breaking Up Is Hard to Do." Howard [Greenfield] wasn't sure about the song, but I persisted and he finished the lyrics. It was fictional. Most songs are fiction and I didn't know how universal that was.

I spent a couple of weeks putting it down and picking it up. I came up with a line with a "doobie-doo down down" that went underneath the whole song, and I went in to sing it in unison with a guitar. I went to the session and I did it that way. This was 1962. It took off, and it was a hit again later as a slow ballad. That shows a good song is a good song.

"King of doobie-doo's and tra-la-la." That became my trademark. I kept it like a trademark and called them the sandwich songs. It starts with an intro—a piece of bread—then came the meat of the song, then it ended with another piece of bread. After I named it my colleagues found it amusing.

Mary Wilson: We went all over but mostly in the South. [*The "Motor-town Revue" was comprised of Martha Reeves, the Temptations, Smokey Robinson, Little Stevie Wonder, and others. It played what was known as the "Chitlin' Circuit," a string of venues throughout the segregated South where African Americans could perform safely.*]

Tour buses. Raggedy tour buses. We were so bad. It was such fun. Real fun. They were like crazy guys, and they'd play cards and we'd harmonize all night—many of the guys were teachers of music and came from a jazz background.

I don't remember my first pay packet. We never got a pay packet. We performed for nothing—for zilch. We didn't even get a weekly allowance. Berry Gordy handled all of that—we were given just a little money for personal items. We were just happy to be out there. We never even thought about it. Looking back, they really exploited us, but we never had to pay for anything—it was like an old-fashioned apprenticeship. We were minors. My parents couldn't read or write. We had no representation. I should have married a lawyer.

Carolyn Hester: John Hammond [*Columbia Records' executive producer and acclaimed A&R man*], who'd signed me, came down to listen to Bob Dylan and I at an apartment in the Village. In the kitchen was a big picnic table and Hammond and Dylan sat next to each other, and he loved Dylan right away. [*Hammond signed him to Columbia after Dylan played on Hester's third album.*] Dylan was just starting to write. I knew he was going to fit right in.

Henry Diltz: A couple of days after we got to Los Angeles in late '62 we went to the Troubadour, and Mondays they had amateur evening. We got up to do three songs—driving chords. I remember the shock of it. What the fuck was happening? Oh, yeah, no one had ever heard anything like it.

Most of the folks played in little clubs to get ready for the Troubadour, but we were—bang—right in there. The result was [that] the very first night we got an agent, Benny Shapiro from International Talent Agency, and within a week we were signed to Warner Bros. Records.

Folk music was huge at that point. It was early '63. And they want us to be in this movie, *Palm Springs Weekend*, with Connie Stevens and Troy Donahue. We had to go to Warner Bros. to meet the director, and we were late. "Well, boys, you are late. He's already at lunch."

So we march into the commissary, and there's the director with some other executives, and we march up to the table. "Pick up, man, we are here for the meeting." No, we weren't smoking [dope] yet.

When we played the Troubadour, the buzz was out. Lots of managers were interested in us, including Bob Dylan's manager. He flew out from the East Coast to meet with us, and we were with Herbie Cohen [*who later managed Frank Zappa, Linda Ronstadt, and Tom Watts*]. That was '63. We did a show with Little Richard, and that was great. We were listening to all the music going on. We did two albums with Warner Bros. We did a single with Phil Spector and we had a couple of singles on jukeboxes. One was "Very Good Year." Before Sinatra. Then we had "Road to Freedom." We were kinda oblivious to what was going on in the real world, the civil rights marches, and this is long before Vietnam hit us.

Carolyn Hester: Even a famous artiste, if she was black, couldn't get a hotel room in those days. I didn't know that my real deep feelings about civil rights would take structure. It was such a surprise because I wasn't a radical. I didn't know I was going to be influencing people or be part of such a massive scene. Thank god for the Village and New York.

[In America] we were introducing to our generation what we thought and the light as we saw it. Our moral outrage was so overwhelming. Sometimes you couldn't sleep at night because it was so exciting. But also scary because of the politics. The bombs had fallen on them already in England. In England they were politically already all there.

Neil Sedaka: Being a performer I had no prejudice whatsoever. My favorites were Ella Fitzgerald and Sarah Vaughn. I lived in the North and had no idea [of the depth of that prejudice elsewhere].

Gay Talese [American journalist and author]: For a lot of people, Vietnam involvement wasn't that much written about. It was the time of the bomb. The space age—very competitive between Russians and Americans. I was following the launches. There was the competition with the Soviets and since they were the first with the dog and then the human in space, they were number one, and both countries had bombs and were thinking about fallout shelters. There was anxiety about the atomic bomb. And that affected all age groups.

Sir Frank Lowe: I spent time in the Village, and I met a very pretty girl. A stewardess. She was English and delightful. And we stayed in touch. She came down one evening and we went to the Village Vanguard. On that night was Lenny Bruce. I had no idea who he was. It was the most acutely embarrassing evening I have ever spent. If you remember Lenny Bruce, he was using language and words which we had never heard.

Our friendship endured in spite of that evening. She was very embarrassed. A nice English girl from Surrey. And then I got a frightful shock—I got a letter from the government: would I please report for my medical to the local recruiting office in New York because I was eligible to be drafted into the American army.

I went along for my medical, which went very well. I was a fit young man. And they sent me a letter classifying myself as A1. I ran over to my friend Jock Elliott and said, "What should I do?"

He said, "Get out. If they serve the papers on you, you are drafted, and then you are AWOL if you don't report. It could come tomorrow or the next day. Get out!" The Agency transferred me within forty-eight hours back to London, to the office in Knightsbridge.

Robert Christgau: There was a sense of rebelliousness in America, but one of the ways it was rebellious was it wanted to enjoy having more pleasure than it was told it could have. This was much more important than the political element, numerically speaking.

Bob Gruen: I had been to a rally with Kennedy, and I was so close . . . I got pictures as he was coming, and he stepped on my foot by accident and he stopped and said, "Excuse me." A very human and polite exchange. I saw a rally where Martin Luther King spoke. I believed in Kennedy and his ideas, that things would be new and better and people would get along with each other and problems would be solved.

Gay Talese: Literature and the laws changed. Books formerly seen as smut and pornography like *Lady Chatterley's Lover* and *Tropic of Cancer*—books that were published underground before were now openly available.

Linda Geiser [Swiss-born actress]: I was twenty-six when I came to New York. I came in October '62. It didn't bother me that I had to bare my breasts in front of a film crew, but they were very respectful. I knew it was the first time a woman's breasts were seen in the cinema and it would be controversial.

The Pawnbroker was a film about a Holocaust survivor, not my breasts. We knew it was an important film because people wanted scenes cut—my scene. But Sidney Lumet was a very determined man, and he wasn't going to let them cut his film.

Remember, I had come from Switzerland. I had been an actress for ten years and nudity was not something we were ashamed of. I knew a very good agent who got me to Sidney Lumet. I got my own apartment. I had a job in a little store in the West Village—Piñata Party. It was a Mexican imports business and the man was smuggling antiquities from Peru. And I made clothes out of the fabric he bought from Peru. We invented everything and anything, and it was wonderful. You could invent your life.

PART TWO

Listen

Do you want to know a secret?

Do you promise not to tell?

Whoa-oh-oh

Closer

Let me whisper in your ear.

Say the words you long to hear.

THE BEATLES

Adolf Eichmann had been hanged for war crimes in Israel. The world had survived the Cuban Missile Crisis. The first James Bond movie, Dr. No, had been released. And civil rights protests were growing larger and louder. When 1963 arrived, Britain was in the grip of the worst winter in living memory—although the political temperature had been raised by sex scandals. The divorce of the Duchess of Argyll yielded, in court, photographs of a naked duchess fellating a "headless man" rumored to be Douglas Fairbanks Jr. And the press was hot on the trail of a scandal involving call girls, politicians, and the aristocracy that would later be called the Profumo Affair.

In the world of music, Brian Epstein was busily trying to boost the impetus of the Beatles' career. "Love Me Do," their first single, had peaked at *number 17 on the British charts. While recording their first album,* Please Please Me, *they prepared for their first national televised performance.*

After repeatedly smoking dope in the hotel's lobby, Bob Dylan had been asked to vacate the room booked for him by the BBC. They had flown him to London to sing in a play that would be broadcast the same night that the Beatles made their big television debut. The Beatles' part-time publicist would soon discover an R&B band called the Rolling Stones, which had shared suburban pub and club stages with a young guitarist called Eric Clapton, among others.

On the heels of their televised performances, both Dylan and the Beatles reached number one on the UK charts. In February, "Please Please Me" became a hit single, and the album charted in March. Columbia was preparing the release of Freewheelin' Bob Dylan *with an album cover photo of him with his girlfriend, Suze Rotolo, huddled against the biting cold on the corner of Jones and West Fourth streets in Greenwich Village. Rotolo would later say, "It is one of those cultural markers because of its casual, down-home spontaneity and sensibility. Most album covers were carefully staged and perfectly posed. Whoever was responsible for choosing that particular photograph really had an eye for a new look."*

So did youth.

3

ACTION

"In Liverpool, the Beatles weren't nothing special.
I got up and sang at the Cavern with the Beatles.
But they weren't the best band in Liverpool."

CILLA BLACK

From Liverpool to London, self-taught musicians who couldn't read a note of music began inventing their own sounds. With begged, borrowed, or homemade guitars, they gathered an audience from among their neighbors and found empty basements and backrooms that became hothouses for their creativity. Their tribal, affluent followers sought new clothes to dance in, to be seen in, and to characterize their identity; and artists, writers, and the media reacted as if a new species had been discovered.

Cilla Black: Brian [Epstein] was very quiet, a shy man, and a perfect gentleman—total gentleman. And smartly dressed—but, then, he had money, he came from a wealthy family. He had a record shop in Whitechapel in Liverpool, and everyone was asking for this one record, "My Bonny Lies Over the Ocean" [1961] by the Beat Brothers, which is what the Beatles were calling themselves then.

But really the Beat Brothers were only playing as a backing band to another guy. I think it was Tony Sheridan—I don't know, you'd have to check back in the history books—who did a rock-and-roll version of "My Bonny," which was a Scottish folksong, and that's how Brian said, "Who are these Beat Boys? I've gotta go see them." They were playing at lunchtime sessions at the Cavern.

Eric Stewart: My first band, the Staggerlees, changed their name to the Emperors of Rhythm. We went to the BBC in Longsight, a studio in a converted church in Manchester, to audition for workingman's club gigs with the Northern Dance Orchestra. At the audition were this band the Beatles, and us. We were playing all our things. We probably did the Shadows numbers [*the Shadows were Britain's most successful instrumental band of the sixties*], acceptable pop, and copies of the American stuff, which was all the men in suits on TV wanted to put on.

Then the Beatles came on. I thought first they were scruffy, but they mesmerized me. They were dressed in their Hamburg gear, not their Brian Epstein–packaged velvet collars and stuff. They were dressed in jeans. Paul had a little leather waistcoat on and sang "Till There Was You," which was originally a show tune. John sang "Memphis, Tennessee." They sung another song, which I presumed was one of the songs they had written because I'd never heard it.

They failed the audition. And we passed. We got paid about fifteen pounds between four of us—no, five of us—but we didn't care. It was fab that someone was paying us to have a ball.

Cilla Black: In and around Liverpool the Beatles weren't nothing special. I got up and sang at the Cavern with the Beatles. They had previously done Hamburg, where they went as a struggling band but came back just so experienced. But they weren't the best band in Liverpool. I was a guest singer with the bigger band in Liverpool, Rory Storm & the Hurricanes. Ringo was their drummer.

There was millions of bands in Liverpool and Manchester and a lot of them were really, really good. We were very insular up there and we were very, sort of, arrogant, ya' know: "Who needs London 'cause we've got our own thing here."

Peter Noone [singer/songwriter, Herman's Hermits]: I was at Manchester School of Music—night school. My dad was in a band. A forties Royal Air Force band. Hughie Gibb, who was the Bee Gees' dad, was in the band. I was emulating Buddy Holly and the Everly Brothers. I had these big horn-rimmed glasses and I used to put them on when we did the Buddy Holly song. I thought just wearing glasses made you look like Buddy Holly, which is really bizarre. I was fifteen. We were already in loads of bands. I was in the Cyclones, and there was a band called the Heartbeats, and one night their singer didn't show up. So they said, "Peter Noone is a singer. He can do it." To be a singer in those days all you needed to do was to know the words to a load of songs.

We were doing pubs, clubs, and bar mitzvahs. There were loads of them and lots of places to play. There was a wave of energy. Everyone was too young to drink, but everyone smoked cigarettes and drank cups of tea. We had a business card that said "Sherman & the Hermits" because the guy who printed the card spelt it wrong. It said "weddings, bar mitzvahs, and clubs." My number was on the card because my family was the only one who had a phone.

I was at school and I knew more about music than my teacher because my family were interested in music. And I knew all the operas. At night school they had all these rehearsal rooms. One time I was in there and they were playing a Chuck Berry song on acoustic guitar. "What is *this*?" I thought. I played the piano, but the guitar changed everything. The piano was a chore. Your mum wanted you to play the piano. Sit up straight and all that stuff.

Picking up a guitar was certainly a passport for picking up girls but it wasn't why I did it. That was total bullshit for me. I'm sure guitarists got laid more because they were in a band but I liked girls older than me. That was a tough one. Twenty-one-year-old girls don't want sixteen-year-old boyfriends.

I remember this girl playing Joan Baez. Boring! What is it about? Everyone was being introduced to new music. Mine was all white. It was a big adventure for kids; there were all sorts of influences.

Georgie Fame: In 1962, I'd been working in the Flamingo in London. I never got a break until finally my manager sent me on a week's holiday. I went back to Lancashire to my mum, and the guy I used to play with in a local band from the factory said, "Come out for a pint [a beer] tonight, there's a band playing and they're making a bit of noise."

We went to our local dance hall and sat in the gallery in the back and all the young girls were screaming. The Beatles were onstage. All the kids were going bananas. They still hadn't had a hit at this time and were still looking for a recording contract.

Peter Brown: They used to come into my shop—John, Paul, and George—to listen to records, because in those days you had record booths, and they couldn't afford to buy the records so they would come in to listen to whatever was new from America.

So they would come into my shop. We found out they were performing at the Cavern down the street. Brian went and saw them and told me at dinner, "I think I am going to manage them."

Cilla Black: They looked great and different. They looked sexy. They had everything that a teenage person wanted, and . . . there was a choice—four of them!

Peter Brown: Cilla says that she remembers me as this guy who ran the record shop. According to her, I sort of told her to piss off because she also wanted to listen to records, but that's a story I don't remember.

Brian obviously saw something in the Beatles. After all, Brian did know about music because we were running record stores; we specialized in the fact that, if you came in and asked for a record we would get it for you within twenty-four hours, that kind of thing, and that didn't happen in those days.

So we knew all about Motown, which was emerging, and rock and roll, and he really thought the Beatles had something that was unique, special. I think he also loved their attitude—ya' know, smart-asses. But in a Liverpool sense. And you know enough about Liverpool, probably, to know they specialize in being prickly, and we knew the humor.

Cilla Black: When Brian saw the Beatles in 1962 he asked John Lennon, "Is there anybody else that you recommend, any other bands?" So John said, "Oh, there's Billy J. Kramer & the Dakotas, the Foremost, Gerry Marsden, Gerry & the Pacemakers, the list goes on." And Brian said, "Any girls?"

"Yeah, there's Cilla." And that's when Brian approached me.

I was closest to Ringo, and I said, "Thank you so much for recommending me to Brian Epstein. He said, "T'wasn't me, I didn't recommend ya'." He was more or less saying, "I'm the new kid on the block, I couldn't do that." And I said, "Well, who did then?" He said it was John.

I did my audition for Brian with the Beatles, but not in the Cavern. It was in a ballroom in Birkenhead, across the water, across the Mersey.

I was eighteen. Brian didn't like me. I was terrible. I was singing in John's key. I did Sam Cooke's version of "Summertime" and it was too high for me and I probably was very nervous. I literally walked offstage and got the next ferry home. I didn't even bother to wait. I knew I was dreadful. But I still had faith in myself. I knew I would make it one day with or without Brian Epstein, that's how arrogant and confident I was. It was still 1962. The Beatles were only known in Liverpool. Liverpool was very insulated; it was not London.

Peter Brown: Brian thought that because we had very successful record shops we were important to the record companies. We were probably one of the very biggest record buyers and he thought that would have some influence on getting them a deal, which turned out not to be true. Every time he took the train to London to see EMI or Decca or Pye, he was coming back unsuccessful.

They would wait for him at the station—George, John, and Paul, anyway—and I would usually end up having dinner with him when he came back. And it was all rather depressing, really. I was slightly ambivalent because I wasn't sure Brian was right about the whole thing.

I was working hard running two shops. Somebody had to order the records, had to supervise the sales, the budgets, and all those kinds of things, and meanwhile Brian was going off, driving them to the next gig. I only really knew when we had our dinners that it wasn't coming together, getting a record contract. The London record companies didn't get the music.

When George Martin actually signed to produce them, in 1962 [*Martin had at first decided the group wasn't promising*], it was when they first went in to the studio and George Martin said that Pete Best, the drummer, wasn't good enough. That's when Ringo was brought in.

Cilla Black: First of all you fancied Paul, then you fancied George, then you fancied John, and then your last resort was Ringo. And who'd have thought today he'd turn out the cute one? I think he looks really great. I saw him the other week and my god he looks great.

Peter Brown: The band really respected Brian. He was knowledgeable. He knew about music. He had access to important people. I think they liked him. He was certainly a very honest person. He was an authority figure as much as they allowed him to be, but of course that was the Liverpool thing, "don't fuck me around" kind of attitude. I think that there is no question that John was undoubtedly the leader of the group and knew that Brian was attracted to him and [that] he could influence Brian's decisions.

Paul was equally savvy in a much more charming way, and he

chose to play the charming one, whereas John was playing the one with the finger. It worked for them both. George, I always felt, 'cause he was the kid, was always not respected as much as the others; there was always complaining like "what about me and Ringo?"

Terry O'Neill: I was really well paid by my newspaper, getting into the music and club scene in between photographing Winston Churchill coming out of hospital or JFK on his way to Berlin—news photos. In those days you really were only as good as your next story, so I was buzzing around everywhere. I'd deliver my film to the picture editor and be off again looking for the next job—sometimes seven or eight every day. You handed over your negatives and never gave them a second's thought. The next job was how you made your money. I can't imagine how many amazing shots from that era have been lost because we never dreamed our backlist would be worth money one day.

It was my newspaper editor's idea that I photographed the young people who were starting to make waves. I was all over town looking and there was this thing happening, a buzz on the street, things seemed to be changing: music, the fashion, young people everywhere having a good time, upsetting the older generation. It was news, and I was in the right place at the right time with the right attitude. I was also the only young photographer. All the others were old guys who just scoffed at the idea of photographing the kids who were into music and fashion and just making people sit up and take notice by doing their own thing. To them, news was air crashes and bank robberies and earthquakes.

I had this idea of photographing this young band I'd heard of. I knew a lot of the bands and the club scene in London. But this one was down in London from Liverpool recording at Abbey Road a single and an album, *Please Please Me*, with George Martin. I think that was late 1962. I photographed them in the studio with George. It was unionized then; technicians in brown work coats, shirts, and ties who had to be paid overtime and took tea breaks. During one of those union breaks, I took the Beatles out back in the yard for a portrait. John seemed to be the important figure in the band, but in the picture Paul's on his shoulder.

Strangely, my picture editor held on to the photo for weeks and then he put it on the front page one day when nothing was happening.

Mike Pemberton [nightclub owner and leisure industry entrepreneur]: I was only twenty in 1963 but I already had my own nightclub in Sunderland, near Newcastle. It was called Club 11. Helen Shapiro was this huge young singing star at the time and she was touring, appearing at the Sunderland Empire in February. After the show she came to the club with this band which was supporting her tour called the Beatles. I turned them away because they were wearing leather jackets and they weren't wearing ties, and being a respectable dive I insisted men wore ties. They hit number one with the single "Please Please Me" two weeks later.

Keith Richards: At that particular time, all the Stones wanted to do was turn people on to this incredible electric blues music from Chicago, and we were a poor approximation of what was really happening. But since nobody was doing it, our attitude was, "Everybody, you should hear this and then maybe you will listen to the real cats like Muddy Waters and Howlin' Wolf, all of our heroes."

Bill Wyman: After I joined the Stones we did some gigs and I fitted in well. But it cost me more money to come into London on the train and then the bus to rehearse or play a gig than what I got paid. But I didn't do it for the money. I got off on it. It was really exciting.

We didn't even dream of making a record. It was so far away as a possibility it didn't even occur to you. We couldn't imagine being on TV or radio, and to think of going to America was pie in the sky. You did it because you liked to play the music. You got fuck-all money. Five shillings. I was working all day; so was Charlie Watts. Mick was at the

London School of Economics, and the other two were layabouts. They were starving, living off Mick's student grant.

Eric Clapton: Keith and the Stones were just in front of me in terms of age and experience. I would go and see them when they were fledglings—when the band wasn't tightened down and was just forming their identities. I spent a lot of time with them when they had their flat in Edith Road in West London, and I would play and sing with them. It was unbelievably disgusting. They never changed the sheets. I thought that was quite civilized, really. Working-class boys didn't grow up to look after themselves.

Georgie Fame: We would play in a club around London or an American base just outside and then we'd throw all the gear into the van at eleven at night and drive back to London and start the all-night sessions. There'd be a jazz band onstage until we arrived. We'd get three pounds a night. We were doing ten gigs a week and getting thirty pounds a week.

We were playing all the time, listening to all the music and rehearsing all week, and we were doing so many sets. Then we'd go down to the Flamingo and do two sets there. But we never repeated ourselves.

After the Flamingo you might stay up for an hour or two and have a glass of wine or bourbon with the GI's and then sleep till three in the afternoon. We didn't need to go to work till seven in the evening.

As a band you were all in it together. We had rented accommodation in Earls Court in West London. There were a couple of working girls there, too. Many times after the Flamingo and at six in the morning we couldn't get a cab and we'd have to walk it back home.

There were very few late-night eateries around. We met the Stones in the Northern Egg or something. That was the only place in West London, unless you went out to the airport, where you could get a cup of coffee.

There were four or five of us living in the same place. It was a ter-
raced house—a few rooms with single beds and hookers living upstairs, and we'd play records. We were so obsessed about the music we
used to walk around talking about music. Our landlords moved us to
Russell Road opposite Olympia [*an exhibition hall*]. An awful, freez-
ing, damp basement.

We came back after the Flamingo one night to our place on Russell Road and there was someone hammering on the door, and the
landlord came in and moved us to Ladbroke Grove. We had to walk
over there. We had very little stuff, some small suitcases and a record
player and all our shit had just been thrown into the new apartment.
That was our next flat for a few months.

Eric Clapton: I was just getting thrown out of Kingston Art. I was
seventeen, playing gigs sometimes. There was a very strong underground. I was more underground. I identified with the mentality of
the Stones or Brian Auger or Georgie Fame and liked it.

Sir Alan Parker: I used to buy my records at Al's Records in Cross
Street, the first record shop in Islington in North London. It was
Buddy Holly and the Everly Brothers. The Tottenham Royal, a mecca
ballroom, was the dance hall of choice—a short bus ride from Islington. There was also the Lyceum in the Strand, but there were always
stupid fights breaking out and it became tiresome as they stopped
the music and we all crouched down one end as the nut cases in their
winklepicker shoes kicked the shit out of one another.

The haircut of choice was a "Perry Como" at the Angel—and further down Essex Road, the same haircut was called a "college boy."
I was mostly buying my own clothes, as I always had a Saturday job
all through my schooldays. I used to work in Jolly's Cooked Meats in
Camden Town. I was in charge of the cooked chicken spit. When I got
home I would scrub away in the bath. Once, at the Tottenham Royal,

whilst dancing with a particularly pretty girl, she suddenly said, "Cor, you don't half smell of chickens."

When I started work I had my first suit made by a tailor in Dalston. "Modernist" was the fashion of the day: short jackets and pointed shoes. I chose a rough black tweed material and insisted on trousers, too. The material was so rough it used to rub the skin of my knees, so I had to wear pajama bottoms underneath so that it didn't chafe.

At the Tottenham Royal we had a live resident band, the Dave Clark Five, on a Saturday. It was odd that the band was named after the drummer. The lead singer was Mike Smith on keyboards. But Dave Clark was also the manager.

Terry O'Neill: London and the suburbs were alive with clubs and dance halls and pubs given over to music. All the emerging bands were cutting their teeth in these basements and backrooms in pubs in front of fifty or a hundred kids. And of course, the boys with the guitars got a lot of attention from the girls, which would upset their boyfriends, so sometimes the bands had to make a run for it out the back door.

Acts like Rod Stewart and Long John Baldry, Jimmy Page—who went on to found Led Zeppelin—playing with the Crusaders, they all did their apprenticeship in these pubs and clubs, and the good ones also got to go and play at the American Air Force bases in Britain, and that was a big influence on them because they were playing to a musically educated audience. A lot of our young bands would hear the records the American airmen were putting on jukeboxes at the bases and they were amazing records you didn't hear in the UK. The airmen would want the bands to play these songs, and that's how a lot of rhythm and blues started in England. I think we were all influenced by America in one way or another—the music, the movies, the cars, the prosperity—we wanted a piece of all that but we wanted to do it our way, in our own style.

Every kid was looking to break the mold in one way or another. It wasn't just music, but art. I'd wanted to be a jazz drummer and ended up learning how to use a camera at art school two days a week. It was in Ealing, just 'round the corner from the club where the Stones and Eric Clapton and all our great bands used to play. At art school you'd find people aged sixteen to eighteen who were just killing time before they had to get a proper job, but somehow the anarchic atmosphere let them experiment and explore themselves and their own interests. You could go to an art school and play guitar for two years—nobody stopped you.

Sir Alan Parker: I went to a great grammar school. I was very good at art and English but we were all being readied for the new "technological age" and so I'd ended up doing pure and applied mathematics and physics. I don't regret not going to university but I would have liked to have gone to art school, where everything interesting seemed to be emanating from. Almost everyone I knew who was vaguely interesting had gone to art school. The art schools had grown up in the fifties as a place for kids who couldn't or wouldn't go to university but didn't want a boring career. They could choose two years in art school to find their feet.

Allen Jones: There was an art exhibition specifically for art students, the Young Contemporaries. It was run by the students from the three major colleges and the work was selected by a high-powered group of critics and students.

The *Young Contemporaries* exhibit was the first manifestation of what is now called pop art in the UK. And you started to realize that something was going on that had nothing to do with art education. [*The* Young Contemporaries *exhibit showed Jones, Hockney, Kitaj, Derek Boshier, Peter Phillips, and Peter Blake.*]

We used to work late, as we were very enthusiastic. We'd go into the senior common room and use their kettle. Hockney would always read the staff mail. But we were all running away from the established art scene. We were all called together and read the riot act: *"Experimentation is for the final year. In your first year you need to focus on nature and life drawing."*

At the end of the summer term the school said, "We are going to make an example and assert our authority," and the example happened to be me. I was thrown out of the Royal College.

Mandy Rice-Davies: We were the first generation of girls who could leave home before getting married. We were a power to reckon with because it was so easy to get a job. Everyone had a job. I was eighteen in '63. I'd been in London about two years. I'd left home in Birmingham at sixteen. You could get off a train and get a job the same day and, if you didn't like it, leave and get another job. And you could rent an apartment for a couple of pounds a week.

The nicer apartment you moved into, the less you ate. Teenagers for the first time in history had power. There were two million of us. It was buying power—money. That's all it was. We never had it so good. It was about indulging ourselves and having a good time.

Clothes were very important. Mary Quant established herself. It was the first time you could buy clothes that weren't your mother's clothes. Teenagers were having a ball everywhere. I was doing TV ads for toothpaste or promoting stuff.

Jackie Collins: From the age of fifteen I'd felt enormous freedom. Being brought up in a family with famous people coming in and out meant I've never been intimidated by anyone. I always felt I was ahead of the game. I never had any fear; I just plunged ahead. I've never seen a shrink.

I got married at a very early age, so I was quite sedate by the time the sixties were happening. But I could see what was going on [in London]. Suddenly one could wear what one wanted, one could do whatever one wanted, screw whomever one wanted.

Pattie Boyd: Modeling wasn't really considered a career. It was something to do. A career would be working in an office. I had fallen into it. I just thought it was fun. It was a means for me to pay rent until I got married. However, the photographers would take three months to pay us, so we would have to borrow from the agency and I always ended up owing them money.

We all wanted to be thin, to look great in the new clothes. *Anorexia* and *bulimia* were words that didn't exist. The doctor would give us "slimming pills" [*speed*] if we wanted them. And there were biscuits that you could buy in the supermarket that would make you feel full. Yeah, I would eat these little biscuits, then I wouldn't have to eat all day.

Peter Frampton: I was only at the art school with George Underwood and Davey [Bowie] for a year because there were a couple of kids that didn't like my dad and he didn't like them. He was a very well-loved teacher but they took it out on me. By that time I was thirteen and academically I was better. I went to the grammar school but I missed the freedom of the technical school where you could do all the creative things.

My parents said, "This guitar lark is getting serious. You need to start thinking about music college." I started going to a lady in Bromley South and she taught classical guitar. I did that for four years. I pretty much hated it but it taught me to read music.

Georgie Fame: We had a little bit of money on the side. Friday was payday and I'd always bump into Charlie Watts on payday. Just down Shaftesbury Avenue there was a shop called Cecil Gee [where] you could buy button-down collars, Ivy League jackets, and we'd spend a little money and buy things. Otherwise, we spent money on rent, food, and cabs. We'd share a cab, three or four of us. Or we'd walk it back all the way. Later on when we had hit records we'd splurge on unnecessary baubles. I've got an old jacket that Michael Fish made for Mick Jagger, but he rejected it and I bought it. Horrible jacket.

Hilton Valentine: Chas Chandler of another Newcastle band, the Alan Price Combo, came and saw the Wildcats, and at the end he said to me, "How serious are you?" and "Would you go to London?" I said, "Where's my ticket?"

The Wildcats and Alan Price Combo had a different following. The Wildcats were playing John Lee Hooker, Memphis Slim, and Muddy Waters. We were a cult band for the northeast. They were billed as rhythm and blues. And they appeared at the Club-A-Go-Go, which was posh compared to the workingmen's clubs we were playing.

We were getting between two pounds and five pounds a gig and they'd be getting fifteen pounds a week. So I joined the Alan Price Combo, and it became the Animals. It was the end of 1962.

Terry O'Neill: I didn't stray far from the jazz clubs and the rhythm-and-blues scene. The dance halls didn't interest me, but for bands like the Dave Clark Five that wanted to make good money, you had to play them. The Tottenham Royal was one of many in London and around the country, ballroom dancing halls where their moms and dads used to dance. Halls were suddenly full of two or three thousand kids out on a Saturday night. The ballrooms nationally could entertain over a million paying kids a week.

They needed hundreds of bands to draw the crowds to all these dance halls, and the bands would earn typically between fifteen and twenty-five pounds. Imagine doing three hours a night two or three times a week—a band gets really good learning not just how to play a song but also how to play the audience, too, and keep it on its toes.

Hilton Valentine: I'd given up the job as a machinist on doctor's orders. We were earning—I was playing with four or five different bands before I joined Alan Price—and it was cash. I earned the same amount of money playing with the bands as [I was] earning in the factory. I didn't think it would last. I was young. It was exciting and I wanted to do it. And I could always get a proper job later.

There was no drugs or groupies then, but there was beer—any beer. A crate of beer and a pack of cards and a sleep on the road: touring. They called me the "human time machine." I would get in the van and fall asleep and sleep until we arrived at the gig. I could sleep anywhere and just wake up ready to go. At this time there was no leader of the band. Eric Burdon was the front. Pricey would do the money—he was the taxman. It was kind of his band—the Alan Price Combo. But no one felt ownership. No one bossed anyone around.

Chrissie Most: We'd been touring South Africa for over a year. Mickie went to a little record company which recorded African music, and that's how he learned to be a producer. He went to the studio and cut the record. We did really well. We made eleven number one hit records and toured the whole country. They crowned him the king of rock and roll of South Africa. We thought of going to Rhodesia. We got there and I called a press conference. I was eighteen.

We got great publicity. We booked the halls, and we got to Bulawayo, to the gig, and there was a riot. The army came in, but they didn't stop it. They had to let it go ahead.

The soldiers were really jealous of Mickie because he was loved by all the girls. There was this rumor that he was going to get beaten up by some of them. So we invited the army's head guy as our guest and we sat him at the front where he was in full view of all the soldiers. We had to duck and dive a lot. Things went wrong. We nearly went over a cliff in Mozambique. I preferred him to play fast numbers, not ballads, because the crowd danced and got hot and we sold more drinks.

By then my parents knew they couldn't stop us, and we'd got married and were living in a flat, and we were so successful Mickie bought a Porsche. Then I got pregnant. It was 1962—time to go back to London.

But Mickie made a big mistake. He was besotted with Gene Vincent and wanted Gene to headline on our farewell tour in South Africa, and we got hold of Sharon Osbourne's father, Don Arden, who managed Gene. We had all our money to come back to England. But Gene Vincent and the tour cost us a fortune on airfares and hotels and we did all our money in. Gene Vincent didn't make a scrap of difference to the ticket sales. Not one extra ticket sold.

Back in London we were broke and had this little flat in North London. It cost us seven guineas a week, no hot water. It was a dump. Don Arden had said to me, "When you get to London, call me. I'm doing these package tours and I'll book Mickie."

Eric Clapton: In 1963 we just closed the door of what went before, like Shirley Bassey or Matt Monro, the sort of postwar pop idol. They were all Frank Sinatra imitations.

When we came along we kind of did a punk thing. The idea of punk, my interpretation, is dynamic, as it let us clear the decks and start all over again. We kind of did that in 1963, but not in a destructive way. We just shut it down [middle-of-the-road pop music]; we ignored it and went straight for Chicago blues and black rock and roll. That was the order of the day. I was listening to Muddy Waters, Chuck Berry—same as Keith. We had a small handful of idols. They were all based in Chicago.

Allen Jones: I was offered a contract in a gallery, which was pretty unusual. So after my first exhibition things happened quickly. The artists began to be seen, as a pop thing, as an entity. But it wasn't seen as a pathway to riches. You hoped it was a pathway to a major museum show and [that] you'd get to sit at the top table.

At that moment my printer, Peter Cochrane, came back with pop art bought in America. We sat in some splendid house—much wealthier than I was used to. Peter Blake was there, Derek Boshier, Peter Phillips, and Hockney, and Kitaj were all there passing 'round these black-and-white photographs. There was a Lichtenstein, a canvas with a pedal can [foot-operated garbage can] with the foot up, and the next picture the foot down.

It was such a release. One shouldn't be constrained by what's right or wrong. It was unbridled. It was the absolute first time; we were all absorbing this. It opened up my horizons. There is no doubt that the only inhibition one had was one's own limits.

Vidal Sassoon: People could get a job anywhere. Good-paying jobs. Once people have an income they have a certain amount of power, and if you have hundreds of thousands of young people with the power to spend money *how* they wanted to spend it and not how Mummy wants, they have the power to change things.

Andrew Loog Oldham [pioneering music industry manager who discovered the Rolling Stones]: It wasn't the Beatles and it wasn't the Rolling Stones, it was Vidal Sassoon, it was Mary Quant, David Bailey, the models, they were the start of it.

Felicity Green [fashion editor]: I joined *The Daily Mirror* in 1961. It was very influential, a very important paper. It sold five million copies to mainly working-class families. I found a place in the paper for fashion, which was new.

My instinct was we needed pictures. One picture is worth a thousand words. In 1962 I introduced photographers like John French, David Bailey, and Terry O'Neill. Before Terry and his like, photographers did football and film stars. What I did was employ fashion photographers for a national newspaper. The reproduction quality was revolutionary. Readers loved it. It had an aesthetic quality that had never been seen before.

Terry O'Neill was one of the first, and we got on like twins. He talked my language and I talked his. The photographers took a particular type of picture, specially sexy but acceptable, never an inch beyond good taste, but it was sexually exciting with beautiful girls.

Pattie Boyd: People started painting their houses and flats. There

was a burst of color, a burst of joy. Color is representative of emo-
tion and mood and I think that's what it was. One minute everything
was gray and the next it was color. It happened almost overnight. The
same with modeling.

Boys started growing their hair longer, and we all just started
wearing different clothes—more free, liberal clothes. Everything
suddenly became a little more sexy. You noticed in *Vogue* magazine
that the makeup was very different.

Mandy Rice-Davies: I came to London with a healthy libido—very
healthy. I was moving in fascinating circles: actors and gangsters and
peers of the realm. A social melting pot.

Whatever I did then is not a tenth of what happened after—not just
me but everybody else. By today's standards it was nothing. I moved
in with Peter [Rachman, the notorious slumlord] at the end of March
of '61 and didn't move out till October '62. I was with him the whole
time. I was his mistress. He was in his forties; I was seventeen. I was
a good-time girl in the real sense of the word. I loved it all. I was certainly not the only healthy young woman with a healthy libido. This
was the teenage party. It was what was happening.

Peter had nightclubs. At one, the Discotheque, above the Flamingo, you'd have the gangsters [the Krays], Julie Christie. I could
dance with Terence Stamp because he had dyed his hair blond for
a part [Billy Budd], and Peter didn't get jealous because he thought
Terry must be gay.

I was acting, dancing, and modeling. I did the Sammy Davis Jr.
show and remained friendly with him till the day he died. I did a
toothpaste ad. I worked for Robert Mitchum when he was in London
filming *The Longest Day* in 1962. My job was to turn up at the Savoy
Hotel at eight a.m., go out to Bond Street, and buy him a bottle of
scotch or two or three. Get him Wilkinson Sword razor blades, the
American version. And now and again go off in search of some pot.
The most important job was to sit in the suite and keep the door open,

and anyone passing by he liked the look of, he invited in. And once he'd had enough I had to get them out. Robert was a lovely man.

Johnny Gold: I have a friend, Monty Marks, who shared an apartment with a guy who made and lost and made millions again on the stock market. We played poker there every Sunday I was in London . . . , and we were playing cards with an American guy called Blackie Siegel and another, Oscar Lerman. Oscar came to London to get away from a girl and had ended up living here for twenty years.

Oscar had this club, the Ad Lib, which was the meeting place of all the young musicians, photographers, actors—they were all jack the lads. It was the most exciting place. And then one day Oscar said, "How would you like to be in this business? I'm opening another club." I thought it was a bullshit conversation because what did I know about clubs? But six weeks later I was looking at premises and suddenly I was signing documents and I was in the club business. We opened Dolly's.

Pattie Boyd: We started going out together, to bistros and cafés and clubs like Dolly's. A crowd of us: Ossie Clark, David Bailey, David Hockney, Jean Shrimpton. You could feel the permissiveness that was emerging, and I think you can see that in the fashion pages. Bailey started being more edgy with his photographs, more sexually daring. He would give you a come-on so you would feel great and sexy. And he was gorgeous.

It was like playtime, really. I had that sense of entitlement, that entitlement of youth, which is blind to other things.

In the fashion shoots, models looked more available and more friendly, more like the girl next door as opposed to models of the era before where they looked totally untouchable and very aristocratic, as though you would never meet them. This shift was more to do with girls that could be your friends, and girls from aristocratic families had to tone down that arrogant look.

When I first started modeling for David Bailey it was a bit scary because I knew that the women at *Vogue* were in love' with him. The editor of *Vogue*, Diana Vreeland, just thought he was fabulous. There had never been such a young photographer strutting around the corridors at *Vogue* with such arrogance, demanding and getting everything he wanted. It had never happened before. But I knew that he was quite shy really.

He was going out with Jean Shrimpton at that point, and we would go to a place called the Casserole on the Kings Road, and I remember one dinner, it was the first time I'd tried an avocado. It looked weird and tasted extraordinary. Bailey kept saying, "It's one of these new vegetables that will grow on you." Was it a new vegetable? In England it was.

Mary Quant: This mother brought a boy called Andrew Loog Oldham 'round to my shop. "I want you to employ him. He won't go to school and I don't know what to do. I can't make him and he wants to work for you. You have to employ him."

Andrew was a gawky thing. I said I didn't need him, but he said he'd do anything I wanted. Anything! And even though I never hired him, he showed up every morning. He worked for us for about two years. He ran about, fetched things. He'd do anything you asked him.

Andrew Loog Oldham: I worked for Mary Quant at the same time I worked for a jazz club in the evenings, and on Saturdays I worked at a really kind of nice mafia basement club called the Flamingo. My job was serving scotch in a Coke bottle because the club had no liquor license. I was the innocent-looking one, if the police came in.

Mary Quant: Andrew worked at one of the jazz places, and we had an arrangement with him. He'd ring us up when American jazz people would come to London and tell us to come and see them. There was a lot of excitement. It was a lovely time.

After about a year, eighteen months maybe, he wrote a letter that he posted from the airport on his way to France. He said, "Thanks very much, it's been great fun, and I see that I can now do all the jobs that you and Alexander can do, so I think it's time I left."

Andrew Loog Oldham: I kind of had my first nervous breakdown. It was too much—I mean, I was seventeen, with three jobs. It was too much, so I then went off to France.

I stayed in Cannes for eight months, begging on the Croisette from English tourists; it was very easy. Then I got involved in a kidnapping, which wasn't very helpful. Very Mickey Mouse—it wasn't dangerous. Somebody said to me, "Listen, this girl wants to be kidnapped," and it was like the gang who couldn't shoot straight. It all went terribly wrong, and it was funny.

So then I came back to England, and Mary Quant said, "I can't give you a job, Andrew. You just walked out. But I'll send you to someone who can," a guy who did the PR for the Queen's dressmaker, Norman Hartnell. He did Hardy Amies [couture fashion designer for Queen Elizabeth II] , he had a model agency as well, at the top of Beauchamp Place in Knightsbridge.

My job was basically delivering stuff to newspapers, you know, photos of models and things like that, and walking models' dogs, basically. I was a gofer. Then my mother said, "You ought to get a real job," so I went and worked for a man called Leslie Frewin. It's got to be, like, the spring or summer of '62, and this man was an industrial PR; he represented things like the British Menswear Guild.

I couldn't stand working for him, and when the office closed at six p.m., I started somehow getting pop music clients, and the first one was this really butch American dancer called Pepe. I can't really remember how I got it. But he was my first client. I was getting five pounds to publicize him—[back] then it was a great ride [gig].

I made a career out of going banging on people's doors when I wanted to meet them, like the guy who managed Shirley Bassey. I didn't get the job, but these people were so intrigued that somebody was fascinated by what they did so they let you in. This guy called Mark Wynter, who had been discovered by Lionel Bart, the guy who wrote *Oliver*, became my first real client. A bona fide singer with a recording contract, and he was about to have a hit, and I was doing his publicity. He had two hits, "Venus in Blue Jeans"—that would have been like September of '62— and then he had another one called "Go Away Little Girl."

I was suddenly now part of the club.

Felicity Green: Vidal and I became friends, and I featured his pictures in the *Daily Mirror*. We had a bond. We were all breaking the rules together and it gave you a very buzzy feeling. It was a time when London exploded. It exploded in every area. It was all youth-based; it started in London and spread all over the world. Mary Quant had arrived. She was queen of the whole scene. She made the clothes she wanted to wear. She opened one shop on the Kings Road and the press beat a path to her door. It was later called the "youthquake," and that was, frankly, exactly what it was.

Fashion is about life. Fashion affects people's lives. People can express their personality through their clothes. Before then you wore roughly what your mother wore. Then suddenly clothes were for you. It gave a sense of individualism. It made people feel good about themselves.

Barbara Hulanicki [fashion designer]: I was terribly style-conscious when I was at art school in Brighton. I would spend hours trying to find shoes like Audrey Hepburn wore, and I would buy clothes and cut them up. I was doing illustration at art school and left home as soon as I could. Moved to London, met my husband Fritz, and moved into this flat in Cromwell Road in West London at the start of '63.

Felicity Green: All the revolutionaries broke out of art school. This is where the energy and innovation and the courage came from. They were rebelling from the formulaic life. They didn't want to pick up where previous generations had left off. They wanted to turn a corner to go somewhere where no one had been before.

Terry O'Neill: I had this feeling that something special was happening and I'd decided I wanted to be the one to record it. Bailey and Jean Shrimpton were the toast of *Vogue* in 1963, from New York to Paris and London, so I photographed them at work and then photographed Jean in the Kings Road and on her parent's farm. Terry Stamp got Oscar nominated for *Billy Budd*, his first film. Michael Caine was making *Zulu*, his breakout film. The two lived together and we were all mates.

I photographed them, their girlfriends. In music, in fashion, in culture, films, writers, artists—you could be what you wanted to be. Nobody questioned it or asked for qualifications, they just let you do it.

I was trying to record this amazing change as a news story; there was a buzz, we didn't know what it was, and we didn't think it would last.

For us working-class lads it was amazing. Suddenly working-class boys like Caine, Stamp, Bailey, me even, were supercool. Posh birds wanted them. They had the pill, we had the accent. Sex didn't kill you in those days. Clubs were opening up, we working-class lads could go in them and mix with toffs [*upper-class men and women*], musicians— even royalty was rubbing shoulders with gangsters and guitarists.

Edina Ronay [actress]: I was at the Royal Academy of Dramatic Art in 1963. I'd made a few films. I was nineteen or twenty, still living at home, and dating Terry Stamp. It was all quite innocent. I was eighteen I think, he was absolutely beautiful, and I wasn't bad myself in those days. I was so used to people looking at me, but people would look at *him* instead of me!

Terry was a lovely guy. He was sharing a flat with Michael Caine, and we would go out with him and his girlfriend of the moment as a foursome.

I was very fond of Terry, and he became a bit like a brother to me. Unbeknownst to me Michael had taken a shine to me. He definitely wasn't my type—sort of blond hair, blond eyelashes, pink face, and very tall. After Terry, I had my first serious relationship with a very nice French guy, and that was clearly never gonna work out because he lived in Paris and I lived in London. It was very tearful when we broke up.

I remember going to a party—it was Terry's brother, Chris Stamp's party, who managed the Who. He was a really good-looking guy, and to be honest, even sexier than Terry—very hip and cool and rock-and-roll. And there was Michael Caine, who made a beeline for me. He was broke, completely broke. He actually said he hadn't dared to ask me out because he couldn't afford to pay for dinner. I remember he picked me up from RADA one day, and he had big holes in his sweater. Terry was doing *Billy Budd* so Terry was making good money. But Terry really admired Michael. While I was with him he got *Zulu*; that was the big break for him.

We would go to restaurants or clubs and the newspapers started talking about us as the "it crowd." At that point, it was the Pickwick, the Ad Lib, or Dolly's. We used to walk in and stop the crowd. I remember once in the Pickwick Club with Joan Collins and she said, "We won't smile because we don't want wrinkles," and we would talk in a way so we wouldn't smile.

Jackie Collins: London started the whole revolution. The music and fashion was an eruption of energy, but 1963 is just a blur to me. I didn't feel a part of that. My first husband [Wallace Austin] was in a psychiatric hospital. The thing I remember clearly about 1963 is my husband's psychiatrist put him on methadrine and that made him an addict. He was bipolar, but they didn't know what bipolar was, then—they thought it was depression and put him in a psychiatric ward. It was scary. He'd hide the drugs—under the tiles in the bathroom—and I would spend my life being a detective searching for them because I had a young child in the house.

I remember walking into the doctor's waiting room one time and screaming, "If this doctor gives my husband any more drugs I'm going to the police."

My whole life then was back and forth to the hospital and my mother dying of cancer so I didn't really find myself part of the sixties until later. But in between my husband had this fabulous fashion business and I would model for him. I felt a little left out of it but I had a lot of friends, and sometimes I'd get a babysitter and go to the Ad Lib Club.

The Ad Lib Club was incredible. The Beatles, Stones, Clapton—everyone there was on the cusp of fame. It was a big club, and as you went up in the elevator you felt you were going to a big private party. It was genuinely fun. You went there to see your friends, and people could have sex with whomever, whenever they wanted—unless you were married with a child, like me. Eventually I got a divorce in 1964.

I guess when you're a young woman in the situation I was in, with a sick husband and a child, I had a lot of responsibility as a wife and a mother, but I had this other person inside of me. I was writing every day. It's always been my retreat, where I want to go and be. I'd start a book, write fifty pages, and then move on to another idea, and another.

I was interested in the sexual revolution. I loved the sixties because women came into their own and could do what they wanted sexually, which was one of the themes of *The World Is Full of Married Men* [*Collins's first novel*]. I was watching it all, taking it all in. In 1963 this was all brewing in what I was writing.

The pill changed a lot. It gave women freedom. The liberation spread right across the world. You'd pick up an American newspaper and it was talking about what was happening in London.

Johnny Gold: Dolly's was pure discotheque. It could only hold a hundred twenty people—it was small. But the energy was electric. Membership was five pounds a year. People weren't *wanting* to be part of a scene, they were [just] caught up in it. They created their own scene, their own way of life, their own fashions. Public school boys adopted Cockney accents because it was fashionable. I'd get stockbrokers in pin-striped suits, loosen their ties, then they'd take off their jackets and suspenders, and gradually they started coming in jeans and T-shirts.

We didn't have a dress code, and they'd be sitting next to someone on the board of a major company or a member of the royal family or the lads from the Beatles or the Stones—it quickly became classless. The snob value disappeared. High-society people wanted to be with the working classes because they were having the best time—working-class guys like Michael Caine, who was sharing a flat with Terry Stamp, and Albert Finney, young kids who were just breaking out. Oscar Lerman met his wife there. He saw her across the room and said to me, "I'm gonna marry that girl over there." It was Jackie Collins.

Two men, James Hanson and Gordon White, built the biggest conglomerate we'd ever seen in Britain. They were ex-army officers, and they both became lords. Gordon was engaged to Audrey Hepburn for a while, and they brought movie stars down. I remember one night getting roaring drunk with John Wayne.

We had to deal with a lot of villains, too. There was one who used to come in—a small guy—he was the most vicious bastard. The story was he was a hit man for one of the mobs. They used to say he wouldn't just shoot you, he'd empty the whole gun into you. Charming!

He only used to drink milk with brandy in it, and for some reason he took a shine to me—and he saved my life because the word was out on a Johnny Gould from Brighton and some people thought that was me. He talked to the right people and set them straight.

It was an unbelievable atmosphere, a melting pot. You just never knew who you'd meet or bump into—it was show time every night. At Dolly's I became friends with the Marquess of Tavistock, whose father was the Duke of Bedford. They had an amazing stately home, Woburn Abbey, and I'd drive there after the club closed and arrive at five in the morning. They sat in order of title, so he, Tavistock, would be at the head of the table, then there'd be a duke and a knight, and I said, "Where do I sit, in the toilet?" I would be with their racing manager, who was an anti-Semitic ass. I didn't feel awkward being in that environment; I didn't feel I shouldn't be there. That's what '63 was all about, but it couldn't have happened prior to the sixties.

Edina Ronay: I suppose I'd fall into the class of posh bird. My family was middle-class, living in Holland Park, London. My father was shocked when I brought this working-class, out-of-work Cockney actor home and was out of his comfort zone.

If I had not been an actor I would not have been involved with working-class people, I would have stayed in *my* comfort zone. I always thought they were very boring, these upper-class English guys who took me out. I was bored to hell. The working-class boys were interesting.

Michael Caine had had this real problem as an actor: he couldn't get the posh parts, and the posh parts are what it was all about. In fact, it was a very strange casting that they let him play an officer in *Zulu*, and it definitely was his making. He was probably the most ambitious person I have ever met in my life and he was gonna make it come what may. At the same time there were people like Bailey around. In fact, Jean Shrimpton became a very good friend of mine because then Terry Stamp was dating her after Bailey. So there was definitely this working-class thing happening, but it's odd because for those boys, certainly Michael, smoking a joint would definitely be out of the question, and getting drunk and all that sort of thing, because they were all sort of straitlaced.

Barbara Hulanicki: The working-class had a voice. Everyone was flocking to London, and by then my husband decided we should aim our price to hit that market. We needed a name for the business, and we called it Biba. I wanted something feminine, and it was my sister's nickname. It didn't mean anything. It was neutral. So we showed this name around and this chap said that it sounded like the name for a cleaning lady's daughter. And that was where we wanted to be.

We began with mail order and a catalogue through word of mouth. They would talk about ordering these clothes from the catalogue. We had to pre-manufacture everything, and it was a nightmare. We were learning as we went along.

Pattie Boyd: I remember somebody told me that there was this fantastic little shop called Biba, in Abingdon Road, it was just one shop, one space, and the clothes were just fabulous. The colors were so completely different to what Mary Quant was doing, Mary's were block colors and very geometric in design. What Barbara was doing was colors in plum and sage greens—muddy colors.

Jackie Collins: I remember this: everyone wanted a Mary Quant miniskirt and Biba's white boots.

Sir Alan Parker: I was nineteen in 1963, a junior copywriter in advertising at the Maxwell Clarke agency and living at home, with my parents, in a council flat in the first flats built after the war. I was earning ten quid a week. My dad insisted I handed over one pound ten shillings to my mother. He was very strict about it, except she secretly always stuffed it back in my jacket pocket when he wasn't looking.

My job was "copy forwarding," and I took the proofs of the ads around to be approved by each department. I befriended the copywriters and the "visualizer" [*Gray Jolliffe, humorist, illustrator, and cartoonist*], who used to give me ads to write at night. They used to mark them "five out of ten—must try harder." Eventually they persuaded the boss to take me on as the junior copywriter at twelve pounds a week.

Meeting Gray was like a crash course in art. He opened my eyes to everything visual, from Cartier-Bresson to Magritte to George Lois. Suddenly the world was full of images—perhaps this was new, or maybe they had been there all along and I just hadn't seen them!

We did five ads a day, and soon I had a portfolio that could fill a medium-sized suitcase. When I went for the interview at the new U.S. hotshot agency, PKL [*Papert Koenig Lois*], the copy chief, Peter Mayle [*later the author of* A Year in Provence], was impressed by the quantity of ads, if not the quality.

"How much do you want?" he said. "Thirteen," I said, meaning thirteen pounds a week. "The job pays fifteen," he said. I accepted. When I got my first paycheck I was amazed. I meant fifteen pounds a week, and he meant fifteen hundred pounds a year!

Terry O'Neill: Two years maybe, tops, is what we figured. We'd have fun, we'd have a laugh, we'd milk it, and then we'd all have to settle down and get proper jobs in banks.

Time magazine didn't coin the phrase "swinging London" until 1966, when they said Jean was the face of the sixties. They were three years late. Diana Vreeland called it a "youthquake"—and Britain in 1963 was the epicenter of it.

Sir Frank Lowe: Nineteen sixty-three was a defining year for me: leaving America, dodging the draft and not going to Vietnam, and coming back here. The whole thing with Biba and Barbara Hulanicki and Mary Quant and Jean Shrimpton, the whole business was just lifting off. I had a flat just off the Cromwell Road and I worked with a wonderful art director who said, "Come on, you have to come to CDP [*Collett Dickenson Pearce & Partners*]. So I went to CDP and there was, of course, David Puttnam, Alan Parker, and Ridley Scott doing the ads.

I left a country that seemed dead on its knees and I came back to a country that seemed exciting. It was a really curious thing what happened. Advertising was the best fun you could have with your clothes on. You could walk into a restaurant and you could know quite a lot of people, and there was no sense of "I'm famous, you're famous" and "I'm important and you are important." It was a very special time.

Felicity Green: There were shops opening that echoed what Mary Quant was doing. Young people could buy clothes that they'd never seen before and that had never been available to them before. There were other designers coming in on the wave of Mary. A whole lot of young designers were coming in and opening shops.

Mary's first shop was in Chelsea, but suddenly there was Carnaby Street. Shop after shop. And of course there was music, and it created this whole atmosphere. We went to listen to music. It was so energizing and stimulating. Everything was directed at youth, which the older generation either went along with and enjoyed themselves or said, "This is dreadful and England will never be the same again and they will all go to hell in a handcart."

Barbara Hulanicki: Fashion was for older people. It was important to buy two good things and wear them for one season. There was no turnover at all. Now the prices went down. Now they wanted something new every week to go dancing in—throwaway clothes. The baby boomers were now earning money so they had, say, eight pounds a week, and they wanted to spend it. First thing was they left home and got a bed-sit for three pounds. Spent no money on food. It was all about clothes. Young girls—and they were very young, fifteen and sixteen—were very rebellious. Anything goes.

Everything was for the young: very skinny and short. They had their own money, they didn't live at home, and there was no dad saying, "What are you doing in that top?"

Edina Ronay: I did shop at Mary Quant first, but she was very, very expensive. It was really very high-quality stuff. But Biba was a revolution, very trendy and sort of the right stuff at unbelievably silly prices, so she was the first one who did that diffusion fashion. Barbara Hulanicki should take a lot of the credit.

Sir Alan Parker: Girls were about relentless chasing and unfathomable optimism, mostly hardly justified by the results. The great badge of honor was when, after having a haircut, the barber would say, "Something for the weekend, sir?" Meaning a packet of three condoms. By the end of 1963 the Durex was out from under the counter and on top of it. This presaged a decade of unprecedented bonking, because everyone was at it.

Edina Ronay: Whenever you went out with a boy they always wanted to sleep with you. I just wished that you could go out with men and not have this dreadful threat that you have to sleep with them. They were very predatory all the time.

Lots of girls, and especially the guys, were sleeping around like crazy. Not me, though. And Michael [Caine] was always a gentleman. In many ways I admired them and felt a bit old-fashioned. I was very faithful, but there were many other girls who were not.

Johnny Gold: The whole of '63 was a feeling of liberation, but what surprised me most was the pill. Suddenly you could go to bed with girls and not be worried. You'd go out and expect to go to bed with a girl and more important, the girls expected it, too. They were determined to enjoy their sexual freedom. Taking away those inhibitions had a lot to do with the atmosphere because we felt we could let our hair down and not worry about consequences. We didn't register *any* fear. The worst thing that could happen was a dose of the clap, and a penicillin shot would sort that out.

Mandy Rice-Davies: I had to say I was married to get the pill. It was only available for married women. But there were a lot of women wearing brass rings. I was eighteen, a single girl, and having sex, and I was a threat.

4

ALCHEMY

"Around six-thirty or seven o'clock one morning I'm
hearing guitar strings. I get up in my dressing gown and
there he is, Bob Dylan, sitting at the top of the stairs,
singing to my two au pairs, 'Blowin' in the Wind'!"

PHILIP SAVILLE

*The revolution starts here. On the night of January 13, 1963—by accident,
not design—the coincidental appearance on Britain's two rival national
television networks by a largely unknown band called the Beatles and a
struggling musician called Bob Dylan sounded the alarm that, within
a year, would sweep away the ancient regime of class and culture on two
continents.*

Bill Wyman: Back then you had a choice. If you didn't have a guitar,
you made one. The same with a car. I made my first car; my dad and
uncle helped me. You had to do it yourself. Then I found all the blues
guitarists did the same thing.

Keith can't drive to save his life. Probably trashed eight of them.
Charlie can't drive. He puts his helmet on and gloves and the scarf
and the goggles and pretends to drive in his garage. But he has never
driven in his life.

We went to gigs in a van with no window, two of us up front and the rest in the back, in the dark, no windows. And when you went 'round the corners everything would fall on you. You'd end up sitting on the hot engine and burning your arse.

Keith Richards: Nobody knew at the time [that] 1963 was a pivotal year. There was a whiff in the air, and I think Terry O'Neill probably felt it as much as I did, but from different angles. Terry was behind the lens, everywhere, *always*.

Norman Jopling [British music critic]: Andrew Loog Oldham had become an established presence during '62 among the music business publicity agents, that fraternity of professionally amiable hustlers who enjoyed a symbiotic relationship—usually over a glass—with any journalist able to deliver column inches devoted to their respective clients.

Andrew Loog Oldham: I had from the age of eight or nine been fascinated by the words *produced by* or *so-and-so presents*—I'd seen these words on show posters on the subway in London and I was fascinated with Bob Dylan's manager, Albert Grossman. I'd heard of him; I don't know why.

A BBC producer had seen Dylan in Greenwich Village and thought, "Oh, I'd like to have him in a play" and brought him over to England before anybody knew who he was.

Phillip Saville [British actor, producer, and director]: I remembered being in the Mad Hatter [*a bar on West Fourth Street in New York City, where the* Freewheelin' *album cover would later be shot*], and there was a place there called something like Tony Pastor's Jazz Club, and it was down in the basement, of course, and I was listening to this man whose name was Zimmerman.

I sat there and I was totally, completely put off my lunch by this young man, by his delivery, the way he played. I just forgot to eat. Also, he had the harmonica strapped to his body and he was very good. Singing all these semi-political songs but in an old blues manner. Anyway, I just more or less introduced myself to him. Bobby hardly spoke a word; it was all in his music.

Months later, I was doing this play for the BBC. It was 1962. We were talking about this play about a man who was fed up with what was going on in the world, who lived in a rooming house and decided to go to his room and never come out. It was called *Mad House on Castle Street*, and in this there was the part of a rather equatious poet who was anarchic, and I remembered Bobby Zimmerman and thought, "That's the guy I want to play this poet!"

So I tracked him down and got through to Albert Grossman, and I told him what it was all about and he said, "Yeah, sure, I think Bob would love to do that." So we sent for him and we put them up at the Mayfair Hotel in London. This is fall 1962. So Bob, like most young people, liked to smoke stuff—cannabis—and because he was extremely anarchic, he used to sit in the lobby, late at night, put his feet up, and light up a joint. Of course, the hotel manager went berserk.

Johnny Gold: There was a lot of weed in London, and later LSD, but no cocaine. Some pills, and this awful stuff amyl nitrate, which was supposed to improve your orgasms, but it was the worst smell—like rotten eggs. I wouldn't have it in the club, and we tried to control it. I had an affair with an American jazz singer and she moved in with me, and she was on everything—I had no idea what was going on but I was stoned off my head for six months. It wasn't a drug culture in '63, the [actual] drug was having a good time—it was carefree.

Andrew Loog Oldham: You would only know who Dylan was if you read the *Melody Maker*. The first LP told you something [*Columbia had released Dylan's first album,* Bob Dylan, *in 1962, in the UK only*]—a big change, a possibility—was coming. It was not so much that the music was new, just that the conveyor spoke for us, not down to us, like the older folkies had. I found out where he was staying, knocked on the door, and they let me in.

Bob Dylan and Albert Grossman—Dylan would say later, "You could smell him coming." Well, that day they were smelling each other and I was smelling them. One rarely remembers the words or actuality of the great conversations that changed your life; it was a physical thing, a conspiracy, a marriage. Grossman was the husband, Dylan the young, all-knowing, attractive wife. Whatever the words were, they started and finished each other's sentences. They had their own code. Whatever it was [that they had], I wanted it. I was probably only there twenty minutes, but it was twenty minutes that changed my life. Because, when in April I met the Rolling Stones, I knew what it was I could have with them, because of those twenty minutes with Dylan and Albert.

I got the job as press agent because nobody in England knew who Bob Dylan was. What was he like? The same he is now actually, very noncommunicative. He already knew who he was. Later, much later in life, you realize that if they can't play with somebody, they'll play with their minds.

Philip Saville: We set up the first meeting, got all the rest of the cast, the heads of cameras, makeup, costume, lots of people calling themselves producers, and the writer of course. Anyway, we're having this reading and it's all going well, and it's coming to Bob, and everyone is turning saying, "Who's this young guy?" and suddenly he says, in front of everybody, "I can't say this stuff."

So I said, "Let's take a coffee break." He said he couldn't "say the stuff." Those are the actual words. There was nothing derogatory about it, he just said he couldn't do it. So we took Bobby aside and said, "You said you wanted to do it?" He said "'Well, I'm not an actor." I said, "Now you tell me!" He had no desire to be an actor. I mean, most people, if they're in any kind of business that does show business, they like the idea of being in front of the camera.

He was nineteen, twenty, he had lots of lines to say, and I don't know if it was the writer or me or mutually, but we said, "Why don't we make two parts, two friends who share a room like students, and we'll give all the words to one actor and Bob can play his stuff occasionally and say, "Oh, yeah." And there was a young actor called David Warner who was rising up the ladder at the Royal Shakespeare Company, very articulate, tall, gangly, so we rushed down, literally that afternoon, and told him about the story. He didn't know who Bob was but eventually they became very good friends.

Finally Bob was more or less asked to leave the Mayfair Hotel because of the pot. I had a biggish house in Hampstead, so I said, "Why don't you come and stay with us?" So he arrived with all his music stuff, and at that time I had two Spanish au pairs, because I had two very young children.

Around six-thirty, seven o'clock one morning, I'm hearing guitar strings. I get up in my dressing gown, wandering along the stairs, and there he is, sitting at the top of the stairs, playing his guitar, singing to my two au pairs, who were looking up from the bottom of the stairs, and guess what he was singing? "Blowin' in the Wind"!

I'd never heard the song; hardly anyone had heard that song. I was one of the chosen few, and afterwards, we were having breakfast, and I said, "I really want you to play that to open and close the play."

Norman Jopling: One dark weeknight evening I happened to bump into Andrew Loog Oldham on the way to EMI House in Manchester Square. As we approached EMI we saw to our amazement it was swarming with ecstatic, semi-hysterical girls. It seemed that the Beatles were there that evening. Neither Andrew nor I were visiting EMI in connection with the Beatles, but there was something slightly awesome about this spectacle. I'd seen plenty of crazy fans before, but this lot were different. There was a radiance about them. We stood and stared at the girls, then looked at each other. We knew instantly something magical was happening. A week or so later I heard Andrew was working as PR for Brian Epstein. He was that on the ball.

Anthony Calder [Rolling Stones publicist]: I met Andrew under a lamppost in Poland Street, Soho. We chatted and we agreed we should work together, and formed a publicity company. We were just the new kids on the block.

Back then they were all smoking weed. There was no hash. I was doing coke in '63. It was available but no one was interested then. There was a club, the Flamingo, the all-nighter, and lots of the acts who started there latter blossomed: Long John Baldry, Georgie Fame, Rod Stewart, Paul Jones of Manfred Mann.

People just came to us for publicity. There was no game plan. None. It was just exploding. If you wanted to do something you just did it. We were out to get publicity.

Andrew Loog Oldham: In January 1963 I was with Mark Wynter recording this television program, *Thank Your Lucky Stars*, and the Beatles were on it. [*It was recorded on Sunday, January 13, the night Dylan appeared on the BBC in* Mad House on Castle Street].

I went up to John Lennon and I said, "Who looks after you?" I walked out of the television studios representing the Beatles in London.

They were promoting *Please Please Me*. I got the job for the simple reason that Liverpool was a long way from London, people didn't make long-distance phone calls, so Brian Epstein liked the idea of having somebody doing the press for him in London.

You see, the great thing with all these people that I had going for me was that I had worked for Mary Quant, I knew how to get into Vogue House in Grosvenor Square. I said, "I probably can get you in a fashion magazine," and I had no idea whether I could or not. Turns out I could. I was bullshitting, bluffing, right?

Well, now I am doing the Beatles as well; I've done Bob Dylan, that was only ten days' work because nobody knew who he was. The only newspaper I could get him in was the *Melody Maker*.

Philip Saville: I thought of Bob as a poet, not a musician. To see this curly-headed kid saying these original things. He said a wonderful line to me: "Why don't you come on the road with me and discover what real life's about. Your intellect gets in the way."

When Bob was in rehearsal at the BBC there was an arts program called *Monitor*. I rang up the head person and said, "Look, I'm working with a young poet called Bob Dylan." It was run then by people who spoke with plums in their mouths [*an upper-class accent*]. "Oh, yes. I'll phone you back." Ten minutes later I get a call. "It's very nice of you to offer this but we've already made a documentary of Dylan." Years later I found out that the documentary they had made was about Dylan Thomas.

When I did that play it caused a tremendous stir because of Bob Dylan and because it was anti-authority. It was so unusual, different. Plays then were still stage plays. It was anti-establishment. It was an astonishing period. I took my wife to Mary Quant. I knew Vidal Sassoon and he cut my hair. I'd go in after hours with a bottle of champagne, and Terence Stamp and Michael Caine would be there.

There was an incredible surge of energy. The Beatles galvanized everyone, but particularly young people.

I remember interviewing a young actor barely twenty years old. He had very little experience. I asked him, "What do you do?" He said, "I'm young." That was the commodity—youth.

Terry O'Neill: The next day, after the Abbey Road portrait landed on the front page, we found out the newspaper had sold out. The editor was staggered—a pop group, not a plane crash, a war, or the Queen, but a pop group—had sold out the paper. Nobody had heard of them then but these good-looking boys with guitars must have touched a nerve—young people buying newspapers—who'd believe it? The editor called me in and said, "Go and get me some more." It wasn't difficult. Every kid seemed to want to be in a band.

Peter Frampton: I met another guy—Terry Nicholson—and we formed a band; we called it the True Beats, and it was basically the Shadows. I was so into Hank Marvin [*the lead guitarist of the Shadows, Britain's most successful band before the Beatles*] that I went to Woolworth's and got glasses and knocked the glass out [to look more like Hank Marvin]. I have a photo, I am the little kid in the middle—it's a classic shot. I'm thirteen. It's my second band already. Then the Beatles hit.

Sir Alan Parker: Nineteen sixty-three was all Beatles. From "Please, Please Me" [*the single released in February*] onwards, I was hooked and listened to little else unless the Fab Four recommended it. As they traveled the UK and then the U.S. in 1964 I would buy a newspaper every day after work to see what they were up to. We lapped up every dopey sentence.

Robert Christgau: I read about the Beatles before I heard them. There was a thing in the *Saturday Review* about this English pop group— and I saw this smart stuff. These people had been to art school and now they were in a rock-and-roll band, and I thought, "These are the sort of people I might like," but I hadn't heard [them]. I bought—and still own—"She Loves You." I heard it on the radio and I bought it in a record shop in '63. It remains my favorite Beatles song till this day. But it didn't generate a shift in my thinking because I was already there.

Norman Jopling: I enjoyed analyzing trends in pop music, and my theory about rhythm and blues in 1963 was simple, as were most of my pop theories. It went like this: plenty of British kids my age hadn't had enough rock and roll—proper rock and roll, that is; rhythm and blues fulfilled that need.

In the UK, rhythm and blues had extra cachet: it was black, it was hip, it was underground, it hadn't really been discovered. It could also be appropriated. And it was, from '63, big-time.

Georgie Fame: That was why Radio Caroline [pirate radio] started—because no one was giving this music any airplay at all. So Ronan O'Rahilly said, "I'll set up my own radio station."

When he first came down to the Flamingo he was fucking terrified—there were all these GI's, whisky joes [*drunks*], and prostitutes. A few white guys used to come down, aristocrats used to come down, but it was ninety percent black GI's.

Ronan came from a wealthy Irish family—he had these architectural drawings [of a former Danish ferry] and he said, "This is parked in a fjord in Norway. I'm going to tow if from the fjord. I'm going to park it in the North Sea and play all our favorite music because no one is playing it." And everyone thought he was a mad Irishman.

Ronan O'Rahilly [Irish entrepreneur, club owner, and founder of Radio Caroline]: I'd opened a club and called it the Scene because no one was playing the kind of music I liked. Eric Clapton, Georgie Fame, and, eventually, the Stones played there. I'd seen them at a club in Ealing and said, "You've got a band here. If you put in the rehearsal time and get serious, come and see me."

Brian Jones was a very, very good musician but Mick couldn't play a thing. He was just saying, "Look at me"—all the pouting and jumping. He seemed more interested in girls and just assumed everything would fall into his lap.

The suits were in charge of television and radio, the record labels owned the airtime: they decided what got played. They and the government were basically saying, "This is the way you do things—our way." They and the assholes from EMI and Decca thought they were in control. I wanted to smash them in the face. That's the Irish way.

I'd read engineering at Trinity in Dublin and I thought about a boat offshore—where they couldn't touch us—broadcasting my kind of music, mainly because of the clarity of the signal across the water.

Norman Jopling: So here was this huge reservoir of wonderful music waiting to be discovered, exploited, and copied, just like white musicians had done all century with music created by blacks.

Eric Stewart: At the end of 1962 my band, the Emperors of Rhythm, had fragmented. I remember the lead singer saying, "We are not going to make it." So the group split. I was down at the Oasis Club in Manchester. I was just hanging out. There were auditions. Record labels were there. That was why I had gone down there. I was sitting there in a coffee bar with a couple of mates of mine and Wayne Fontana comes around the corner.

He was big locally, Wayne Fontana & the Jets, but they didn't have a record deal or anything. They were doing functions and bar mitzvahs. We all were. He comes over and says, "Can you help me? My guitarist has had an accident and his car's broken down and he can't do the show. I have to audition; can you help me out?"

Okay, so what? We were all doing the same songs. The gear's here and there's the guitar, right diddley doo-da. So we played. It was rubbish, but it was what everyone wanted to hear. I came off and went back to the coffee bar and thought, "Okay, I did him a favor and he'll buy me a drink."

Wayne comes skidding 'round the corner of the coffee bar and says, "Eric! Eric! I've got a deal. They've given me a two-year contract, but they want you as well." I said, "Hold it. What do you mean they want me? I'm not in your group." He said, "Well you are now. You are now in the Jets." The drummer [had] turned up just by accident, he wasn't even in his band either, and he got the gig as well. The guy watching, the A&R man of Phillips, saw these four guys and thought, "They've got something."

We released our first record, "Hello Josephine." We did a rock-y version and it got to number 46 in the charts. Our money went from fifteen pounds to fifty pounds a night. We were working nearly every night because we had a hit record.

Walking down the street one day there was a big poster for the Dirk Bogarde thriller *The Mind Benders*, just released. I said to Wayne, "*The Jets* doesn't sound very exciting. What about Wayne Fontana & the Mindbenders. So we became the Mindbenders in mid-throw.

We were still touring and doing these little support gigs. We were on the bill with the Detours somewhere. Then they became the Who.

Graham Nash: We were the Hollies by December of '62. Oh we were good. We were doing a show at the Cavern in early 1963. The Beatles had been discovered and were selling millions of records and [the record companies] must have thought, "They can't be the only fuckers up there, let's go and have a look."

They smelled money, because don't forget, the Beatles were only getting a penny a record. We were just making music, getting fed, and fucking.

Terry O'Neill: The record companies were all chasing this new market, kids with disposable income spending it on records and portable players, so they needed young bands because the kids wouldn't buy Elvis or Sinatra. You look at a band like the Dave Clark Five. Not a lot of talent other than Mike Smith, the keyboard player and singer, but they were playing to thousands in the dance halls, so obviously the record companies got interested in them.

Norman Jopling: The Dave Clark Five? Hmm. Well, Mike Smith had a good rock-and-roll voice but other than that they had nothing to offer. Two years earlier I'd landed my dream job. The paper wrote about new records and the acts behind them, like the Dave Clark Five, but I wanted to write about serious music. I'd found my mission: to write about rhythm and blues, to spread the word in print in the *Record Mirror*. I didn't need to be any great shakes as a writer; all I needed to do was a lot of raving and shouting about the artists and music I liked.

I was nineteen, opinionated, and one of my opinions, never reflected in print but which I certainly didn't keep quiet about, was that the British so-called rhythm-and-blues movement was useless. The previous year I had regularly checked out Alexis Korner's Blues Incorporated at Ealing Jazz Club and at the Marquee, followed the comings and goings of the various vocalists and musicians who wandered in and out of his troop, kept checking them out, and after a while even stopped being disappointed as one contender after another just didn't hit the spot—and not for lack of trying.

One afternoon in April 1963, the editor, Peter Jones, began subjecting me to a haranguing on the subject of Giorgio Gomelsky, a Russian émigré, who had been an important figure on the fifties UK jazz scene. His latest in a series of mostly short-lived club ventures was the Crawdaddy Club, held on Sunday evenings at the Station Hotel, Kew Road, Richmond.

The club's latest attraction—resident attraction, in fact—was a rhythm-and-blues combo called the Rolling Stones, who Giorgio had met the previous year and had featured once or twice at his Piccadilly Jazz Club off Great Windmill Street, now reincarnated as Ronan O'Rahilly's Scene Club. Giorgio believed in the Rolling Stones with missionary fervor and was also acting as their unofficial manager although no written agreement was in place. The problem was that Peter wouldn't write about rhythm and blues. He left writing about rhythm and blues to me.

Peter stood there looking down on me as I tried to hide myself, pretending to be completely involved in designing some exquisitely difficult layout. I knew what was coming. Giorgio pesters Peter, Peter pesters me.

"Peter, believe me, all British rhythm and blues is crap."

"Why don't you just go down there and see them?"

"I know what they'll be like. They'll be rubbish."

Keith Richards: The Beatles had suddenly appeared out of Liverpool and we realized we were not the only bunch of guys in England that actually tuned in to black American music. They were the voices of soul-orientated vocals. We were into the instrumental blues stuff, but at the same time we suddenly realized that there is something happening across the country—and it's not just us. We thought we were hip. We thought we were it. Liverpool? Go fuck.

Norman Jopling: The editor turned his biggest gun on me. "You're supposed to be the rhythm-and-blues expert." The "supposed to be" got me. I capitulated.

When we arrived in Richmond, late, there was a crowd of kids outside the Station Hotel who couldn't get in—the place was packed full. We elbowed our way to the front, flashed various press cards, cameras, demanded to see Giorgio. The noise was already fantastic— Giorgio appeared and just pushed us into the room where the Rolling Stones were already playing.

It was one of those Bo Diddley songs with a Bo Diddley beat. I'd never heard anything like it in a live act. I'd never felt anything like it. The place shook, everyone in the audience was wet with sweat, the sound was bouncing off the walls, throbbing, utterly irresistible. It lifted me up and swept me along, song after song.

Keith Richards: You want to play the blues. You are a white kid from London and you got the hang of it pretty much but you ain't from Chicago; you ain't Muddy Waters or Chuck Berry.

All we wanted to do was interpret other people's music and turn people on to it: "Now, listen to the real shit!" It was some nihilistic missionary bullshit—just turn other people on. "Now you've heard us, you like that? Now you're *really* going to dig the real cats!"

Eric Clapton was the same. Jeff Beck was the same. All the cats were here. [Pete] Townshend was the same. We just wanted to turn England 'round to this incredible music they were not hearing . . . and we would give them our best shot at it.

Eric Clapton: I joined the Roosters in January '63. I was seventeen. There was a very important character in the band, Ben Palmer, who had very, very strict, severe principles about what we were doing and why. The others were more than happy to have fun.

We all liked the same thing so our repertoire was based on that, but when you put that stuff onstage it's very easy to start sacrificing principles to get a response. How do we liven things up and get back in touch with the audience? That's what pop is about. This guy didn't give a shit. And as I was joining he was making up his mind that he didn't want anything more to do with it. There is a point when you make a decision—am I going to stick to my principles or sell out in a minor level?

I've survived on what I learnt from him. Do what you know best and you love, and you will be alright, and that's been my very simple philosophy, and I learnt it from him. He left and became a woodcutter.

I was ready to learn but we caved in because we couldn't really cover the costs of what we were doing. Paul Jones, the lead singer of the Roosters when I joined, had already gone to Manfred Mann, and he became a star.

Then I joined Casey Jones & the Engineers. We played fun fairs [*amusement parks*] and god knows what. Those six months seemed like an eternity. It was trite, end-of-the-pier pop. I thought, "I can't do this." My friend Ben had been banging on: "Why are you doing this?"

Famous wasn't even a term then. It wasn't even a concept. *Famous* was the people we loathed already. The Beatles were trying to be famous. They weren't yet but they were on the edge. It looked like they were going that way. People who were famous were game show hosts and people like that. Fame wasn't part of the program or the agenda.

Norman Jopling: The personnel in the Stones were not entirely unfamiliar. I recognized a couple of them from playing on and off with Korner, and the singer I'd seen several times in the Star Café off Old Compton Street in Soho.

Jagger was known to everyone there simply as "the rhythm-and-blues singer." I thought it was a joke till I saw him perform. But the sound they made together was nothing like Korner's worthy troop. This was alchemy. It was perfect—rhythm and blues in Chicago couldn't have been any more exciting than this. I was almost in a state of shock. After the initial rush my brain switched back on and my first thought was, like, "We could do it. White people could do it."

Keith Richards: You got this incredible buzz going on. We realized we were not in some esoteric backwater. The Beatles were the same generation as us within a few years of each other, and it was bubbling everywhere else. All these other bands like the Detours [*which became the Who*] and Gerry & the Pacemakers. There was a burst of energy in England at the time. It was very welcome. We'd been waiting around for quite a while.

Norman Jopling: After the gig, as the crowd melted away, I hung around chatting to Giorgio, being introduced to the Rolling Stones one by one as they ambled offstage. Brian, the most intense character, was the chattiest, doing a PR job on me. "What can you do for us?" he asked. What could I say? Anything they wanted, really.

We jumped in the group's van and made our way to the house of a "producer." All the Stones started picking up the instruments and playing around on them. Drinks were poured, everyone relaxed, unwound. I started chatting to the guys. I was surprised to see Mick, the singer, adept on several of the instruments. He had the hardest job in the band, fronting that incredible sound and holding his own. He was polite, distant, not just from me but from everyone that evening.

I spoke mostly with Charlie and Keith, who, like me, was a big Mary Wells fan—we shared our disappointment with "Laughing Boy" but hoped that "Your Old Standby" would be a return to form. (It was.) Those were the kinds of conversations everyone had in those days.

Next day, Monday, I told Peter how wild and great they were, told him I'd write a rave story on them, and how wrong I'd been. This pleased him.

When I got back to the office that Wednesday, I sat down to write the article having the distinct feeling that I should be very careful in what I said. This had more to do with the fact that there were certain expectations attached to the article: Peter's, Giorgio's, the group's. Also, it was the first time I could remember a feature article written in *New Record Mirror* about an act that didn't yet have a record: after all, that's why we were called *Record Mirror*.

The chronology of what happened at that eventful time in the career of the Rolling Stones still doesn't make sense to me no matter how many times I read everyone's reminiscences, go over and over the dates, and who did what, or saw whom, or said what. But the most important thing, as far as helping the group, had little to do with me or my article. Peter Jones, sitting on his favorite stool and holding court that week in De Hems Bar in Soho, was being harangued by Andrew Oldham, whose clients included Brian Epstein's burgeoning NEMS [*North East Music Store*] stable. As usual, Andrew was hustling for coverage, and Peter advised him to check out the Rolling Stones, mentioning that they were about to get a rave write-up—the first group without a record to be featured in our columns.

Andrew Loog Oldham: At that point in England there wasn't in the air the feeling of "things are changing" the way they were in the United States, which had [the] civil rights [movement going on]. In England it seemed much more about adventure.

It is absolutely amazing how music and culture in the U.S. went up in direct proportion to the carnage in the Vietnam War. But that's the spike. In England we had the pill, I was nineteen, I didn't have any goals, it was all just a lark.

Sir Alan Parker: At the start of 1963, I don't think we were overly politicized. We were more interested in the new Beatles album than what was going on in Vietnam or Alabama.

Images of Ursula Andress coming out of the water in *Dr. No* were more appealing than a monk self-immolating in Saigon. I think up to then there was a real disconnect between the realpolitik of our lives and the Macmillan bloke [*the British prime minister*] with the dead rat on his top upper lip. If you had a duffel coat you maybe went on CND [*the Campaign for Nuclear Disarmament*] marches.

The big scandal of the time was the Profumo Affair—our minister for war was sharing a girl with the Soviet naval attaché and it was the height of the Cold War. But Profumo lying to Parliament and shifty Cold War naval attachés weren't too interesting to us. However, we *were* all mesmerized by all that shagging at Cliveden [*the stately home of Nancy Astor, the first female member of Parliament*] where the girls met the politicians. I thought that was what all the upper classes got up to all the time. My dad scoured the *Daily Mirror* every day for each salacious tidbit.

Mandy Rice-Davies: The thing that broke the story was the fight outside the Flamingo and then the shooting. Then there's the trial of Stephen Ward, who introduced us to his influential friends in London society. [*The police charged Ward with "living off immoral earnings"— basically pimping Rice-Davies and Christine Keeler. He took a fatal overdose the night before his trial's final day.*]

It was a window in time. You could park a car and not get a ticket. But the establishment were out to get someone, someone had to pay for the embarrassment to the government and the upper classes.

I was in jail for seven days—for an out-of-date driving license, which wasn't criminal. The police were dying to get me. Then they tried to charge me with theft of a television set—before Peter [Rachman] died, I'd left the house and there was a rented TV in it. I couldn't get back in because they'd changed the locks.

After delving deep, the police only came up with five men in two years with whom I'd had a relationship. I moved in with Peter at the end of March of '61 and didn't move out till October '62. I was his mistress and not a call girl. I was a good-time girl. A mistress one hundred percent.

I got really angry with Stephen Ward's trial judge when I said I had had the bonk with Bill [Lord] Astor. The judge said, "Do you mean to say that you had sex while the defendant [Stephen Ward] was in another room in the same house?"

This was the point I lost my temper and he threatened me with contempt of court. I have some residual anger but it didn't defeat me. I immediately showed a clean set of heels [*turned over a new leaf*] and got myself a job. I began singing almost immediately. The attempt by the establishment to surround me with shame didn't work. I didn't feel ashamed.

The public were delighted that sex had come out in the open. The upper class, who had always had the upper hand, didn't seem to have it anymore.

Keith Richards: I really loved to play with the other guys. You had the sense that if we applied ourselves, there was something kind of unique going on. We were working in an area where just to get a gig was difficult because the jazz guys had all the clubs stitched up. The Inkpot [for instance], was a damn basement. It used to rain on you through the ceiling, and it was next to a subway station and a train would go by and it would drown out the music. It was a great breeding ground. Those cats were serious, 'cause no one would go down to this dungeon unless you got something out of it.

The stage had just room enough for a piano and a couple of amplifiers. Tiny. Condensation dripping down on you. It was a great learning ground, if you could play in places like that.

We also played [the Crawdaddy at the] Richmond Station Hotel. It's where I think Andrew Loog Oldham came to see us. He went scouting and found us, and Andrew was basically the sixth Rolling Stone, or seventh, or whatever.

Bill Wyman: I was twenty-six in 1963, older than the others. I had flown. They had never flown and I had to calm them down. We had all these people doing stuff around us and we'd see things changing, like the miniskirt and tights instead of stockings, but you were in the midst of it and you couldn't see it coming.

We were all entering into something that we didn't know what it was, how long it would last, or how special it was. It was amateur hour. We just took it day by day. We didn't plan to be rebels and neither did the fashion people or photographers. They were just doing their normal job with new ideas. It wasn't preplanned or organized; it just happened.

Well, we went into a recording studio in March '63 and we cut five songs in five hours. Great blues tracks. They were sent to seven record companies. And they all turned them down. They weren't interested. We were distraught. We loved the recording and no one liked it. Oh dear, we are back in the clubs again. Then the Beatles came to see us and we became friends and they talked about us to promoters, the media—they were a great help to us.

Andrew Loog Oldham: When I met the Rolling Stones in April of '63 they were almost an inconvenience because I was very happy being a press agent. I had all the clothes I wanted. A social life didn't really interest me. I had the work life I wanted. Now I had to be responsible to these people, you know, but I couldn't help it—I mean, I had to do it.

Peter Jones told me about this article by Norman Jopling on a band that had not got a record out—which was very strange for them to be printing—and [that] I had to listen to them. I really didn't care, I mean, I didn't care about R&B, it didn't interest me in the slightest. And it was on a Sunday that I would have had to go and see them in Richmond.

This is like April, end of April. Bill Wyman and I argue whether it's the twenty-first or the twenty-eighth. I cross the zebra crossing [*crosswalk*] to get to the room in the Station Hotel where the stuff took place, and you had to walk down the path next to the railway tracks, and there was this very attractive couple fighting.

They stopped fighting when I walked past, then they continued fighting when I walked on, and after I finished standing in line to go into this place and this group came on, I realized that one of the couple fighting was Mick Jagger.

I just thought it funny that these middle-class students [in the audience] could be so into this sharecropping music in a grotty [*gross*] club. It was just a big—reasonably big—room, with middle-class art students with holes in their sweaters.

But I knew I wanted to manage [the Stones]. I wasn't really qualified because the whole idea with a musical act is you got to be able to get them work. I mean, you know, I could say, "I can get you in the newspapers," but what good is that going to do? I wanted the lot, I wanted the publishing, I wanted the management.

Georgie Fame: We didn't know about finances or publishing. People told us, "If you want to record a song you have to have it published," which is true, but what they didn't tell you was that you could be the publisher. You thought you had to go to an established publishing house, so the normal course of events was that they said, "Here's the deal: you have the song, we publish it, and we take 50 percent and the copyright and you take the other 50 percent." If you were two writers like Lennon and McCartney you had to split it and you got 25 percent.

No one told us you could get 100 percent. John Lennon and McCartney don't own the copyright of their early stuff.

Anthony Calder: Andrew came back and said he was going to sign a blues band, and I said, "What the fuck do we want a blues band for?" It was the Stones. They were living in filth, Mick and Keith, dishes piled high, unwashed for weeks.

Andrew Loog Oldham: Brian Jones was the apparent leader so he's the only one I spoke to.

I hunted around to find someone who could be a partner with me. First of all I went to Brian Epstein, but he wasn't listening; he wasn't prepared to entertain someone he had employed as a publicist as a potential partner in managing another act. Then a journalist of the *Melody Maker* told me where I could get an office for four pounds per week in Regents Street from this agent Eric Easton.

I brought Eric Easton down to see them, and then the next Wednesday they were rehearsing in a place called the Wetherby Arms, and Brian Jones signed for all of them.

Keith Richards: For me what was important in 1963 was getting into a recording studio for the first time. In those days the hardest thing to do was to record, and from a musician's point of view the most difficult thing was to break into a recording studio.

There was also a feeling of doom, that feeling that if you got a recording contract, a recording career lasted only two years. That was basically it. So in a way you were thinking at the time, "How fantastic [we're] making records. But we have only twenty-four months."

But we had not felt the power of the LP. Everything up to that time was predicated on a hit single. Every tune. Every six weeks you came out with a new hit. And by the time you threw three or four, nearly everyone goes down the tube.

Andrew Loog Oldham: Keith's got it right, but he's also got it wrong. Okay, what you looked for, what the record company gave you, you'd have a single, and if that did well they'll let you have another single, and if that did well they'd let you have an EP: it's the same size as 45 rpm, costs twice as much, and it has four songs on it because it goes at a slower speed—45 down to 33-and-a-third, right?

Then if you were good—and the Rolling Stones were very good because the first time they had an EP it went to number 9 in the singles chart, which means people were paying eleven shillings as opposed to six shillings—then they'll let you have an LP. The LP saved artists. An artist could be appreciated for his total quality as opposed to have it nailed down on a three-minute single.

Eric Clapton: We all felt part of something. Everything was plugged in and there were clubs we all went to, the Ealing Club or the Marquee. That was great. It was about the music, not about being seen. I'm a pretty snotty character. There was a great moment for me when the Stones were playing at the Crawdaddy where Andrew Loog Oldham saw them.

They played in Richmond every Sunday. They were playing Bo Diddley and Chuck Berry. The Beatles came down to see them. We were all individualists and watching the Stones, and these guys came in all wearing the same thing—black leather gear and the same haircut. We all had different styles of hair, and there's these guys—they all had to look alike. They all wore the same clothes. Someone was telling them what to wear: Brian Epstein. I felt contempt. They wanted the big pie and they knew how to get it.

The Beatles came down to see what the competition was about. But what held us all together, and it still does more than ever, was the love of music and the music we were listening to. That made it okay. My contempt was silly. But it was based on what they looked like and how they behaved, but if we sat down and talked we would discuss Chuck Berry and Muddy Waters.

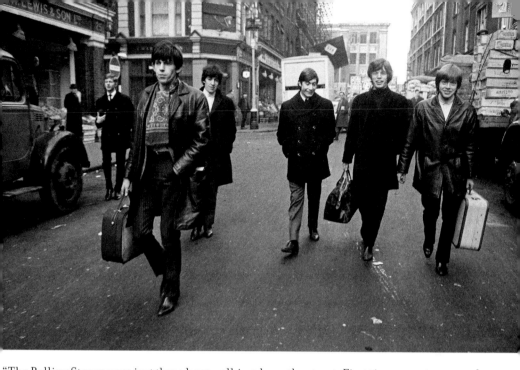

"The Rolling Stones were just these boys walking down the street. First time we got some cash we all went out and bought new guitars and Beatles boots."

Keith Richards

The photographer Terry O'Neill chose harder, edgier style to shoot the Rolling Stones in London's Tin Pan Alley to differentiate them from the clean-cut Beatles and other bands.

BOTH PHOTOGRAPHS BY TERRY O'NEILL

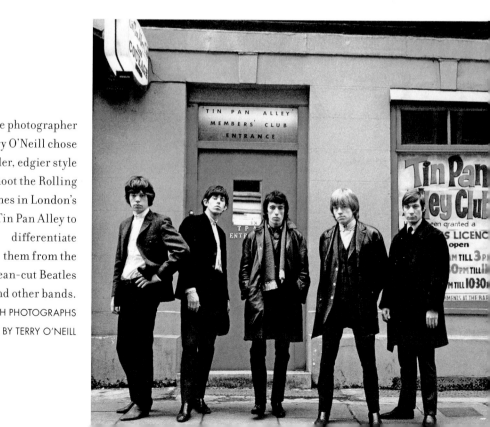

In 1963 television appearances, the Rolling Stones were expected to conform to a smart dress code with jackets and ties, but they soon shed that respectable image—it didn't match the music or the act.

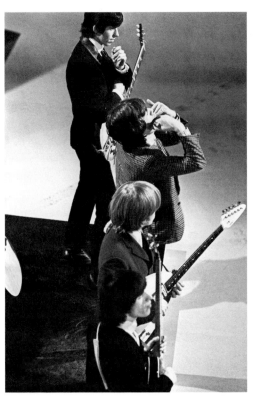

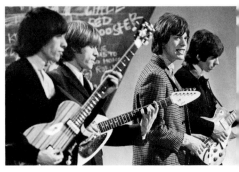

"We hated our first record. We refused to play it live. It didn't sound good to us so we just didn't do it. We were not that kind of calculating money machine."
Keith Richards

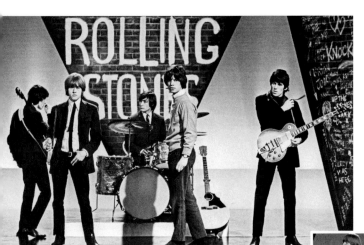

ALL PHOTOGRAPHS
BY TERRY O'NEILL

"Jagger was known to everyone simply as 'the rhythm and blues singer.' I thought it was a joke until I saw him perform. It was alchemy."
Norman Jopling

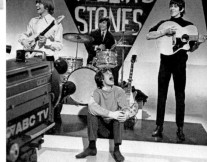

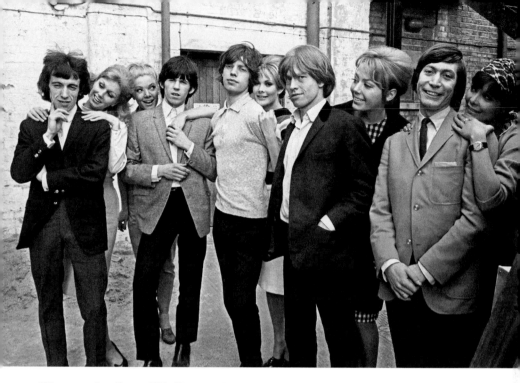

"Photographer Terry O'Neill remembers the Rolling Stones were 'immediately cool.' I was just trying to be polite and not get busted." **Keith Richards**

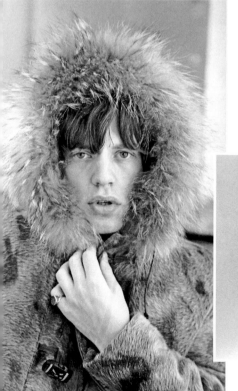

"When I sent the Stones photographs to my picture editor, he went berserk. 'They're ugly— get me a pretty band like the Beatles.'"

Terry O'Neill

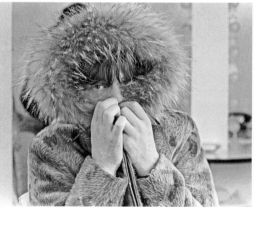

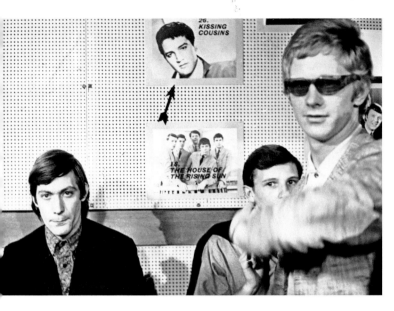

Keith Richards called the Stones' young manager, Andrew Loog Oldham (pictured here with Charlie Watts), the sixth Stone. "I do love that man. He forged this thing."

"Brian Jones felt threatened because he had control of the Rolling Stones until I came along. In any band there's a group leader until there's a manager." **Andrew Loog Oldham**

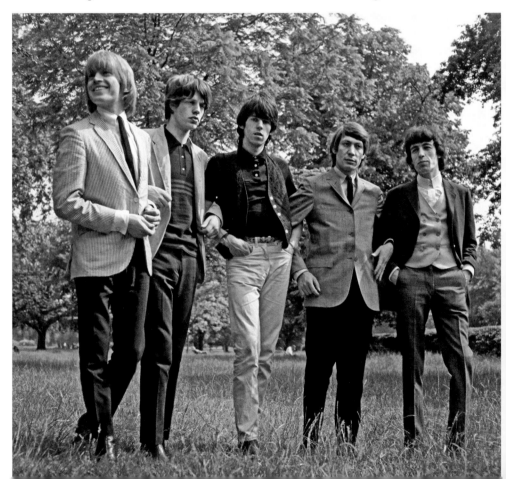

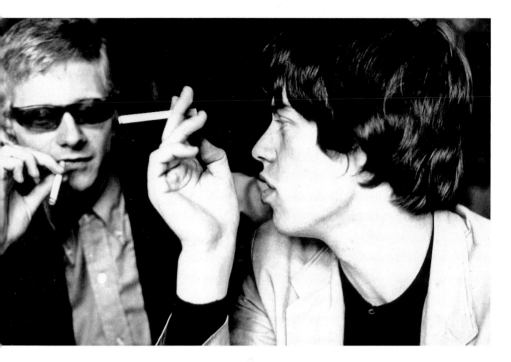

Stones manager Andrew Loog Oldham and Mick Jagger. "The big difference between the Beatles and the Stones were [that] the Beatles made it in America. The Stones were made *by* America."

Andrew Loog Oldham

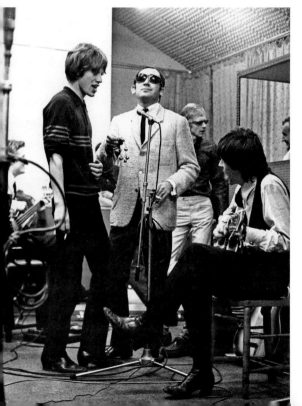

Jagger, Richards, and Loog Oldham *(background)* in the studio with Lionel Bart, songwriter, pop impresario, and composer of the hit musical *Oliver!*.

ALL PHOTOGRAPHS BY TERRY O'NEILL

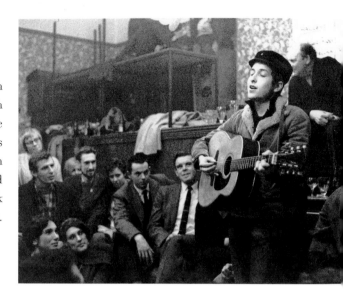

Spotted by a British producer in a Greenwich Village folk club, the unknown Bob Dylan was flown to Britain to perform in a televised drama and honed his act in London folk clubs after rehearsals.

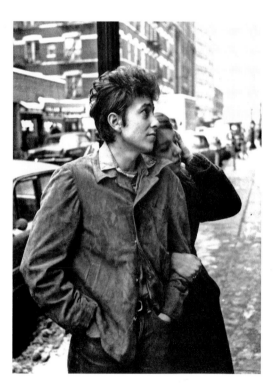

An outtake from the the now-iconic album cover of *Freewheelin' Bob Dylan* with Susie Rotolo, taken on the corner of Jones and West Fourth Street in Greenwich Village. The album reached number 22 in the United States but hit the top spot in Britain.

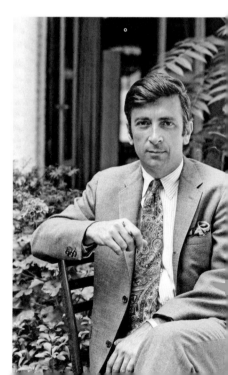

"When I first heard the Beatles it had an impact. You were aware of new music and new people. I was breaking boundaries in journalism. I always felt it could be an art form. Literature and the laws changed."

Gay Talese

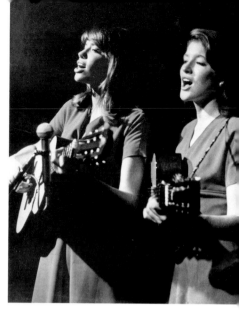

Carly and Lucy Simon toured Greenwich Village clubs and Ivy League campuses with their folk-rock repertoire but scored only one minor hit before Carly's solo career took off in 1971.

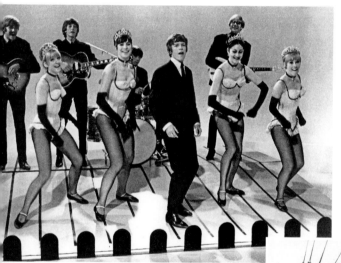

'When I saw the Beatles, that was my eureka moment. Less than a year later we were in America. We did 365 concerts in one year. The Beatles thought we were fluff. We weren't in the same league." **Peter Noone**

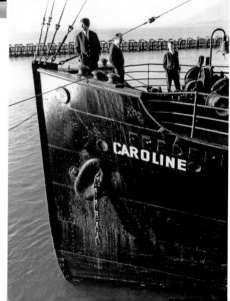

"The suits were in charge of television and radio, they and the assholes of EMI and Decca. I thought about a boat, offshore, where they couldn't touch us, broadcasting my kind of music." **Ronan O'Rahilly**

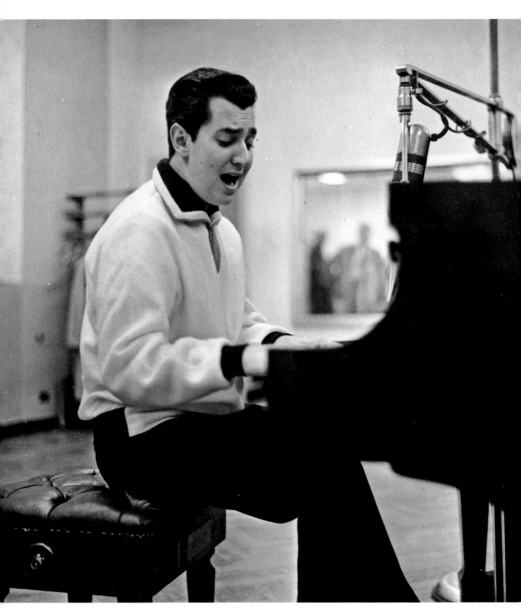

"The mood was new music. It was more rebellious, more evasive writing, more metaphorical. I'd had ten hits in a row and then the Beatles and the Stones came in and … I was the outsider. My records stopped selling."

Neil Sedaka   CREDIT: GETTY IMAGES

Bill Wyman: We were so naïve it's incredible. That was what it was like. The same with the photographers. Same with the artists and with pop art. The Who. Carnaby Street and Kings Road and all the shops. We were trying to be professional. Going from amateur to professional. Suddenly there was a bit of money around. Brian and Keith weren't so destitute. Charlie gave up working, June or July, so I gave up work after I met Andrew Loog Oldham.

I became professional. I thought, "I am going to do it and if it don't work I can always go back to another job. I have qualifications and I was good at math and I'd done my national service in the Royal Air Force. So I am going to go for it." Everyone I knew said, "Don't! You are risking everything. You have to have a pension and a steady job." But I went against everyone. It was a great risk as I was bringing up a family.

George Harrison had also told Andrew, "There's a band in Richmond you need to see." We signed to Oldham in April and a record deal and recording contract. But we didn't even dream of making a record or being on TV or traveling around the world. We did what we wanted when we wanted and how we wanted. We just came out in our normal clothes and played like that. The promoters said, "We don't want to book you again. You don't play the music that girls want to dance to, there's no makeup, and your guitars are all different colors. You are useless."

The first time we got a big article in the *Record Mirror* and I sat on the train with the magazine open on my lap expecting someone to notice. I was so proud of it. I waited to be recognized, that's how naïve we were.

Norman Jopling: The Beatles, myself, Andrew Oldham, all saw the group during April at the Crawdaddy. Andrew then moved quickly. By the time my article—their first national write-up and the first by a music reporter—appeared early in May, Oldham and Eric Easton had already formulated their master plan, signed the group to a management contract, and would shortly sign a lease-tape deal [in which the copyright of recordings is leased to the record company for a period of time] with Decca Records, who were still smarting over rejecting the Beatles.

New Record Mirror hit the streets on May 8th with the Rolling Stones article on page two, and that afternoon three of the four major record companies phoned me to find out where they could contact the group. I told them to talk to Andrew Oldham, who I now knew was involved in their management, although I was still under the impression that Giorgio was also involved.

Andrew Loog Oldham: We found out that Giorgio in fact had a recording contract with the Stones, or an option, right? And I had to get him out. When I went down to Richmond and fell in love with them, nobody said, "By the way, we've got this problem." They made sure we were really in love with them and wanted to sign them, *then* they said, "By the way, we've got this problem: Brian signed on our behalf."

Brian is the only one who signed it. We rehearsed Brian Jones to say that he had this big opportunity to join another group that would make money and he had no future with the Rolling Stones.

"I can't be tied up, here's the ninety pounds back," he said, and Giorgio released it.

Norman Jopling: Whether or not Giorgio was deliberately ousted by Andrew is a matter for conjecture. Somehow I doubt it. Backstabbing wasn't Oldham's style—he would have considered it beneath him. April and May 1963 were seminal months in the group's career, when Andrew signed the band and got them in to meet Decca.

Keith Richards: The guy that we got to meet [at Decca] and who signed us up, he actually turned the Beatles down. He could have had them for a song, but he blew them out. He hated us! He had no idea what this music was about—or what was happening. He was of that generation that was not about to move ahead, but when we turned up I think what happened was that he dared not make the same mistake twice.

Andrew Loog Oldham: Everybody knows Decca turned the Beatles down. Mind you, if you heard the tape, you might have turned them down too.

They were also turned down because the guy who made the decisions was either going to sign this band from Liverpool [the Beatles] or a group from Essex, Brian Poole & the Tremeloes; it was easier to deal with a band from Essex than from Liverpool.

We had no demo tape for the Stones. We did a deal, an independent deal, meaning we would pay for and supply the record and therefore get a bigger royalty. The Beatles were signed direct, which means they were getting, like, one and a half or two percent; we would get six or seven percent and we paid the Rolling Stones out of what we got.

How did I know about that? Because some of the people who I admired were people like Phil Spector, and that's how it was done. There was an artist called Chris Montez—"Let's Dance." When he came to England I represented him and I met his manager, and his manager wrote the song, produced the record, he published the song; all Chris Montez did was sing.

I'm not saying it was new; it wasn't the first time it'd been done in England, but we went and made the record at the old Olympic studios in a mews off Baker Street. I told them, "Give me the three or four songs you think are the most commercial and we'll record them," and they picked "Come On," a Chuck Berry song.

Bill Wyman: Every band at the time—Beatles, Searchers, Animals, Dave Clark—we all thought [they would last] two or three years if we were lucky. Brian [and] Keith had never had a job. I wasn't too worried.

I thought down the line I'd need to get another job; [the band would be] a nice temporary diversion, and then we'd move on to a normal life. Everyone, Lennon or McCartney, we all thought it was temporary.

It was like being in the eye of a hurricane. Looking back, we were right in the middle of it and we weren't really aware what was happening around us.

Mary Quant: The Beatles were very good customers. They bought lots of clothes and hats and miniskirts, everything. They were very nice, very friendly. Funny.

Well, we had this rather fabulous flat down the road. It had been the ballroom of one of those houses. A great place for giving parties. And they'd all come and perform and dance and play. They'd drop in quite often.

The parties would just sort of happen. Lots of friends were musicians and photographers. We couldn't help but feel part of an exclusive scene. Everything was brand new and completely different. People had fabulous cars—E-Types and so on. I was designing collection after collection and selling them. I was always working on my next collection, next pieces, and having them made.

It was a time of permanent excitement and a sort of terror, really, how one could keep up with it. Anybody working in it—the music or whatever—would feel that pressure.

Norman Jopling: That spring, the word *"Merseybeat"* [the name coined by the music press for the bands emerging in Liverpool, which was built on the banks of the River Mersey] was dominating UK pop. The Beatles' second single, "Please Please Me," had reached number two, and "How Do You Do It," [the] debut single by their NEMS stablemates, Gerry & the Pacemakers, had beaten the Beatles to number one.

Then that was displaced when the Beatles' "From Me to You" rocketed to the top spot early in May. Then the Beatles' song "Do You Want to Know a Secret" was poised to chart.

That April, our photographer, Dezo Hoffmann, managed to persuade our editor that something was happening up in Scouseland [*Liverpool*]. The evidence had been piling up: the Beatles had already scored a chart-topping LP, a number-two single, and, from being the supporting act on the Tommy Roe/Chris Montez tour, they'd been promoted to bill-toppers. Their girl fans were already screaming wall to wall.

So the little NRM team caught the train to Liverpool. Dezo took reels of iconic shots which even today resonate with the down-to-earth charm: Paul ironing, John making tea, down in the Cavern, having their hair cut. Plus dozens of pictures of fans and many other Liverpool bands, the known and the unknown.

Peter Noone: I was in my grandmother's house in Urmston, this suburb of Manchester, and me and our bass player hear some music in the background, in a field. We walked out of my grandma's house and we cross this field and go over a hedge, and there are the Beatles playing. The council had booked them to play the annual summer show. They were already famous. They did their repertoire. And I am like, "*shit!*" *Wow* wasn't invented then, it was still a comic book word. And the bass player says, "We are fucked." He was ready to hang up his gear. I say, "Let's get the guys and rehearse every day."

When I saw the Beatles that was my eureka moment. Less than a year later we are in the U.S. charts. That's the moment when I went pro. That's how it got to be. It was the way they presented themselves that inspired me. You knew all the music. That was bloody good. It was slick. Everyone was dancing and shit. In those days John Lennon was the leader of the band. He was Herman and they were Hermits. They were suited and booted [*all dressed up and ready to go*]. They came in a van. They were just mind-blowingly enthusiastic. "Shit," I thought, "that's the way to do it."

After that eureka moment, I rehearsed every day. I found guys who were so stupid they thought I knew what I was doing. We got serious, and other people got serious around the same time. I said to Keith Hopwood, who was the lead Hermit, "You have to quit your job." "What are you talking about? I am a telephone engineer," he says.

I didn't have a job. I was still at school. We were dead lucky. We had this woman called Mrs. Tittringham who let us rehearse in her front room, despite all the neighbors and everything. One of her daughters was a police officer so we were left alone. I was just a sixteen-year-old kid, but I am bossing older guys. It's always like that in boy bands. Someone takes control of it all. Because I was a little bit better educated and more feisty than the others—and I had a bank account my parents had set up for me. We would do two gigs a day sometimes. Then there was a lunchtime thing at the Manchester Plaza, and girls would go dancing for lunch! We'd do that, then get to Liverpool in the evening for a gig. I drove all the time [even though I didn't have a license]. It was my van. We sold newspapers all day Saturday and [football] match programs at Manchester United to raise money. We could go pick up newspapers and deliver them, pick up programs and deliver them, and still get to gigs on a Saturday night. It was really northern working-class shit.

Graham Nash: We drove down to London from Manchester in the van to record a BBC radio spot somewhere near the end of May 1963. It was live; there was no, "Sorry, I fucked up the verse, can we do it again?" It was, "You're on live now. *Now!*"

We stayed in a room that had seven beds in it—we didn't have money then, and the BBC didn't put you up. Parlophone had signed us.

We only stayed about three days. We were recording in Abbey Road. There was a three-hour morning session and a three-hour afternoon session with tea breaks. At the end of the session a lady would come out with a tray of tea and little packets of money in it. You actually got money, a wage packet, from Abbey Road. It was a favorite thing of our time—we would make music, then get tea and be paid for it.

At Abbey Road, all the engineers had work coats on and everything was sanitized. It was insane to be in Abbey Road and actually record. We recorded our first hit song in our first recording session there. Actually, we recorded the entire album.

Peter Noone: We go to London to meet a producer and we play him our live tape. But our tape played backwards. He says, "Look boys, go back to wherever you come from and figure out how the fucking tape works before you come and waste my time." It was really offensive. I almost quit the business it upset me so much. We were made to look like idiots, real chumps—which we were.

The next time we do this I say, "Let's not go to them, let's bring them to our thing." Mickie Most says, "No, I'm not going to Manchester to hear you play."

So we said, "We'll pay your ticket and book you into the Midland Hotel." We thought that was the Plaza of Manchester. We'd never been in it but we knew it was *the* place. And Mickie says yes and he comes to the Beachcomber Club in Oldham and we tell all the girls that this famous American record music producer is coming to see us. He's not American, of course, but we knew he'd come looking like an American because that was his thing. "So scream," we say [to the girls]. So they all scream in all the wrong places during the songs. It was pathetic, but Mickie kinda liked it. He saw this attitude, and he brings us to London.

On the road south there is a café, the Blue Boar, that's on the A5 between Coventry and Birmingham. Once you made it past Birmingham on the road to London, that was like enlightenment.

A lot of the bands would meet there. The Blue Boar Café is where I got to know Jack Bruce from Cream, and Robert Palmer. Forty years later I run into Robert Palmer. "Do you remember when we used to stop at the Blue Boar, all these people making sandwiches and such?" Up north it was a bacon "butty"; down south it was a sandwich. We all had this in common.

In my band, we had one really tough guy. My mother had a coffee table with screwable legs, and we had four of those, and if anyone ever messed with you, those would come out. We'd stop at a fish and chip shop, and everyone wanted to beat you up because we had longer hair and were musicians. It was unbelievable. "Are you boys or girls?" And we'd say, "How many girls do you know with these [table legs]," and we were the ones the cops wanted to talk to.

Anyway, when we got to London, "How about the studio next Sunday morning?" says Mickie. "Wait a second. I have the Animals at midday. Can you be there for nine a.m.?" So like schmucks we say yes. We should have said three. It would have given us time to bathe and everything. We finished the gig somewhere in Manchester, drove all night, went into the studio at nine in the morning, and at noon the Animals come in.

Hilton Valentine: We did an album and a half in one session—three hours. We were en route coming down from Blackpool [in northeast England]. We were doing Saturday night concerts, and the next gig was in the Isle of Wight [on the south coast of England] on Sunday night, so we drove down from Blackpool into London overnight, and after six hours in the van, we recorded and then continued to drive down to the Isle of Wight to get the ferry for the next gig. When we were recording we would take time to get the balance levels and we would record something. We wouldn't even hear back what we played. And Mickie would go, "Right. Next?"

PART THREE

Come on, I gotta see you, baby
Come on, I don't mean maybe
Come on, I've gotta make you see
That I belong to you and you belong to me

THE ROLLING STONES

*The world was in flux in the summer of 1963. President Kennedy prom-
ised to deliver a civil rights bill in the United States and traveled to Germany
to denounce the recent construction of the Berlin Wall in front of half a million Berliners. Martin Luther King declared, "I have a dream" on the steps of
the Lincoln Memorial, and the Kremlin sent the first woman into space. Zip
codes were introduced in America, Marvel Comics created the X-Men, and
Cleopatra, the most costly and beleaguered movie ever, was finally premiered. Britain remained in the grip of the Profumo Affair, and the public
marveled at the audacity of a gang that pulled off the Great Train Robbery.
And the youthquake was in full force.*

Bob Dylan's Freewheelin' *had been a huge success in the UK in the
spring, and while it languished on the U.S. charts, he himself rose to national prominence, walking out on* The Ed Sullivan Show *over attempts to
censor his music; appearing at the Newport Folk Festival; and singing with
Joan Baez at the March on Washington in August.*

Ready Steady Go!, a subversive new pop show, was launched on British commercial television and literally rocked convention. The Rolling Stones released their first single, the word Beatlemania was coined, and the not-long-ago conservative record labels finally woke up to the tectonic changes in the industry and began scouring provincial towns for talent that didn't wear suits and ties and eschewed covers of middle-of-the-road American music.

5

ALACRITY

"Suddenly you are on, up there onstage, and before you
know it young ladies are throwing their underwear
at you. A year earlier, you couldn't get laid."

KEITH RICHARDS

*Throughout the spring and summer of 1963, an unstoppable force of inspired,
aspirational, and lustful youth elbowed aside convention and conformity
in Britain. Parents, politicians, and businessmen frowned and fretted but
were eventually overtaken by the inevitable. Conservative record labels
sought to exploit a new market, television stations vied for the best ratings,
and filmmakers swapped swords and sandals for sex and short skirts.*

Norman Jopling: The Flamingo was an exciting club, but somehow I
was never fully at ease there. But I discovered a club I loved. That May,
the Scene Club was a month-old basement dive in little Ham Yard,
off Great Windmill Street in Soho, not five minutes from the *Record
Mirror*.

The premises was run by an Irish entrepreneur and idealist,
Ronan O'Rahilly, and his business partner, a genial South African—
Lionel Blake. It was unlicensed, featured live attractions, with the
music policy more or less based around rhythm and blues.

I mooched along [*wandered over*] to Ham Yard, found the dingy entrance to the Scene, and announced myself to the two guys on the door. The Scene wasn't big, it was seedy, and full of darker corners. There was a bar which didn't serve alcohol, a dance floor, and not much else. The atmosphere was almost always low-key, relaxed, modest, and completely unpretentious; the focus was on the music so there was no brazen hip, no blatant cool. Everyone was digging the same thing and that was all that mattered. You didn't have to dress up or dress down, but you could if you felt like it.

It wasn't a pulling club [*pick-up joint*]: there were generally far more boys than girls. For the next year, maybe eighteen months, the Scene Club was red-hot, the hottest little club in London. The live nights at the Scene could be brilliant. Chris Farlowe—arguably Britain's best-ever blues voice—with the Thunderbirds; Georgie Fame & the Blue Flames, also resident at the Flamingo.

In June the Rolling Stones played a four-week Scene residency on Thursdays; the Roosters, featuring Eric Clapton and Tom McGuinness, also performed, albeit somewhat irregularly. Eric also played there during his brief stint with Casey Jones & the Engineers. That autumn when Bo Diddley toured—a god come down to earth—he, too, appeared at the Scene.

I used to come into the office most Saturday mornings, and one Saturday, at that time Guy, the Scene's DJ, brought up Eric Clapton, who just sat around saying not very much at all. Guy took me aside and whispered that this guy was a brilliant blues guitarist. I took an immediate dislike to Eric for looking so great.

A day or so later I felt very ashamed of myself, so when Eric got stranded a couple of times after gigs at the Scene, I'd give him a lift to wherever it was he lived in South London on the back of my scooter.

Bill Wyman: We made our first record on 10th May. We were still all working then. We did it in the evening. Took two hours or something. It didn't take long to make a record, and we were a good little band.

Andrew Loog Oldham: It was pretty awful, the recording; it wasn't good. It was done in three hours—in those days, everything was done in three hours.

They were so nervous, you know, and I certainly wasn't a record producer, right, but we sent it to the record company, and the record company used to have meetings every Tuesday to decide what they were going to release, and very cleverly, the man who had turned down the Beatles, this guy called Dick Rowe, said the recording is not good enough, we want to make it ourselves again, at the Decca Studios.

I thought, we're fucked, because if they made it and made it successfully, then the independent production deal and the control over the recordings would be out and there goes my dream, you know, they would be like the Beatles, we'd only be the managers and they'd be direct Decca recording artists, and I'm sitting there going "oh god," because I wanted to be an independent producer and tell the record company what to do, deliver the record and say, "Hey, this is the next single."

Fortunately, the attempt to rerecord was a failure—it was actually worse than the one we made, you know? So they took ours and we had the independent deal, it shaped our immediate future, it shaped the rest of the Rolling Stones' future.

Norman Jopling: My own UK R&B faves, the Rolling Stones, now had their first record out, the predicted "Come On," and to my ears most disappointing. Brian Jones had taken to visiting the *Record Mirror* offices regularly, and in addition to picking his brains on all matters R&B (on which he was *the* expert), I got some up-to-date Stones info from him for a feature.

In contrast to my first article on the Stones, it was a stilted piece of PR. "Come On" simply didn't capture their magic and it was impossible to pretend it did. I couldn't slag it off in print but couldn't enthuse, either. I wrote, "It's good, catchy, punchy, and commercial, but it's not the fanatical R&B sound that the audiences wait hours to hear. It's a bluesy, very commercial group that should make the charts in a small way."

Keith Richards: We hated the first record [*released June 7*]. We refused to play it live. It didn't sound good to us so we just didn't do it. We were not that kind of calculated money-making machine.

That's what I do. I make records. If I think I can't play it live I don't do it. We were always anti in that way. We felt ashamed about our record, but it was in the top twenty. We had made a record. And after all, we would have sold our souls to get into the studio, and we did. We were at the crossroads right then.

Andrew Loog Oldham: So then the next stage was how do I get them, in terms of publicity, out of these little rhythm-and-blues mentions. I wanted to open the door with one of the most powerful people in Fleet Street, who was a journalist called Pat Doncaster, who had a column every Thursday in the *Daily Mirror*, and he was like God then, you know, he was like Walter Winchell.

Keith Richards: We were deliberately set up. Stunts. You know if you go to the Savoy without a tie on you are going to get thrown out. As predicted, we'd get thrown out and they'd get their pictures. It was a game with the press. It was a laugh. Andrew was just colorizing what was there. Just get it out there!

Terry O'Neill took this picture of us in Soho, we are these boys walking down the street, "Oh look at these sharp kids." We all have the Beatles boots on. First time we made substantial cash we all went down to the store and bought new guitars and Beatle boots. That was the kicks. That was it. You've made it! I had a brand new suitcase. It was the very first suitcase I ever owned, and we used it in the shoot.

Andrew Loog Oldham: The other trick we used to do was get all of the diehard fans, the girls, and have them come 'round the office.

At that time you had to buy yourself into the charts. There were only forty-six record shops in England that reported to the charts, which made up the top 20 or the top 30. You only had to buy three or four in each of them, on a Thursday and Friday and Saturday, then the record stores would report to the musical papers on a Monday and you could be in the charts.

The girls were great, man, you know, we'd give them money to go and buy the records and some said, "No, no, no. We love the Stones. We'll pay for it ourselves." It would only get you in the bottom end of the chart, but it was the beginning, because it meant that the record company would go, "Wow, we should press some more records."

You can call it cheating if you want, but it was just a way of getting attention for your artist. [*"Come On" reached number 21 in the UK charts.*]

Jeffrey Kruger: Mick Jagger would tell you that he couldn't even get an audition at the BBC. We had them play in the [Flamingo] club, and there was one producer who heard them and said, "What is this rubbish? They will never get anywhere. You can't play stuff like that on the BBC."

Terry O'Neill: I'd seen this band called the Stones in Richmond, and I could see they were really cool. Andrew wanted publicity for them and my editor wanted more bands.

But I was so busy around central London I didn't have time to go out to photograph them. So they came to me. I took them in the park, walked them around Soho streets and into Tin Pan Alley to photograph them near the studios there. I got a bunch of office girls to drape themselves over the boys, and put them on the banks of the Thames or up against graffiti, which made them look even edgier in those days. Dangerous was what I was looking for, because they kind of *were*—rebellious, different.

Anthony Calder: One great picture for the tabloids [*a group shot, close-up, in casual clothes and unsmiling, made the band look mildly menacing in 1963 compared to others like the Beatles*] put them straight on the road to number one. It was Terry's idea. Then everyone copied us.

There would not have been the Stones without [Andrew and the publicity]. They would have broken up.

Keith Richards: Terry would say, "Let's throw a few dolly birds [*girls*] into the photo. I always had a girlfriend somewhere but they always got fed up with me. I was always playing music, always on the road, and then another girlfriend, and another one.

Terry O'Neill: I didn't have to work too hard. They were just immediately cool. Keith in particular. He was just naturally cool in a nonchalant, "whatever" kinda way.

Keith Richards: I didn't try to be cool. I didn't think about it. I think the minute you think about being cool, you ain't. I know a cool guy when I see him. But at the same time, if *other* people say you are cool? Okay! [But] I was just trying to be polite and not get busted.

Andrew: I do love that man. I always loved to work with him. He forged this thing together. And Terry was a very important part of it.

Terry O'Neill: When I sent in the pictures the editor went berserk. "They're ugly—get me a pretty band like the last one [*the Beatles*]."

He spiked the pictures, so I went back out looking for another band and found the Dave Clark Five, who looked smart in blazers and polo neck side-buttoned shirts. I forget where I photographed them—it was near the newspaper office. I think it was behind the Savoy Hotel. They were very clean-cut, actually a bit square. They had these naff [*unfashionable*] white shirts like dentists or continental waiters. In fact, I heard Dave Clark got the idea while on holiday in Spain.

The next thing I know they are on a double-page spread with my picture of the Stones under a headline "Beauty and the Beasts." The Dave Clark Five were really an antidote. First the Beatles and then Dylan looming—television needed some boys who were middle-of-the-road, respectable in America, where television shows like *Ed Sullivan* were censoring lyrics that were deemed provocative; then happy-clappy songs like [the Dave Clark Five's] "Glad All Over" were tame and didn't offend advertisers. So much of the music of the British invasion was about sex, but America wasn't ready for it. National television wanted the happy smiley faces. Meanwhile, the ground had been broken in Britain, and while British bands were invading America the scene was already changing in England. Rock and roll was getting harder, sexier, more blatant, and it was the Stones who were leading that charge.

Norman Jopling: There was only one center of the UK music business. If you wanted to make it, you came to London. But now that London had discovered Liverpool, London also discovered that there were lots of other great British cities—mostly up north—that not only boasted great football teams but also boasted great Beat groups. By now, most of the myriad Liverpool groups were signed up.

The next city to invade the charts was Manchester: Freddie & the Dreamers were top 3, and the Hollies were scoring with their debut single "Ain't That Just Like Me" [in May 1963].

We took the train up to Manchester and straightaway met the Hollies. I got on particularly well with Eric Haydock and Graham Nash, and there was something about their quality of enthusiasm I liked. They were proud of their city and proud of the whole Manchester pop scene, taking us to a club called the Twisted Wheel and to a clothes shop called the Toggery where the local groups bought their clothes.

The Hollies, though, were trendy dressers in the Beatles' style: Chelsea boots, tab-collar shirts, dark suits, leather-and-suede gear. The first six months of 1963 had already transformed the UK record business and moved the talent focus from solo stars to groups, expanded the horizon from London into the provinces, the music itself from pop to white rhythm and blues, sounding the death knell for the old Tin Pan Alley establishment.

Bill Wyman: The newspapers called us Neanderthals. We opposed everything that was then popular. Oldham tried to smarten us up, but we wouldn't do it. After the first appearance on TV [July 7, 1963], there was a public outcry. We had to go through the same prejudice every time. It was a huge deal. It was the only way to sell a record. You were seen by the whole of England. Andrew got us on *Thank Your Lucky Stars* [*a TV show in which a guest disc jockey and three teenagers would review mimed performances and singles*]. But the producer tried to stop us being on the show because we came in all casual, and he tried to give Andrew money to go and buy suits.

"They are scruffy and dirty and they smell, and we can see the fleas jumping off them."

Keith Richards: *Thank Your Lucky Stars* was the first experience of doing a TV show. We had to wear houndstooth check jackets—uniforms—just for that one show. Mysteriously, the next day all the jackets seemed to disappear.

Bill Wyman: We got into these jackets and trousers, with a pale blue shirt and narrow knitted ties, and we just mimed. We came offstage and then there was an outcry because of our long hair. Well, originally we couldn't afford to have haircuts. The look was all accidental.

Charlie had long hair because he was working [as a graphic designer]. The rest weren't working and in bed all day long. Mick was a student. Once it even got me in trouble at work. I did a show with a pink shirt and a pullover and next day I was called into the manager's office and told, "You can't wear pink shirts and you need to get your hair cut." I got a bollocking [*reprimanded*] like you were in school. I had a year-old kid, I'm married and trying to hold it all together and paying off the hire purchase [*installment payments*] and debts. Having a job was serious for me.

When we did the TV show it was already in the music press that something extraordinary was happening with us. We got recognized after the TV show. It was kinda exciting because it was all pretty girls. Girls started to ask for autographs. They used to hang out with us and make themselves available to us. They were the girls that dressed all trendy, like the girls Bailey was shooting for *Vogue*. Hardly any makeup; long, straight hair.

The other Stones were more clued in because they were living in London and were more part of what was going on. But I was out in Beckenham [*a London suburb*] with my family, not hanging out in London and walking the streets.

Keith Richards: Suddenly you are on, up there onstage, and before you know it young ladies are throwing their underwear at you. A year earlier you couldn't get laid and now they are throwing underwear at you.

Anthony Calder: Back then there was no such thing as AIDS or herpes. No fear. We had the pill. The girls were fucking everyone and everyone was fucking everyone else. That's when Andrew [Loog Oldham] started this thing [story line], "Would you let your daughter marry a rock star?" and it became a tabloid theme.

Keith Richards: This is the amazing thing about the human race, the male and the female, to be one minute, "Who the hell are you?" and the next minute suddenly girls are screaming and dying and throwing things on the stage.

I felt so normal; I was boring. I always had a feeling that there was something in store for me, but at the same time, everybody dreams, and you can dream your life away. It's a weird thing to think about. Yes, in one way I did think I was special. I did think I had something special, but in what field? Musicianship? No. I can't read a note.

I suppose in that year I was hearing in my head what I wanted to put across, what other people might want to hear, I just thought I was crazy. I am hearing these sounds. I am trying to translate them and trying to learn in musical terms how to paint the picture. The silence is our canvas. I was learning on the run. You really never have the time to philosophize where you are going.

There has to be some other thing going on here. I didn't suddenly turn charming overnight. Weird energy—we happened to be at the vortex of it. Other people would tell it the same, I'm sure. We all went through it the same.

Norman Jopling: Nineteen sixty-three was a good year for meeting like-minded music friends—similar age, similar wavelength—who'd started hanging around the music business. It was the year British music finally began reflecting the sixties instead of the fifties. It was the year my personal taste proved in tune with the zeitgeist.

I should qualify the bit about being in tune with the zeitgeist. I appreciated the phenomenon of the Beatles and everything that followed, or wallowed, in their wake, but the sounds of the Beatles and Merseybeat and the beat boom were never on my record player [and] were seldom played at the clubs and dives where I hung out.

And all the UK groups and solo artists I interviewed or socialized with in 1963 knew they weren't as good as the Americans. It wouldn't be for another year till British music would evolve sufficiently to stand in the same artistic arena as the Americans.

Bill Wyman: We would have made it without the TV show, but it made us known countrywide, and then we got offers to play outside of London. Before that we were just a band in a jazz club. Then when we went there we were still playing blues and the kids would just stand and stare because they couldn't dance to our music. Most was slow, bluesy stuff. They were dance ballrooms and we realized that we had to play faster numbers and more popular music. People said we were copying the Beatles. Nonsense. They were tidy and we were scruffy. They were nice boys—we weren't.

Andrew Loog Oldham: As I got closer to Mick and Keith, Brian Jones felt threatened because he had a position of control over the Stones—until I came along. I mean, in any band there's a group leader until there's a manager. And then that group leader either goes, "Oh, thank God I don't have to do that anymore," or else he gets a bit mental or he doesn't handle it well. Brian didn't handle it well. He liked the idea of having control over the rest of the band, of making Mick and Keith sit in a teahouse while he had meetings with me and Eric Easton and then he'd go back and report what had happened.

Bill Wyman: There were divisions in our band. Mick was middle-class. Well-off family, living in a nice house, detached, gardens. Went to grammar school. Brian Jones's father was an aeronautical engineer and was highly qualified. Keith was working-class. Same like me. We were poor and smoking at the age of seven and burglarizing. Charlie was working-class, living in a prefab until he left home. [*So many British houses were destroyed during the Blitz that the government constructed hundreds of thousands of inexpensive homes—or "prefabs"—for returning soldiers and their families.*] There were class divisions in the band. Two upper-class and three very poor, working-class kids. But we were unified musically. We were creating a platform for people like us. We didn't abide by the showbiz rules—gloss, outfits, uniforms, and makeup and all that stuff going on around us. We were against all that. And then people started to copy us. You had the Pretty Things and the Animals, and things slowly changed.

We had that one record, "Come On," written by Chuck Berry. It was a bit more commercial. We were the only band who wouldn't play their single; we wouldn't play the fucking thing live. We hated it. We wouldn't publicize it or promote it. Andrew was going loony: "Play your fucking single!"

"No, we don't like it and we won't play it." We had to do it sometimes if we knew he was coming to a show to see us.

Then we did another TV show where we went on casually, in our own clothes—*Ready Steady Go.*

Terry O'Neill: A lot of us, like Andrew Loog Oldham, were really into our clothes. We liked to dress smart—Italian suits and shoes, kind of cool and continental, single-breasted jackets, plain knitted neckties. Others, like Justin de Villeneuve or Andrerw Loog Oldham, would go to tailors where you could buy a suit and pick the style, how many pockets, buttons, et cetera, and have it made up for five pounds—a more dandified look. The tailors got wise to it. Some guys were picking so many features from the style book the tailors were losing money.

The Stones just wanted to be very casual and they were the first really cool dressers: dressing down, creating their own laid-back, we-don't-give-a-damn style. And it wasn't contrived. They were the real poster boys of this revolution that was taking place—a revolution in identity and individuality.

They'd go on television wearing a polo shirt or just a woolen [*a sweater*] over an open-neck checked shirt. Mick would be casual, preppy even, like a university student. Brian or Keith would be more Bohemian and have on leather jackets, but Bill liked to dress up—he was really smooth. They didn't wear matching uniform suits like the other bands, but just looked like they'd been picked out of a crowd and thrown together at the last minute, which was great because it was the music that unified them. That look really changed things. Some people, in the industry and television, for instance, were really confused by it, but the kids who were following them just felt this was how to be cool—dress for yourself, dress to stand out in the way that the flappers, the women in the 1920s, changed fashion, rejecting the post-Victorian, Edwardian, puritan look of their mothers. World War One had changed things. Women had the vote, power, a lot of men had died, the girls had to change things. It was the same postwar reaction in the early sixties—a new generation wanted to announce they had arrived.

The girls wanted to look mod-ish. Marilyn Monroe and figure-eight bodies were how their mums wanted to look; this generation wanted to look sophisticated but naughty, like *Vogue* models, like Audrey Hepburn's rebellious little sister, short skirts they could dance in, boots they could sashay down the street in, clothes they looked sexier in, that they could advertise themselves as part of the scene, and people like Mary Quant and Barbara Hulanicki were the only designers they could buy from until the rag trade started copying their style and churning out short skirts and gamine dresses. And they needed a home, away from the Main Street retailers—that's how Carnaby Street started, a place in Soho you could get a cheap rented space to open your own boutique. In 1963 it really started to become a destination if you wanted to buy cheap and hip clothes.

Mary Quant: By 1963, the Chelsea store had really taken off. It wasn't for the working-class girl. It was all Chelsea people. They came with their parents and saved up, and some of them were artists and designers and sculptors, and some of them had money in their own right.

Everybody came: Audrey Hepburn, Leslie Caron, Brigitte Bardot. They all came. I would work with them personally. Leslie, she was so beautiful and everything that I liked and wanted to design for. Legginess. It was all about legs. Much more about legs than color. The miniskirt we started very early—end of the fifties. But by '63 it had become very popular. It caused such havoc. People were outraged.

I couldn't understand how people could be so shocked by the miniskirt. It was always covered up with opaque tights. It was difficult to understand why they were shocked. The mini was a way for young people to assert themselves. Youth was changing forever. It hadn't had a voice till that point. The clothes and fashion freed them from the claustrophobic clothes from before. They could go on from work and dance all night. In the past they thought they had to change several times a day, and they thought they had to wear corsets and things like that. I think the miniskirt was the impetus for it all—and the jazz. The two together were a combination and a catalyst. It was a badge of honor to be able to wear the mini. It took courage, because it hadn't been done before, and it was very short, and you could dance in it.

Pattie Boyd: I went shopping one day with a friend, a male friend, and this woman was walking towards me and said, "Do you know what you look like? That dress is disgusting!" And I just burst out laughing, as I was sure she had never seen such a short dress on anyone.

Mary Quant: Lots of people were very angry because our shop was so sexy, it was "obscene." We caused absolute havoc in Chelsea. The smart suits would beat on the window with rage because the skirts were so short and sexy. It was extraordinary.

Alexander and I were working day and night. People would beat on the door in the evening. It was marvelous. I loved it. It was such an extraordinary, electric success. The Kings Road became like a catwalk. There would be one American magazine shooting on one side of the street and then another magazine shooting on the other side of the street, and they'd get each other in their photos.

Justin de Villeneuve: The Kings Road really took off, long before it became "swinging London." I became an antiques dealer, and that's when I changed my name to Justin de Villeneuve. I'd stopped working for Vidal by then and done other ducking and diving. I took a stall in the antiques market. I could acquire things. Don't ask where they came from! My partner was upper-class. We made a good team. Me, the East End boy in the sharp suits, and he, so terribly English— ex-captain in the army, father was an admiral. He had the knowledge, and I could acquire things.

I was friends with Marc Bolan, but he wasn't called that then, he later became T Rex. And Cat Stevens. I used to hang out with these kids, and by then I was known as a bit of an entrepreneur. I could do things. If you wanted something, I could arrange it.

These guys were just starting, I'd know a record producer. It was all a bit bibbly-bobbly [*amateurish*] then. Not high-powered like now. They'd bring them to the stall or the flat. I always had a flat. I had a fab flat in Linden Gardens in Notting Hill. In those days it was scruffy and dangerous, not posh like now. Then it was pimps, hookers, and drug dealers.

I always knew something was going to happen. Then I met Twiggs [*Twiggy*]. And I knew I was going to crack it [*be successful*]. She was working in my brother Tony's hair salon—I called him Antoine—and he told me he knew this schoolgirl who wanted to be a model. She was only thirteen then—too young—but by sixteen she was the biggest model in the world.

Terry O'Neill: Everybody thinks Twiggy is the poster girl for the 1960s, but she didn't really burst onto the scene until 1966. Justin approached me and I took them both out shopping on the Kings Road in 1966. Justin was a brilliant entrepreneur, like Andrew Loog Oldham, wise guys with panache and a boldness. He made Twiggy a superstar through chutzpah and his ability to wheel and deal in any circle.

But it was Jean Shrimpton who really opened the world's eyes and put swinging London on the map. She was the first supermodel. David Bailey photographed her for *Vogue*, and the two of them were the toast of New York, Paris, Milan, and London. They were the [Mario] Testino and Kate Moss or the "Posh [Spice"] and Becks [*Victoria and David Beckham*] of their day. I dated Jean for a while; so did Terry Stamp. And Mick Jagger was dating her sister, Chrissie. I guess this was the birth of the age of celebrity. Before that, celebrity was Hollywood and royalty. After 1963 it was us, we were the news, the photographers, the models, the actors, the footballers, the hairdressers, designers, and of course, the bands, the Beatles, the Stones, and others. Fashion, the arts, music, were all separate, and suddenly in 1963 they fused and became indistinguishable. I mean, think of Burton and Taylor. That's the way it was before 1963, one actor married another. Suddenly it was a rock star and a model, a photographer and an actress. Their world's collided and coalesced. It was one of those moments in history when there is an alchemy. Historians can have their theories but for me it was just evolution, it was our turn, young people, to turn on the world. Nineteen sixty-three was the Big Bang for us.

Norman Jopling: Nineteen sixty-three was the year that UK pop really took off, and the second half of the year did not disappoint. The Beatles were still number one in the LP and EP charts. "From Me to You" was falling after five months in the singles chart, but their new just-released single, "She Loves You," was about to blow away all opposition and top the charts globally. Summer 1963 was when surf music broke into the charts: the Beach Boys crept into the top 40 with "Surfin' USA."

From May 18 to June 9, 1963, the Beatles embarked on a major UK tour for the first time as headliners with Gerry & the Pacemakers and Roy Orbison. "From Me to You" was number one at the beginning of the tour. There were twenty-one venues spread over twenty-four days— three days off—and the itinerary was crazy. The M1 was Britain's only motorway—and only sixty miles of it. The traveling was grueling.

Andrew Loog Oldham: After "Come On" we had nothing to record, I mean, all of these groups that had been created and were coming along, there's, like, so many of them, they're all raiding the potential R&B songs that the Stones knew.

I'm by now sharing rooms with Mick and Keith—my mother had kicked me out again. Not in that Chelsea flat, no, no, no, thanks, ooof, no, that was terrible. So Mick and Keith had moved and I moved in there and took the couch; that's where I start working on them to write songs based on the premise that if Mick can write postcards back to his mother he can write lyrics and if Keith can play three chords he can write songs. They laughed, because they didn't think they could, but they recognized how important that would be.

Cilla Black: The Beatles were doing their own stuff when they recorded their first album. They changed the face of the Earth because they had written their own songs. They weren't relying on Americans anymore; they were writing their own songs, and that was the difference, and there was a knock-on [*catalytic*] effect.

Vicki Wickham [English manager, producer, and songwriter]: In 1963, everyone knew everyone. There were only a very few clubs, so everyone was there that you knew.

I came from BBC light entertainment, which was radio. And I worked for a producer. I was his secretary. We had music, bands, actors, and sound effects. And I got really good at how to put a show together and edit it. After a while I thought, "This is great." I tried to get on at the BBC but couldn't. I was twenty-one.

My girlfriend was going out with Elkan Allan, the head of Reddiffusion TV [*London's commercial television station*], so she introduced us. He said, "You have to start at the bottom. I have several programs that we are piloting, and if we get one off the ground I promise you that you can move up." So I went to work for him, and one of the pilots was *Ready Steady Go*.

The very first show [*August 9*] was Brian Poole & the Tremeloes. They did "Twist and Shout." It was a cover. I don't think they ever wrote their own material. Billy Fury—England's Elvis—his record was doing well on the radio. He was really sexy, small, and just had a real aura about him. Girls loved him. Huge as hell.

Terry O'Neill: *Ready Steady Go* was the first really truly classless entertainment show on British television; it got rid of the dinner jacketed, Oxbridge, lead-crystal accents and formality, and just mixed up the acts and the audience—it went with the flow.

Keith Richards: Class was one of those things you could burst through. . . . "That's got to go." Everybody was thinking and saying the same thing. In a way, you started to feel that you were the voice of all this energy.

In 1963, the Beatles were far more enormous than us, but we were great mates. We were all part of the same energy. We all felt that we were lucky to be on this first big tsunami. No competition. Fantastic.

It was rare and innocent. No one was old enough to be anything but innocent. It was all done from sheer heart and pure thoughts—if you can imagine me saying that.

Terry O'Neill: Can you imagine today two bands helping each other, swapping songs, jamming together, even giving up their gigs for each other? No. They'd lock themselves in their dressing rooms arguing with the management about the lighting, the sound, or who got the top billing, or why they had banana Twinkies and the other band had orange. In 1963 bands weren't rivals, they were pals—probably because they didn't see music as a career but as an interlude in their lives before they had to settle down. There wasn't that commercial competition, which is what drives egos. Then it was exciting just to think you could get out of your hometown and play another, go on a road trip and see if what you had could turn on a new audience.

Georgie Fame: Ronan O'Rahilly told me one day that he'd been up to Newcastle and he'd found this fantastic band and he was going to bring them down to play at the Scene Club. I walked in there and the Animals were in full form, jumping up and down and singing. The Animals were tough cookies. Very suspicious. Alan Price was very smart, and Chas Chandler was physically hard. Geordie boys [*a regional nickname in coal-mining communities that describes working-class youth from around the northern city of Newcastle*]. We became great friends.

Hilton Valentine: Ronan O'Rahilly, who had the Scene Club in London, came up to see us play in Newcastle. Jeffrey, our manager who owned Club-A-Go-Go in Newcastle, was booking in bands like the Stones, the Yardbirds, Sonny Boy Williamson. O'Rahilly managed the Yardbirds and Georgie Fame in the beginning, so they agreed to put the Yardbirds in the Club-A-Go-Go for a week, and we were going to London to do the Scene. It was a swap.

I don't know when we changed our name to the Animals. But I think it was our first journey to London, our first gig as the Animals. Mickie Most came to see us in London. It was our first trip to London. We were a new band and it was a big thing.

Chrissie Most: We were broke and had this little flat, no hot water. It was a dump. And I was pregnant. Mickie's mum said, "Leave the baby with me and go on the road with Mickie." He didn't want to go on the road without me because we'd done everything together from the start, but really he didn't want to go on the road at all—he wanted to concentrate on being a producer. That's when we found the Animals, and Mickie came to me and said, "We have to book the studio, and they are coming down from Newcastle."

We either had to pay the rent or pay for the studio, so we paid for the studio. Alan Price wore a cloth cap and a donkey jacket. They were so badly dressed. But Mickie saw them and signed them because they were so good.

Terry O'Neill: I heard about this band the Animals coming into London from Newcastle and organized to photograph them straight off the train. I took them shopping first, then to a studio because they didn't look the business in cloth caps and donkey jackets—they looked like laborers. But it was just one big working-class lark to them, fooling around with bowler hats and stuff.

Hilton Valentine: It was on Oxford Street, and it was really a rehearsal place where violinists went. We didn't last long in there. They told us to leave 'cause we were so loud. I don't know what happened. It was certainly not a place where we should have been.

It was unusual in the beginning, being photographed. And it *was* the beginning. We didn't have a recording contract. That came later. We did the Yardbird gigs and went back to Newcastle and then back to London to live. We moved to London because there was work. It was all starting to happen.

We lived in west Kensington—sounds posh but it was unfurnished—and we had camp beds, and the only heat that we had was little electric heaters.

Vicki Wickham: We all knew each other. There was no question of someone not taking your call. Nobody hugged each other at home, and suddenly everyone was giving you a big hug. That was absolutely fab. It was affectionate and tactile. It was a very nice time. People were friendly. It was nice and easy and didn't make a statement about your relationship.

Andrew Loog Oldham I would see out and about. He'd tell me where he was getting his shirts made. It was really significant and important, in the same way when you bought an album you wanted to carry it around on a Saturday so that people could see the design and the artwork and discuss it.

Artists were beginning to dress—except the Animals, who didn't dress. If the cover was great and exciting—like the first Stones record—it was making a statement about the music.

Terry O'Neill: None of us had any time to think about where we were going. We were just too busy having a good time, working hard and playing hard. For some it was looking for the next song or the next recording contract; for me it was the next story, always the next headline photograph.

Pretty soon I was the highest-paid and probably youngest photographer in Fleet Street. Young people, film stars, bands, singers, models were the news, and I knew them all, clubbed with them, ate with them, and in some cases *made* them by getting them on the front page.

I wanted to chronicle them in their own time and space; I wanted to treat them as a news story. It just seemed that being young, doing what we did in our way, was suddenly what the world needed. There was no plan, no artifice, no career mapped out. We lived and drank and shopped and loved in the moment, for the buzz—and the money. Money meant we could leave home, get a flat, buy cool clothes. You could rent a flat and buy a new suit every week for five pounds.

Vicki Wickham: I was living in Knightsbridge with four other girls, sharing a flat. I had the worst room there. My roommates were very conventional, doing very conventional jobs. None of them did more than get married. I was the only one that was doing something a bit different. I was only being paid seven pounds and ten shillings a week.

The studio was at the bottom of Kingsway in the West End. I was there early. Get on the phone. See who was in the charts, who was interesting, and every single night we would be out to a club. We didn't get home till two or three in the morning. There was a lot of drinking. Some people were smoking some pot or hash, but nothing stronger than that. Ginger Baker was the only person I knew who was doing heroin or something stronger.

None of us realized we had power. It was just what we did. People would chat us up, take us out to eat, but we became friends with Andrew Loog Oldham, who was one of the first managers I met.

Andrew Loog Oldham: This is August, the Stones are rehearsing in a basement in Soho, and they've got nothing, no songs.

They're in those Terry O'Neill photographs. In the photos, I'm wearing sunglasses. I'm copying Phil Spector—not in the sound, not the look—I couldn't look like Phil Spector—I mean the whole fucking mystery.

Aristotle Onassis said when we were very young, all you need to make it is a good address—it doesn't matter whether it's the basement or the attic—and a suntan.

I kept going to France, to get the tan, or I used face cream. You looked orange if you put too much on.

Look how young they look in Terry's photos! Bill Wyman is always a little bit apart from everyone. He was the only one who'd done national service; he probably was the only one who was actually raised with an outside toilet. He's twenty-seven in 1963; we're nineteen or twenty.

Terry O'Neill: Andrew was just a kid really, but he was smart, he was savvy, and his youth worked for him. The Stones let him manage them because they thought, "He's worked for Brian Epstein. He got the Beatles publicity. He can do the same for us."

But Andrew was a worker. He never stopped hustling and pushing and networking and making things happen for the Stones. Keith's right when he says he was the sixth Stone.

Andrew Loog Oldham: So in rehearsal there's nothing to do, there's no song that's working. I leave, because I'm not contributing, and when I come out, I turn right, and by turning right, I change all our lives. If I'd turned left, it wouldn't have happened. I get outside the rehearsal room, turn right, I go to the corner, and I run into John and Paul getting out of a taxi by the Talk of the Town, [a theater] on Leicester Square tube station, and they're inebriated. They've had free drinks, because free drinks were still very important as drinks were very expensive, and they said, "What's wrong, Andy?"

They'd just won their first Ivor Novello Award, which is the songwriter's thing, right? So they were very happy, and I said, "You know, I've got nothing to record."

"We'll sort it out man, we've got a song for you."

So they come down [back to the rehearsal room] and they actually play a song to the Rolling Stones called "I Wanna Be Your Man." They pretended it's half-finished and they're going to finish it off there in front of the Stones. They said, "We haven't written the bridge yet." Yeah—they'd recorded it ten days before, with Ringo singing the lead. So they're coming down and giving us their crap, because you know, it's not John and Paul singing lead, it's Ringo.

They were great hustlers, they really were, I mean, I thought I was good, but they were an education to the Stones. John and Paul could sell a song to anybody. I mean, they had the gift of the gab. They were a double act. They were hustlers, pure and simple. Brian Epstein didn't peddle their songs. That would have been beneath him.

They could sell a song to a deaf mute. John glared at you and dared you to be stupid and say no. Paul was the charm geezer—good cop/bad cop. They were on tour with Helen Shapiro in early 1963. She was topping the bill. John and Paul gave her "Misery." Her A&R man turned it down. On the tour bus the next day they flogged [*sold*] it to Kenny Lynch.

But with "I Wanna Be Your Man," it was magic! Brian Jones picks up the guitar, and the way he plays "I Wanna Be Your Man," he makes the song belong to the Stones. I got the same feeling as the first time I saw the Stones. Immediate! It almost gives me a nervous breakdown. I mean, I am just so fucking overwhelmed by the whole thing that I go off to Paris for three days and buy shoes—no really, because I was just so overcome [with excitement].

Vicki Wickham: The first time I met Andrew Loog Oldham, the Stones were on *Ready Steady Go*, and I went around the corner to the pub, and Andrew was outside in a beautiful Mr. Fish shirt with his red hair, and a drink in his hand. He managed to say hello, and slid down the wall. He just passed out he was so drunk. That was my first meeting with Andrew. He was an absolute baby. Nineteen years old.

I loved Andrew: he was arrogant, a pain in the arse. He was the first person who had a Mini with tinted windows and a chauffeur. We got on great. We had nothing in common so we had everything in common. We hung out and would go out and see artists. We'd go to restaurants. I couldn't afford it so I would go with Andrew and people from record companies, and they always paid.

Andrew Loog Oldham: Somebody who Terry O'Neill knew well, the fashion photographer Terence Donovan, had already said to me when I worked for Mary Quant, he said, "Oh, Andrew," he says, "you're an alcoholic, right?' I said, "What are you talking about, I don't even drink." He says, "You got the isms" [*Cockney slang for the shakes associated with alcoholism*]. Terry Donovan turned out to be totally right.

Hilton Valentine: Free booze was always welcome. We were all working-class boys and alcohol was part of our diet. [If] you didn't drink, you weren't a man. We hung out with Georgie Fame, Eric Clapton, when they were at the clubs after gigs. There was a club in Ealing, and in the center of London, the Marquee, the Cromwellian. The Beatles and Stones were there and at the Ad Lib. We'd talk about music and women and get drunk.

I loved the Beatles. There was no jealousy. We were all in this moment together. It was a working-class thing, and the shackles were broken. We were all out having a bloody good time and partying like hell. It was a very hedonistic time. And we were getting paid. There was that feeling you could do anything you wanted to do.

Vicki Wickham: The first time the Stones were on *Ready Steady Go*—absolute magic! There's a lot of hanging around and lots of cups of tea, and it was a great opportunity to talk to them a bit. They did "Come On," I think. They just were just, like, "This is what the music should be. This is where the bar should be, and we should go above it and not below it." It was no big deal. It really wasn't. They were comfortable, amongst people they were used to.

Bill Wyman: We went on casually—in our own clothes.

Sir Alan Parker: I never watched much television but the breakout shows of the year were *Ready Steady Go*—"The Weekend Starts Here" was its billing—and *That Was the Week That Was*. [*The latter was a satirical news and politics show hosted by David Frost and starring, among others, Dudley Moore and Peter Cook. John Cleese and Roald Dahl were among the writers.*] Both broke the mold of staid British TV and set the pattern for a decade.

Terry O'Neill: The Stones just turned up at the Kingsway Studios to do *Ready Steady Go* in their regular casual clothes. And it worked. I was backstage with them mucking about: Mick under a hair dryer, Keith shaving from a light socket, Bryan messing with Bill's hair, Andrew and Keith sharing a cup of tea. I shot some great reportage that day. Mick turned up in a coat with a fur hood and a pair of corduroy trousers, and pulled faces. Keith just looked cool—always did, always has. At that time they couldn't have got away with it anywhere else but *Ready Steady Go*. It was the first TV show for kids, by kids, with kids doing their own thing. Radical!

Vicki Wickham: We were so low-key. My job was to make sure that people were onstage when they should be. I had to remind them that they had five minutes and put your hair dryer down. Yes, there were close calls. Sandie Shaw [*1960s British pop singer with seven top-ten hits*] managed to miss it completely one time. She was talking to someone in the dressing room and just missed the entire thing. It was just no big deal.

The idea was that the audience were part of the set and that the artists were interspersed with them. People wanted to dance and not sit.

At that point my job was everything. Just putting it together.

Doing the script. Booking the artists. Making sure we had everything we needed for the show. We truly did just about everything. I was made editor, and to this day I don't really understand what being an editor actually means. It was live: there was nothing to edit. But editor meant helping select the audience, booking the artists. We'd go 'round the clubs and invite people to be in the audience. Everyone looked great, danced great, and the bands and artists were people we liked at the time.

No "Here's your mark, don't move outside it." In '63 we were miming. They didn't have to worry to tune their instruments. None of them were very good at lip-synching. That was what television was in '63.

Terry O'Neill: Because everything was so laid back and all the rules went out of the window at *Ready Steady Go*, I got in amongst the audience and during rehearsals; that's when I noticed Mick was already becoming the major focal point of the band, and not just because he was the lead singer. I mean, it was Brian's band, but Mick didn't have an instrument so he seemed to use his body—make it work with the music, act out the song, striking poses, pouting, pushing himself. He was very charismatic already. He was a showman. Other bands, the guy just stood there and sang. Mick *moved*.

Vicki Wickham: From secretary to editor took just three or four months. I was so bossy and loud no one questioned my position. The artists were all the same sort of age so they didn't think it was strange that this bird was saying, "Get yourself together."

The first time the Beatles were on I think they came on with Dusty Springfield [*British blues and soul singer whose album* Dusty in Memphis *is ranked one the the greatest of all time by* Rolling Stone *magazine*] as host. She interviewed them about the music, hair, and their look. They mimed their song. We didn't realize how big they were going to be, but already there was a queue to get in right down the street all the way to the tube station.

Kids tried to get in. Police had to come. It was incredible. The Beatles didn't really know how big they were at this point ,and *we* certainly had no idea. It was '63. It was fab and dangerous, which was lovely. It was dangerous in a way that was exciting. Not like anyone would get hurt, it was just, "Wow, people are really prepared to break down this door or try and get in through the boiler room."

Cilla Black: Brian Epstein wanted me to go down to London to record with George Martin. The only time I could get down into the studio was in my summer holidays because there was no way I was gonna give up my day as a clerk typist—that wasn't gonna happen. I was quite a sensible girl.

Where I came from in Liverpool, which was a very poor area—I mean, much poorer than the Beatles—my dad was a stevedore on the docks and my mother sold secondhand clothes in a market, so my work ethic was theirs. I not only worked in the office five days a week, I worked in clubs in the evening, in coffee bars serving coffee, and I would sing, and I was getting really big money then, half of my wages for the week.

I was singing at the Blue Angel Club after that disastrous audition, and Brian Epstein came in and saw me again. He said, "Why didn't you sing like this at the audition?" I told him it wasn't in my key, so he sent George Martin up to see me from London.

I was nineteen when I went down to Abbey Road Studios to record "Love of the Loved." It was Paul's song; he used to sing it as part of the Beatles' set at the Cavern. To sing a Beatles song that had never been recorded was probably a big plus. But it wasn't a big hit.

Brian took us all on, so you had to have great faith in him. I always believed, like in the Cinderella story, that one day my prince will come or fairy godmother, and both of them came in the shape of Brian Epstein. Yeah, I did believe that there was something, but I didn't know which way to go about it, and in those days, to crack London was a bit like cracking America, really. Brian knew everything down from Bach to the Beatles. I did *Ready Steady Go* in September. My next song, "Anyone Who Had a Heart," went to number one.

Norman Jopling: Brian Epstein's new press officer, Tony Barrow, called me about Brian's latest hit-maker, Cilla Black, and asked if I'd like to interview her. I was curious. I had no real opinion about her record "Love of the Loved," but there was something about Cilla that seemed interesting. So I wandered up Shaftesbury Avenue and met her in a little café close to Monmouth Street.

Peter Brown: Brian was a paternal figure, totally involved with their welfare. The Beatles were family, Cilla was family, Gerry & the Pacemakers were family—but all of those other artists, none of them had the cheeky panache of Cilla and the Beatles.

Norman Jopling: She was there with her boyfriend Bobby [*her husband and manager after Epstein's death*], and we sat at one of those little chipped Formica-topped tables with cramped bench seats facing each other, over a coffee and a bun. Cilla was very much alright, bright, down-to-earth, instantly likable.

Cilla Black: I didn't like London at first because I found the people unfriendly. But then Felicity Green sent me to Vidal Sassoon to get my hair cut.

He was Cockney for a start; he came from nothing, he was very working-class, and I kind of quite liked that. Then you had your Terry O'Neill, who still sounds Cockney to me—he came from a working-class background. Everything came together.

It was like a jigsaw puzzle: you had the Beatles, you had the Liverpool explosion, you had the Cockney explosion. All of a sudden, working-class was really in. Even radio had to change, and television certainly did. When we came down from Liverpool, you had broadcasters reading the news on radio wearing a dinner jacket and a bow tie, I mean, why? Nobody could see them anyway.

On the news you had to speak the Queen's English—I've never quite known what the Queen's English is, but everybody spoke in a different way. Everything changed: skirts got shorter and shorter, it went from the fifties thing overnight.

Barbara Hulanicki: We had a few things [we] were making for Cilla Black: stage clothes for five pounds, [and] we had transparent T-shirts. She came in and we talked and we said, "We don't know whether to go for five pounds or go for the cheap end." She said, "Go for the cheap end. That's what it's about." She knew what she was talking about. She was wonderful.

We started getting all the elite coming in. But we had all the others too, who weren't elite—the Stones and the Beatles—they came in to date the shopgirls because they were so gorgeous. They were just bands. They weren't that big. They weren't worldwide.

Felicity Green: I loved the way Barbara Hulanicki dressed and the look of her. And I had an idea: would she do a pattern for me? So she did this pattern and we got fabric and it was made up and I was so smitten that I gave it this huge space in the newspaper. But I totally underestimated the response.

Barbara Hulanicki: We had the huge hit with the gingham dress. Felicity Green, the fashion director of the *Daily Mirror*, called and asked us to do a mail-order dress for the *Mirror* and said, "I'd like a gingham, like Bardot in St. Tropez."

We had the samples made up, it was photographed. It was in one size only. They were all tiny. Very small. We only made two sizes in clothes generally, eight and ten. Girls were minute since the war. There was no meat. English girls had very long legs like sticks. I can never forget the day the gingham dress came out. We had an address where all the mail went to and when we went to collect it my husband Fitz [*Stephen Fitz-Simon*] came 'round the corner, and he was dragging two sacks, and he said, "There's more." It was all money orders.

The dress was twenty-five shillings. By the time we finished we made a halfpenny on each dress. There were thousands of postal orders [*money orders*] all over the kitchen. We went to a bank and tried to set up a business account and we brought along all these postal orders, and they wouldn't process it. You had to fill in forms; it was lots of work.

Vicki Wickham: It really came back down to the music—if it was good it didn't matter how you spoke, how you acted; it was just down to the music. It was a common denominator.

There were no labels then, though I suppose Biba was the first label that anyone got to know. There was a picture of a brown-and-white striped skirt and jacket in the paper. I thought it was great. I called up Barbara Hulanicki—"Do you still have it in?"

Barbara was too busy to go out. She was always sewing. I'd only see her when I'd go over there and drink copious amounts of tea waiting for the gear to be made.

It was a time when young people cared about how their hair was cut [and] who cut it, though a lot of mums still cut hair. The clothes were cheap and fashionable. You didn't need to have a lot of money for people to say, "Wow, that's great."

Barbara Hulanicki: We had lots of bits left over from the mail order. Odd dresses and things. I said, "Come on and let's make a shop out of our flat." And I'd ring up a few people. We had one or two girls working for us. We turned the music on and we sold out everything. And for weeks after, people would arrive in the middle of the night and they would come in and we would have nothing left.

Once you've got something that's really pulsating, you don't give up; you keep on supplying this very hungry market. We'd get a delivery in the late afternoon. The assistant girls would say so-and-so dress and so-and-so blouses are coming in. And girls would sit and wait for the delivery for hours. Sometimes the vans would come and it wouldn't have the right stock. The girls were desperate. They wanted something new and they had to have it to go dancing. They would be furious. They had hot money—cash. And then the Beatles came in.

Sir Frank Lowe: A lot of us used to meet at the original Biba shop. Well, it was fantastic. You'd go in there and sit on the sofa and have a cup of coffee and chat to your mates, and all these girls would come in and out of the changing rooms, and it was just an extraordinary thing.

Vidal Sassoon: The British public wanted and needed change so badly. When I walked down the Kings Road on a Saturday afternoon the whole street seemed to be an atelier—not just Mary Quant's shop, the whole street. Everyone with super haircuts and all wearing Mary's clothes. And everyone jumped to it and came to London.

6

AUDACITY

"The mood was new music. I just had five years of top-ten
records all over the world, and then in 1963 the Beatles and
the Rolling Stones came in and changed popular music.
I thought my career was over. I was twenty-three."

NEIL SEDAKA

*The second American Revolution, nearly two hundred years after the
first, was being fought not only for equality, enfranchisement, and civil
rights but for the abolition of laws and strictures that enslaved creativity in literature, film, and the arts as well. From folk festivals to film
sets, on printing presses and celluloid, the nation was ready to bare its
breasts.*

Gay Talese: In 1963, I was thirty, and I was married—we pretty much
eloped. My wife was a junior editor at Random House, and I had joined
the *New York Times* back in 1953 as a copy boy and became a reporter.
Also, I was writing a lot on the outside. I needed the money, as I was
living beyond my means on a newspaper salary. *Esquire* was paying
me the most and not editing me.

I was ready to move but I was also worried about paying the rent.
The *New York Times* was a steady income, and we didn't have any chil-

dren in '63. One of the stories was an assignment in London in 1963 to do Peter O'Toole [*who would soon star in* Lawrence of Arabia].

I don't know when I heard the Beatles first, but they were still in London and I knew about them. They were a little group, eccentric in appearance, with their long hair and dress. I was aware of that. When I first heard them it had an impact. You were aware of new music and new people.

We had the same feeling when Kennedy was elected. When you have a young man in the White House, my generation were very much feeling that our time had come, with Kennedy as our youthful figure with international power. The Cuban Missile Crisis was a good testing ground for him.

Kennedy was a master of language. He was wonderful. I covered his speeches. I was interested in the sidelines. I covered Cape Canaveral, writing about the astronauts; they were stars, Kennedy was a star. And now this new music personified by the Beatles was in the air.

Sir Frank Lowe: In a sense '63 was the greatest year of my life because I came back from America, and if I hadn't come back and they hadn't wanted to draft me I would have stayed there.

Britain had been dull and America exciting. But it had all changed, driven by the working-class because they had nothing to lose.

Gay Talese: There was a change in fashion—you saw this in the streets. The Beatles had their own fashion. There was a youthful look, a new style in almost everything. It was really propelled by the presidency in the U.S. The president, Kennedy, made a tremendous impression, and it was augmented by his advisors, who smoked cigars and didn't wear a hat. Everyone used to wear a hat, but Kennedy didn't wear a hat. My father told me that a man is not fully dressed without a hat. But Kennedy changed that.

We knew about his sexual appetite, but it seemed at variance with his bad back—it was public now that he had a bad back. He had a sexy wife who probably wasn't sexy, but she looked sexy and well-dressed—the suits and the pillbox hat—and fashion was very much coming in, especially for women. You had the miniskirt—the anti-fashion fashion—and the classic fashion that Jackie personified: the well-designed suit or coat. The knockoffs were accessible to young people. Fashion—who could afford the designer suit? The economics always affect fashion. I felt the emphasis on youth. Kennedy was possibly the youngest president in history and it affected the whole culture.

Norma Kamali [American fashion designer]: I had just graduated from FIT [*the Fashion Institute of Technology in New York City*] and all the jobs were superficial, so I thought, "I am going to travel." I saw an ad in the *Times* for a position at Northwest Airlines. At the time, working for an airline was like working for Apple. That was the desired place to get a job.

I didn't know I wanted to be a designer. Absolutely not. I hated the whole fashion thing at FIT. Everyone looked like *Mad Men*. Matching hats and handbags. I just didn't fit in. I was so miscast. I thought they were all so superficial and so someone at the airlines said to me, "When you go to London"—I was going to Paris first—"this person said there are some boardinghouses in this area in London called Chelsea, and you can stay for six dollars a night. It's a nice little area, and it's really pretty.

So I meet my friend Betsy in Paris and I'm waiting for her in the lobby of the Normandy Hotel, and there are these British guys who obviously are in some kind of a group in the hotel. Steve Winwood was in the band, and they were all thinking that I am French and made jokes about me and my friend Betsy.

We started talking in English. And they went, "Oh, gosh, why don't you guys come with us. We are doing a tour around Paris and just outside." So we went with them, and they said, "When you come to London there's this club called the Speakeasy, and you have to come. Everyone's there."

We didn't know anybody. Nobody was anybody yet. It was still so early. The Stones and Beatles hadn't come to New York yet.

Allen Jones: We lived on one floor at the Chelsea Hotel in New York, and I had a studio on another floor. That was very exciting. Wow, this is America and I'm here. We were so excited, and we didn't know that back home, London was becoming an epicenter, too. We knew Warhol enough to say hi, but he was still just another artist on the scene then.

What I was really worried about wasn't being sent to Vietnam but that I'd come back to my parents from an American airbase wearing an American uniform, which might upset them. [*British nationals who were permanent residents in the United States were eligible for the draft.*] I did get called up for the draft. But the recruiting officer said, "You're wasting my time." I was twenty-six, white, and married. [*American men between eighteen and twenty-six were drafted; Jones was already at the upper limit of the age range. In addition, men in college, as well as married men were often excused from the draft or received a deferment.*]

I had lived there for a year, but my wife got homesick—and pregnant—and I couldn't afford to bring up twins in private education in New York. So I returned to London.

Norma Kamali: Our first night [in London] we went to Margaret Street where the Speakeasy Club was. You went down to this place, it was like a coffin with drapes. Silent and dark. And you get led in through these drapes, and there was everybody who was a musician at the time. I mean everybody.

But I wasn't impressed—I didn't know who they were. I would come back to my job at the airline and no one had a sense back in New York who they were. It was English Motown. It was the music of choice. British music was happening. I met Jimmy Page [*later a member of Led Zeppelin*] and all these guys. Kids. I was Norma from New York, and I didn't know who I was.

This shaped who I became. The moment was so big and we knew it

was different from our parents, but I don't think we knew how pro-
foundly different it was till ten or twenty years later. So it was highly
charged living in that moment, and I was stimulated every day. Every
day in London there was something new that had never been done
before. And every day since then, it's been a take on or a look back or
a nod to things at that time.

Carly Simon: My sister and I were touring the second year I was in
college, which would have been '63. Lucy started to play the guitar,
and there was some guy David who was a folksinger, and he was all I
ever wanted and could ever have dreamed of, and he was on Martha's
Vineyard and his parents were friends with my parents.

It was David who taught Lucy some chords, some picking. They
had gone to school together when they were very little. They were
friends from Martha's Vineyard and from school, and he taught her
the chords, and so she learned and I copied off her.

So by 1963, the summer, we both knew about three or four chords,
and we thought we'd get a job singing in a nightclub with our two guitars. And we hitchhiked to this place called the Moors in Province-
town, and nobody would pick us up on the way up, they just passed us
one after another. We were yelling at people who passed us, "We'll see
you at the Moors. We'll be the stars and you'll just be the little plebs
and you'll wish you knew us."

We went up to audition, and the band that was playing there were
just drafted to the war in Vietnam, so we were hired on the spot because it was the same day that the guys had left. We had about four or
five songs. We did some folk songs by Joan Baez—she was so popular
then. There was a song "West Virginia." We both did vocals. Everyone
thought we were gay! They thought we were a gay act. We were called the
Simon Sisters. We didn't really know what gay was.

We spent the rest of the summer gaining ground on our repertoire,
and then that fall Charlie Close, our manager, had us audition at the
Bitter End in Greenwich Village. That was my sophomore year. We

were getting our repertoire stronger, and we had fifteen songs. We were the opening act for a lot of people that fall—Woody Allen, Joan Rivers, Bill Cosby, and Dick Cavett.

Gay Talese: I was hugely ambitious and driven in 1963. But I wanted to live freely. I wanted to be a writer. I didn't want to be beholden to the *New York Times*, but I had to pay the bills. I had to have a job. I left the *Times* completely. I was writing all over, getting extra money.

I was sent to London to interview Peter O'Toole. He was the most interesting man I had ever met. While he was an international movie star, he was also very smart. His frame of reference was amazing. He knew art, opera, poetry; he was a very intellectually curious person and a nice person.

I stayed at his big house in London after I wrote a profile of him; he invited my wife to come over and we spent a week or so after I'd done the research for the piece for *Esquire*. He convinced me that I was being a little too cautious as a person with regard to my personal life. Just stop practicing birth control. Don't worry about the money. You'll make it. And I was persuaded by this because [of] the person who was telling me. This was a guy who was taking chances being an actor. He had lots of small parts before he got big parts.

Norma Kamali: I was going to London the tail end of '63. I walk along the Kings Road and looked around, and all of a sudden I see shops, and they are really interesting and different, and I see people dressed in a different way. People in short skirts. We had our knees covered and we wore stockings. Oh my god this is unbelievable, and I was so excited, like, totally excited. And I think the Beatles song ["I Wanna Hold Your Hand"]—I think they had just released a record, and I can't remember when I first heard it but I know I heard it when I was walking down Kings Road because the song was blaring out of the shops. The sound was so new and this was so new. Everything was so new—the contrast from this, the radical new color explosion, to little old ladies all dark and gray—it was an explosion from black-and-white into Technicolor. I couldn't believe what I was seeing. I had chills the whole time. I was in awe. I knew I had found my star. I fit in here. I knew I didn't fit in at FIT. But all of this was like coming home: this is where I belong. It was the freedom—it was very liberating for me. My mind was exploding with ideas.

Henry Diltz: We were still in our suits—our uniforms. It was jazz and folk and comedy, and we had four station wagons and we went to all the colleges. We played with Nina Simone and Herbie Mann. We were the folk music. We signed on to a bus tour and it was forty-one nights on a bus, and there was a gospel group—the Gospel Pearls: three-hundred-pound ladies who sang amazingly. In the South there was one hotel who wouldn't let us stay there because of the black people. Should some of us stay there? No—hell no. We are going to stick together.

We all smoked grass at the time. We got forty-five dollars a week and everything was paid for. It was fun as hell. Our generation, we thought we were up-and-coming and we knew all the answers. We were smoking grass, but as the guy from the Doors said, we weren't taking drugs, we were taking sacraments. We wanted to get insights. I was taking acid, just starting, in New York in '63.

Robert Christgau: I was part of the political wing but we were outnumbered by trippy self-indulgent hedonists who by then had never known a year in which the GDP went down or the income of their parents went down—never in their lives, ever. We had experienced nothing but economic expansion. I could go get my little crummy job, live parsimoniously, save money, and take five months off.

What encapsulates the mood of '63 for me is that someone is able to put a pack on his back with the collected poems of W. B. Yeats and a few other books and spend five months on the road with nine hundred dollars in the bank. That is freedom, and it was just *there*. If I needed to get a job I could just go get a job tomorrow. It was not an issue. No anxiety whatsoever about employment. And that is why the economic factor is so important. Getting a casual job to get you to the next place was an absolutely assumed thing.

Gay Talese: I remember in '63 one of the pieces I wrote was about a movie actress named Romy Schneider. The lack of resistance to sexual impulsiveness you followed up with infatuation, and you just did it. It was in Vienna. And I remember us talking, and she was not aggressive but during the conversation with her, where she was very forthcoming about her hatred of her mother, we went to bed, just like that. The world had changed. And a couple of days later my wife came over, and the film was moving from Vienna to Rome, and we went to dinner with a lot of people from the cast, and I was dancing with Romy, and it was so easy when you have had a sexual experience with a person, and my wife noticed it. The spirit of the time was just fulfill your impulses. There was no resistance. It was the sexual revolution beginning.

Linda Geiser: If I saw the director or leading man seducing the girls, I would admire the girls but I thought it was a bit yucky to sleep around. We used diaphragms because we didn't like condoms. When I cheated on my boyfriend once or twice I didn't feel guilty, but I felt it wasn't worth it. I wanted to be free all the time and do what I wanted. I knew one thing: what I wanted was to be an actress. I didn't want to be married.

Robert Christgau: In my world, if you had a girlfriend, you slept with her [even though you weren't married]. And that was the way it was, and everyone I knew did it. There were not a whole lot of libertines in my group of friends. And it's the candor about sex that changes. Not what you do.

But in the early sixties I don't believe there was a lot of casual promiscuity. It seems very important that you can sing about sex in songs. That's a big deal, that there is a certain amount of sexual explicitness in sex songs that wasn't there [previously], and it ought to be. I do think it was a big deal. There was a level of prudishness that was being exorcised from the culture. *Lady Chatterley's Lover* and Henry Miller—those things are really important. It was ridiculous for those books to be banned.

I was having sex at least every two weeks throughout that entire period. I partook of some of that easy casualness. It seems to me that one of the main things of '63 is not that sexual mores were changing but that sexual practice was being acknowledged.

Gay Talese: In '63 I wrote a piece for *Esquire* about [the Broadway director] Joshua Logan, a homosexual who was married. I knew that. I didn't mention that, but in one scene I did say he was having a fight with an actress, Claudia McNeil, who was the star of the show *Tiger Tiger*. Claudia got mad at Joshua. He was saying, "You are acting like some queen up there." And she said, "You're the queen." That was the term for being a homosexual. And *Esquire* was worried about a lawsuit and said, "We are not ready to use that."

I said, "Let me see if I can get him to give me permission." He was on vacation in Mexico. I called him and he said, "No. I would rather you didn't use it."

"So what do you want me to put in there?" And he said "Why don't you put in 'empress.' "

Gay wasn't even in the language. They were queens and faggots, if you are talking crudely. But '63 was the beginning—a forerunner of the sexual revolution.

Terry O'Neill: So much was changing around us in 1963. In our young crowd we knew people who were gay, like Brian Epstein or actors, but we didn't address it or draw attention to it; it didn't seem to matter, unless you were a raving heterosexual and a gay guy came on to you.

But they didn't. Gay men had their own way of being discreet. They kept themselves to themselves because the rest of society was so rampantly, violently homophobic, from the cops and politicians down.

It was only young people who were casual about it, almost unconcerned, not the least bit threatened. It was the same with sex, fidelity, and adultery. There was very little guilt, not many boundaries. Your girlfriend's best friend would sleep with you. You'd pick up with your best mate's girl if they'd split and you fancied each other. There didn't seem to be any issue. Sex was fashionable, like music and clothes. Mind you, I think this was still very much a London scene. Out in the provincial cities you'd still get a bottle in your face if you slept with your mate's girl, whether he was with her or had split with her.

Gay Talese: I don't think infidelity was part of the fashion in America but it went uncondemned. Kennedy's affiliation with Hollywood is what appealed to young people like me. Kennedy's affairs were common knowledge, and not just because I was a journalist. [But] my father and people like him wouldn't believe it, but I knew people and it was common knowledge among my circle, and it wasn't scandalous.

We had our flings, and sometimes it led to divorce. In my case it didn't.

Linda Geiser: A whole bunch of people, including Warhol, we all went out together. Soho opened up for the first time. It was in the days when you weren't allowed to live in the lofts. They were commercial rooms, and the landlords would come at night and throw you out. That was one of the biggest changes—it was when Soho changed to living quarters for living artists.

I was in a group of young people that was doing all kinds of things. Andy Warhol was part of it. One day he told us to put on leotards, and then we were painted by him and his group. We had to make these funny movements. We were a train or something. We did it on the [subway] platform at West Broadway. Then my agent called me and said he had an audition for me. It was a movie. My agent said, "So-and-so star doesn't want to do it. This part doesn't need a well-known actress, it needs a face."

I knew immediately *The Pawnbroker* was going to be a controversial movie because of the nudity, because it was the first movie about a concentration camp, and because I knew nudity couldn't be shown. But I was fine to show my bosoms for a few seconds.

Sidney Lumet only wanted to do it his way. Sidney had been to Hollywood, and he said, "I don't want to work in Hollywood, where the producers are cutting my film and telling me what to do." They had the cutting rights, not the director. He said, "I am going to do it in New York," and he started shooting.

Rod Steiger didn't want a salary. Rod got a car, a Cadillac—this crazy idiotic car that he was futzing around in—and then a percentage of the film later. He was driving us crazy with this car. We all had to take a ride in it. He was so proud of this thing.

I was paid three thousand dollars a week! For six weeks! At the shop I was making two-fifty an hour, no more than a hundred dollars a week. On Broadway we got a hundred twenty a week.

I was not aware that I was making one of the great movies of all time. He told me about the nudity from the beginning. My father was upset, but I said, "Papa, it is revolutionary." We had to wait. We were filming in the fall, in September. It didn't take very long to shoot that scene. The whole thing took maybe an hour.

I knew right away that the film had a problem getting a release date 'cause I knew it couldn't be released that usual way and Sidney was not giving in. There was the feeling of rebellion against the old establishment. The young people wanted to do things their way and do new things.

Bob Gruen: I was eighteen in '63, trying to graduate from high school. I lived on Long Island. I wanted to go to [the] Rochester [Institute of

Technology in upstate New York]. I was interested in photography and I knew they were the best photography school.

I was starting to listen to folk music in high school, and my friend was playing guitar and he taught me how to play. I remember the Weavers and I remember my friend came over with a Dylan album sometime that year, saying, "You have to hear this record, this guy is amazing." I fell down on the floor laughing. I said, "This guy is not a singer. Are you kidding me?" But he said, "Listen to what he says."

Robert Christgau: Till April 18, 1963, which was my twenty-first birthday, I am living in my garret in Manhattan, and I set off on a hitchhiking trip around the country and it lasts till the middle of September. It takes me fifteen thousand miles, and I slept on people's floors—I visited all my friends all over the country. I spent some time in Berkeley and in LA—I had never seen California before.

The whole notion of America was very important to me. At Dartmouth I read British literature, and I was reading American fiction at the time because I felt I didn't really know it and I wanted to see America as I read about it on the road. And so I was listening to the radio all this time.

My musical experience was delivered to me by AM radio. "Surfing USA" by the Beach Boys—it was just starting to come up during that year. It had a utopian vision of America. It was a utopian time.

I liked pop art for the same thing: the edge, the incongruity. Some people think pop art was satiric. I didn't and never have. I liked it. They knew they were doing something outrageous. But was Andy Warhol satirizing or was he celebrating? Yes, sometimes there was a satiric element, but essentially it was a celebration, and that was what it grew out of. It was a rebellious time and yes, there were certainly things to get rebellious about. There was a civil rights movement, of which I was extremely aware.

Allen Jones: I did a drive for three months with my friend from college, Peter Phillips. He had a Harkness Scholarship—very prestigious—that allowed him to live in America for two years, and you had to travel for part of the time beyond your hometown. So Peter rang up and said, "I've got this car and it's free, how about doing a road trip?" We drove for three months down to Key West and the West Coast and through Salt Lake City and Niagara. We never went down to Alabama: freedom riders, civil rights—you don't want to go down there in New York license plates.

We stuck to the coast. In South Carolina you'd go into a diner and there'd be two walkways—one for whites and one for blacks—and we walked down the black one because we couldn't take it seriously, but we soon wised up to that. It wasn't very funny.

A car had broken down, there's a white woman in the back and the driver, who is black, has the bonnet [*hood*] up. We stopped and asked if we could help. He was stunned. The American woman in the back said, "No! Just tell the people at the garage in the next town."

Gay Talese: Civil rights began in '63 with the freedom riders. I was covering some of it. We had race riots in New York. But there was no "we shall overcome" spirit. [Martin] Luther King hadn't emerged as the leader yet. He was around. But there was fear and mistrust of black people.

Henry Diltz: We weren't really tuned in to what was happening outside, other than the Vietnam thing. We were only interested in the music. On the West Coast there was Scott McKenzie, who later sang "If You're Going to San Francisco." Beautiful high voice. There was another guy who played the banjo so beautifully—one of the Clancy Brothers, the Irish folk band. The Troubadour was the mecca. I didn't have to worry about the draft because I was technically in the reserves. I just dropped out of sight. It added to the college atmosphere. That added to the "us vs. them" attitude to authority. It fed it. Why would we go to a foreign country and shoot someone we don't know? For no good reason? More evidence of the wrongness of the people in charge and the rightness of us who were opening up to life. We were taking acid. We rejected the old world. Yeah, it was self-indulgent. I never did a nine-to-five job.

And two streets away from the Troubadour in LA was the Tropicana Motel, and everybody stayed there. We lived at the Tropicana and played at the Troubadour. But we used to play a whole week, not just one night. It was the clubs and the college concerts. We'd travel in a van across the country from state to state and do a folk club for a week and a few colleges and then move on, and we'd go to New York and do a couple of TV shows. I remember that young dude Dylan coming out.

Al Kooper: Folk and rock and roll were very differentiated from each other. They didn't like each other. I liked both and that made it tough for me.

I heard Dylan in the Village. His voice was tough for me. Paul Simon said, "Have you heard Bob Dylan?" And I said, "Yes, but I don't get it." He said, "Forget the singing, it's the guitar playing that's really good. Forget the singing."

Carly Simon: I miss how easy it was to learn songs from each other backstage. You'd just take out your guitar and no one was self-conscious and no one was a star in those dressing rooms at the Bitter End [*a club in Greenwich Village*]. You just felt so comfortable teaching each other songs. It was collegial and it was like a college campus, and you'd just go from one room to another: "Hey, I've got this new tune, dig this."

The big difference for me and everybody was being a singer/songwriter. That was a new cult—to be your own person through your music. I really think why Dylan was so important was not just because of his talent, but he took Woody Guthrie a step further. It wasn't only songs about the Depression, it was songs about inside your heart. It was a new energy.

Dylan, singing by himself in '63, was the road being paved for the great soloists and the Woodstock era. They weren't political. He was singing about "tonight I'll be staying here with you."

Stevie Nicks [singer/songwriter, Fleetwood Mac]: I had been transferred to Arcadia, California, going into tenth grade. I was sixteen in 1963. I got this magical guitar teacher. After one month of lessons, this guy leaves for Spain and sells the guitar to my mom and dad, so that guitar was laying on my bed—I still have it—and I wrote a song that day.

I'd just broken up with a guy who started going out with my best friend. My first great love, star quarterback, he was great at everything. I was the new girl, I was kinda freaky 'cause I'd come from Salt Lake City. Arcadia was very society. I was dressing Hicksville. I had a straw bag; I stood out. England hadn't crossed over, but I'm me and I'm cute, and I meet Steve.

We went out for a month. Nothing happened, but being with him was fantastic. If it wasn't for this guy I might never have written this song. I was as in love with him as I've ever been since. There was nothing like the pill, but things were changing. Nobody was sleeping with anyone, but making out in the car—I'll never forget that, it was fantastic.

And I get this guitar, and my first song goes, "I'm sad but not blue, boy loved another," et cetera. I remember it like it was yesterday. At home at that time I was very close to my parents. I played that song to them, crying tears over my guitar. My parents were totally supportive as long as I went to school.

I've learned ten chords, which is all I know today. I didn't feel I needed any more lessons, and I started writing all the time. It was my joy. I wanted to chronicle what was going on in my life, but by then my best friend had broken up with Steve. My memory of him is pure even though he betrayed me. The girl became my very best friend. I didn't get mad with them. I knew writing songs would be my path.

It was a musical happening. This was something very different from Elvis and Sinatra—they were entertainers. Fifteen-year-olds were inspired, involved. It was a revolution. Young people had a voice, had something to say, dancing in the streets and cafés.

Neil Sedaka: The mood was new music. The mood was something more thought-provoking and the culture of the time was changing—clothes, the arts—and I was not part of it. I was an outsider. I had just had five years of top 10 records all over the world. I had ten hits in a row from '58 to '63, and then in 1963 the Beatles and the Rolling Stones came in and changed popular music.

The first time I heard the Beatles [in April 1963], my wife and I were on our honeymoon on a cruise, and there was a jukebox on the *Queen Elizabeth* and I heard, "Is there anything that you want . . . " [*from the Beatles song "From Me to You," released in April 1963*].

Al Kooper: Neil got spooked. Many of his teammates had their songs recorded by the Beatles and made a lot of money, but Neil didn't. They were all writing the same kind of songs. They had their songs in the top 10 every week. We were all in the same building [the Brill Building]. I was nineteen and living with my parents in Queens and commuting to New York every day and going home at night. We wrote for a living, me and two other partners. We were nicknamed "the Three Wise Men."

Neil Sedaka: I listened to the Beatles and the Stones. I preferred the Beatles because Paul was smiling and looked very wholesome, and the songs were well constructed. The Stones were a little more turning their back and sticking their tongue out. I preferred the Beatles and started writing in that kind of style.

The rebels versus the nice lads. Contrived a bit. John was from Liverpool and an outsider type. Jagger was from the suburbs. It was a switch. It was no longer the solo, smiling American singer. It was more rebellious, painting pictures, more evasive writing, more met-aphorical; mine were more happy-go-lucky, tra-la-la songs.

I was fascinated. It was the next step. The Beatles music was an English take on the American Brill Building, and Paul has told me that he was very influenced by the Brill Building.

Carly Simon: Nineteen sixty-three was such a splendid year because that was the year I went to the South of France. I was rebelling against my mother and sister trying to push me into being a Simon Sister when I wanted to go off with my boyfriend and back to school. I was being pushed into show business. I got into a lot of French music, and [DJ] Johnny Holliday and I bought a lot of 78s and listened to them.

I knew that I had a good voice. I was confident about that, but get-ting onstage was another thing. I had such a bad stammer, and when I was asked to read out loud at school I would stammer terribly, and that carried over into being in the limelight, anyway. I felt pulled in two directions. I liked the ability to meet and make music with people like Judy Collins and various people. But it was never fun for me. I didn't like to perform. I felt like I was being dragged along by my sister. I was very nervous to perform.

I wanted to marry my boyfriend, a writer. I had a picture of myself, in the kitchen with a lot of intellectual people sitting in the kitchen, and I'd be making coffee. I was being very quiet.

But that was not what happened. We [*the Simon Sisters*] weren't making very much money, and whatever we got as an allowance from my parents. I was probably getting about twenty-five dollars a week from gigs, and when we were at the Bitter End it was fifty, but that was for the two of us. We'd been on for a week, and then we'd be off for a month. And then we'd play the Gaslight [Café, on MacDougal Street in Greenwich Village]. We were always the opening act.

Al Kooper: Paul Simon's story is amazing. They were rock and rollers when we met, and for about eight years. They had a hit R&R record as

Tom and Jerry. Then he and Art reinvented themselves as folk singers in 1963. They called themselves Simon and Garfunkel—their real
names. I think they reinvented themselves because of Bob Dylan.

Paul Simon started playing stuff on an electric guitar, and it
sounded better on an electric guitar to me. He was finger-picking,
and he taught me how to finger-pick, and that changed my life. I'd
seen Bob Dylan perform. I bought tickets. Paul Simon had got me interested. Seeing him in concert I had a reformed opinion of him. I
didn't let the voice deter me and I got into the other aspects. He filled
the Town Hall, and he was getting bigger.

Bob Gruen: This was the beginning of what we called the "protest
movement," which involved the [Vietnam] war. This is the time of
the civil rights movement. Phil Ochs was singing songs about civil
rights. Rock and roll was a rebellion. Civil rights was more serious.
It had a purpose.

Neil Sedaka: People would come up to me and say, "Oh, didn't you use
to be Neil Sedaka?" At twenty-three! I was able to write in that rock-
and-roll style but people wouldn't buy me. The time wasn't right. At
that time in '63 the most influential musician was Dylan. Folk music
was bubbling. I went to clubs in the Village. It was funky, floppy,
druggie—not my scene. The Brill sound was on the way out. My career
slowed, each record sold less and less. Then my records stopped selling or playing.

Carly Simon: We did a show with the Carter Family [*a traditional
American folk group*] and they all wore matching clothes, sitting down
and playing their mandolins and their accordions. I think it was the
trend.

Our image was confused. We met with this woman who was a
choreographer who taught us movement with what we sang like the
Supremes and Motown groups. I objected to those strange dance

movements because it didn't go right and it wasn't me. There was something studied about it. I reacted very negatively to it. I thought I was being pulled along to something I wasn't attracted to. I had a sense it wasn't us. We'd meet in this dance studio and do these dance steps. We got to dance with Burt Bacharach, and they were all confused about what we were. Bacharach was a great hero of ours, along with Dionne Warwick.

We were on our way up to Newark. We were doing a college tour in '63. We'd got back to the Bitter End, and then the rehearsal studio to learn these dance steps, and then we'd meet with Bacharach. In fact, he gave us a song called "Once." There were odd influences that came from a lot of different places.

Chrissie Most: Mickie used to fly to America every second week, and he would go to the Brill Building—where all the songwriters worked on Broadway. He met Carole King, Neil Diamond, Neil Sedaka, and all the others. That's how he got all the songs. They wrote songs to order.

Allen Jones: The experience of going to New York—it's the city for me—the energy level there is spectacular. During the sixties I still had the green card and I kept going back and forth. There is this feeling of breathing deeply. If you have anything to offer in America you have a chance. In Britain they'd always want to know which school you went to.

I'd come back to London after the first trip. I said, "I simply have to get a green card." I had to move to New York. It was seminal. I was just married to a beautiful blonde—after I was thrown out of the Royal College, I'd started teaching, and I was taking out the beautiful blonde, the best student; this was a cardinal sin. She was nineteen and four years younger than me.

I went to the American embassy for a green card, and I swore [to] something and then they said, "Within six months you're eligible for the draft." The Vietnam War was really getting going. It was a sobering thought. Hockney, who was going to and from New York, said, "Wear different-colored socks [to your draft board interview], and if it doesn't work, take a bus to Niagara [so you can cross the border to Canada]."

Neil Sedaka: I thought my career was over—and I was twenty-three. I had had my run. The Everly Brothers, Fats Domino, they [had] all had five years, and it seemed to be the pattern. I was no longer salable. I was entranced by the Beatles and Stones. But my audience wouldn't accept the tra-la-la's and doobie-doo's and the happy songs I was associated with.

Carly Simon: I had heard the Beatles' album. (I got all the Beatles to sign it for me—it was given to me by a friend who was a DJ. I've since given it away. Horrific. I can't believe I did that.) I'd heard whatever they had out there on the radio. Everybody was into the Beatles.

Neil Sedaka: We were all discussing it. We knew we had to change and be more introspective and get out of that comfortable atmosphere or we'd just write the same thing over and over again. In '63 in England it was more hedonistic, and no one really understood what was happening. They were young. They were kids. I knew there was more in me and that I was a creative person and that I wanted to change styles and develop and grow. I was still going to the Brill Building. I had a much more career-minded sensibility.

Norma Kamali: When I was [in London] I would bring back clothes from Biba and from the Kings Road, which was fantastic. I would spend the eighty dollars I made as a flight attendant each week and I would bring back clothes for friends. And then it got that I was bringing back so much with a big cloth garment bag, and that's how I started my business. I opened a little basement store on Fifty-first

Street and I started selling clothes I bought in London. It kept growing from that, and I started to make my own clothes. But it was that
experience in London that made me think of fashion in a completely
different way. I understood that anything was possible. I had permission to do anything I wanted.

You would relish the fact that you came up with something new.
The way you dressed each day was an expression of something that
no one had seen before. People were like a piece of art every day. I
remember when I arrived back from the first trip. I always had needle
and thread with me. I was wearing a skirt to my knee and I remember literally sewing the hem of the skirt all the way 'round so it was a
short skirt.

Cars stopped, and I was talked to as if I was a prostitute. No one
had seen legs before. And forget legs—that didn't have stockings and
garter belts. It was unheard of. You had to be brave because no one
dressed that way in New York. They thought I was nuts or crazy. Not
even stoned, just crazy—no one was really stoned yet.

It gave me permission. I had the inclination, but I didn't have permission before. You didn't have to dress like your mother. Everyone
could be fashionable. Anyone with a sense of style could do it, and it
started the first concept of democratic fashion.

Carly Simon: There was a convergence of a lot of images. You are
trying to work out who you are and which mannequin you were. I was
already becoming the hippie, and we all went down to the Village and
had our ears pierced, and had long hair, and the antiwar movement
was building a lot of steam. People were talking about it in coffee
shops. People were going to Washington [to protest].

Bob Gruen: My parents were brought up in the Depression. At my
age it was a much more difficult time. In 1963, it was pretty affluent:
people were building houses, and it was a different world financially
and opportunity-wise. I just thought about not wanting to work nine

to five. I didn't really know what I wanted to do. I had no plan. I just wanted a life where my parents wouldn't bother me and I could sleep late in the morning.

I liked songs that had meaning. Rock and roll is the freedom to express your feelings very loudly. And that is what I lean towards. Bob Dylan. "Like a Rolling Stone" is a much deeper and a stronger sentiment. On guitar I would learn how to play Dylan songs. That was what I wanted to sing. I didn't want to be anything. I was playing guitar and taking pictures for fun.

Neil Sedaka: With the death of Kennedy it was a shock and a big change. We recognized our mortality. The civil rights movement was playing out.

Stevie Nicks: I had a song I wrote about the Kennedys—[the song is about] a dream, I'm putting on my makeup and someone knocks on the door and says, "They're ready for you," and a man takes my arm, and it is Martin Luther King, and the Kennedys are all there and one says, "There's a piano."

When he was assassinated, I was playing music. I was listening to the Beatles' "I Wanna Hold Your Hand." I was very taken with that particular song; it was different from anything I'd heard—folkie and rock-and-roll.

I got a truckload of singles—lot of country, lot of Everly Brothers. At the end of that year I all of a sudden find myself flipping to R&B. We're driving along, I'm in the backseat, and I'm singing along to "Be My Baby" [by the Ronettes], a Phil Spector thing. My mom and dad said, "Where did you get this love of R&B?" 'Cause my grandfather was a country singer on the road. When I gave him an album [later], I saw a flash of jealousy in his eyes—we knew I was going to make it.

Robert Christgau: Supposedly it was teenagers listening, but I was not a teenager and neither was John Lennon. The Beatles didn't change this [music] and neither did Bob Dylan. This shit was happening without them. What were the Beatles showing us or getting ready to show us? The British invasion was about the Beatles and the Stones and a lot of other people going back to American music that had been forgotten or dismissed. The songs I'm talking about are mostly from African Americans.

7

AFTERSHOCKS

"No one expected it to go on and on and on. It just
got bigger and bigger. It took over our lives."

BILL WYMAN

By the fall of 1963, the revolutionary and self-indulgent exuberance in Britain was giving way to a new reality for youth's prophets: success, fame, and notoriety. But these came at a price—responsibility, hard work, and the loss of innocence. The evolution raised their expectations, and hormones could only get them so far. Commercial demands and a new careerism took the form of ambition—something this generation had once eschewed.

Bill Wyman: By autumn '63 we'd only made two singles. No album. The first one, "Come On," went to number 20. "I Wanna Be Your Man" went to number 12. That's all we had. We were a big band for the public, but no clout, no backup, no history.

The Beatles had number ones. We were better and more exciting than other bands, so we outsold everyone for the live shows. Except for the Beatles.

We got the same crowd as went to the Beatles. We were on tour when that second single ["I Wanna Be Your Man"] came out.

Peter Brown: They were boys, they were such kids. I mean, in 1963, George [Harrison] would have been only nineteen. Andrew [Loog Oldham] was nineteen in 1963 when he took on managing the Stones, and he'd already worked for Brian. We were doing all our own stuff, and Terry O'Neill was taking all the pictures. There were no boundaries.

You should talk to David Puttnam—he's now a lord. He was a boy from the suburbs of London. I remember him telling me the story that because he didn't speak properly or appropriately that he was always in the back office, and when this thing happened in 1963, he was put in the front of the office because he was "cool." He was in the advertising field when it blew up so he was very much aware of the changes because he was watching.

Terry O'Neill: Advertising was very quick to pick up on the sudden changes in society. Some big names, like David Puttnam, Ridley Scott, Alan Parker, all cut their teeth in advertising and went on to do great things in other creative areas.

One minute you are young and insignificant, the next that youth makes you an asset. In 1962 the *Sunday Times* in London started a weekly color supplement. It was a bit of a disaster at first but by 1963 it was suddenly the coolest magazine on the planet. You'd have a Jean Shrimpton fashion shoot followed by a photo essay from some African war zone followed by a profile of a hip young band followed by a piece on furniture design or an investigation of life behind the Iron Curtain—all this was revelatory at the time, all designed in a very hip, cool way.

The clever agencies picked up on this new opportunity to make advertisements conform and reach out to the new audience. So if you were selling a washing machine, you didn't pose a middle-class housewife next to it, you found an artistic fun way of selling it. And the agencies needed to mine the mind-set of young people.

Lord David Puttnam [film producer]: I was twenty-two in 1963. I'd left school at sixteen, and I was an assistant account exec at the advertising agency Collett Dickenson Pearce & Partners. In 1963 I was earning twelve hundred pounds a year, which wasn't bad. I was married with a one-year-old daughter and living in a rented two-bedroom flat. We had a Dansette [record] player and some 45 rpm records, a black-and-white television set, a radio, and a Grundig tape recorder on which I recorded and played back music off the radio.

I had a white suit and longish hair, but generally they kept me hidden away, until one day the office door opened and there was the head of the agency showing some clients around, and he said, "And this is our young man."

Sir Alan Parker: I was very "under-read" in 1963, and was continually reminded of this by my smarter, older colleagues, whose quotes I couldn't reference—so I had a lot of catching up to do. However, by mid-1963 I could comfortably quote Yossarian's witticisms in *Catch 22* and Alex's ultraviolence in *A Clockwork Orange*, and I even knew the ending of *The Ipcress File* before the film came out.

David Ogilvy's *Confessions of an Advertising Man* [a how-to book] was required reading for us young advertising turks in our Brooks Brothers button-down shirts and wide-welted brogues. We were a long way from Madison Avenue, but at least we looked the part. We spouted his aphorisms in the toilets and in the pub. We were particularly fond of "If you pay peanuts, you get monkeys" and "People are more productive when they drink." "Two or three brandies improves my copy no end." This, of course, became the mantra for an entire generation of advertising folk.

Lord David Puttnam: Suddenly, youth was fashionable; the bosses wanted to show us off. Looking back, that's when it became apparent something was happening, that 1963 was a pivotal year. The world was changing, and changing in our favor. We mattered. Nineteen sixty-three was the greatest year of my life. I was working with Terry Duffy, the *Vogue* fashion photographer, David Bailey, Tony and Ridley Scott.

Sir Alan Parker: David Bailey was the epitome of "working-class Cockney boy made good," and I had his photographs taped to my wall in Islington.

Suddenly it was OK to have an accent, which until then had de-noted class and stuck you at the bottom of society. Traditionally, if you spoke [with an accent] you had to be thick. All this changed, not least of all because of the Beatles, who made not just Scouse [*slang for people from Liverpool*] and their dialect, but all regional accents, acceptable and even attractive.

Also, I was lucky to land in advertising, which was a new and an entirely egalitarian business. In advertising, no one cared about ac-cents in the creative department. No one cared if you had a degree. All that mattered was the portfolio and how good the work was. My contemporaries, like David Puttnam and Charles Saatchi, were all misfits who were not conventionally schooled but soon caught up.

The account executives in advertising were a different breed, and being posh was a prerequisite. They had to meet the clients, after all, who were kept away from us oiks [*people of a lower class*]. Many ac-count men were ex-army officers, so it must have been odd for them, as the creative department would have been decidedly "other ranks," but now we were suddenly in charge.

Considering my eventual profession, I don't remember too many epiphanies at the cinema in 1963. I was not a smart film student. I had tried to catch up with the art stuff I'd missed, and was urged by the senior creatives in the agency to see Fellini's *8 ½*, which was too clever for me. Similarly, the social realism British films of that year seemed very unreal: *This Sporting Life* and *Billy Liar. This Sporting Life* was particularly baffling, as it seemed to have very little accuracy to the North, the working class, or, indeed, sport. Mind you, I did see

Lawrence of Arabia three times, which probably made up for my lack of inspiration elsewhere.

Terry O'Neill: I don't remember going to the cinema much in 1963. That's what moms and dads did on a Saturday night, or we used to do with a girlfriend. I remember photographing Elizabeth Taylor on the set of *Cleopatra*, which was premiered in 1963, but by then we had clubs to go listening to bands and hanging out. A lot of the young bands were breaking into the established touring scene where promoters would package acts and take them around the country. Mainly they had been American middle-of-the-road mainstream acts, but the British bands like the Stones were getting on the bill too.

Norman Jopling: The Everly Brothers were touring the UK that autumn, and Don Arden [*Sharon Osbourne's father*] was the promoter. He brought over Bo Diddley, hired the Rolling Stones for their first major tour, and filled the cracks with Mickie Most. It still wasn't enough. When ticket sales for the first few dates looked disappointing, he brought over Little Richard to share top billing.

Chrissie Most: Mickie was producing as well as playing. We'd booked the studio for the Animals, but we still had to pay the rent. We began touring with Don Arden, Mickie Most, and the Motormen. We used to drive in the Porsche. Mick Jagger would ask for a lift back to London to see his girlfriend—then it was Chrissie Shrimpton, the sister of Jean, the model. We got him in the back of the Porsche, somehow—it was a two-seater. After we dropped him off Mickie said, "Shame that boy is so ugly."

"No way," I said. "He is sexy."

"Sexy?" he screamed.

We had murders [*heated arguments*]. Mick had a bad complexion but he still had sex appeal. Andrew Loog Oldham was a brilliant manager and saw that Mick had that and [Andrew] played it up. Girls screamed for the Stones but they also screamed for Mick, and he started to play it up himself onstage.

Don Arden had paid a fortune for the Everly Brothers, and Bo Diddley was a big draw, but Don didn't need them once he'd sold the tickets, so he organized people who screamed for the Rolling Stones and he got others to boo the Everly Brothers offstage.

Georgie Fame: I played a few gigs for Don Arden, but he never gave me a hard time because my manager was harder than him.

Norman Jopling: Every week of the tour, each of the Rolling Stones wrote a longish column for *New Record Mirror*. Mick reported "Little Richard played to two packed houses and drove the whole audience into a frenzy. . . . [H]is hypnotic hold on the audience was reminiscent of an evangelist meeting. . . ."

Next came Bill: "We took a day off to record our new single, which the Beatles offered us some weeks ago. Brian plays steel guitar on "I Wanna Be Your Man," and it is an entirely new sound for a British disc. . . . Our new van arrived last week and already it has been attacked by eager fans, and bits and pieces disappear every night."

Keith: "We should like to thank the girls who sent us the cigarettes. Brian announced he has given up smoking—in fact he has only given up buying them. . . ."

Charlie summed things up: "Mickie Most always gives a tremendous opening. . . ."

Charlie was right: Mickie Most was a tremendous opener, a good all-rounder, and a convincing rock and roller. Mickie was a shrewd, likable guy—he'd been around since the late fifties, cut singles for Decca as the Most Brothers. But no chart action. Then he met a South African girl, Chrissie, and decided to try his luck there. Mickie managed to notch up eleven straight number ones in a row in South Africa.

Mickie was now doing something similar to what Andrew Loog Oldham had pioneered—producing his own records and selling them to the major companies. He added that he wanted to be a producer of good records. His wish would shortly come true, in spades.

Keith Richards: The Everly Brothers and Little Richard and Bo Diddley. That was an education. Six weeks on the road. Superb!

We had just come out the clubs. We could barely hack it. But we had this great groundswell, and we ended up finishing the show by the time it got back to London. The Everly Brothers said, "You better finish the show. It's your time." But listening to Little Richard, listening to him every day, and Bo Diddley, especially—so superbly professional, and those voices like angels.

Andrew Loog Oldham: Keith is quite right when he says that tour was like going to university, I mean, come on, six weeks with Bo Diddley, the Everly Brothers, it was great. Mickie Most was an act on that tour. He and the Stones were bottom of the bill. They were only getting fifty pounds a night on the tour, so it's less than ten pounds a night each. They got to pay for bed and breakfast, getting around in a van which Ian Stewart was driving—except Brian, the parents of his girlfriend would lend him their car.

There was no money, remember this: even if you sold a record, the way the record companies had the contracts is you got paid in about a year, and then if you happen to be selling any records in France and Belgium or anything like that, you wouldn't get that for eighteen months. And the Stones hadn't written any songs.

Bill Wyman: The Everly Brothers were booed. Masses of fans were there to see us. They didn't like the Everly Brothers anymore. A great shame, as they were magnificent. We came out the heroes. The press said we were fantastic.

Keith Richards: Unbelievable! We were playing black music and being black cats. We learned how to play the audience a little bit, we just got to hang in the rafters and watch Little Richard and Bo Diddley get off and we'd say, "We learned a bit today."

We would crawl high up in the theater. These were all old cinemas—two-thousand seaters. We'd find a way up, look at the stage and watch Little Richard—he was outrageous. He is one of our greatest friends. I always got great encouragement from those guys. They starred, but backstage that's where we learned what counts from them.

What goes on onstage is one thing, but what goes on backstage and how everyone reacts to each other? There was no hierarchy backstage, and you could walk into any one dressing room and say, "Show me how to play that. Show me that note. What's that link you've got there?" Bo Diddley was the same. Absolute gentlemen.

Then I met Muddy Waters, and that's what sealed it for me. These guys, they changed me. I saw how they conducted themselves and the respect that they got—that's what I want to be like. Of course, my image was totally different. Keith Richards, nutty dope addict—you live with it. What I'm saying about these times is Little Richard would be totally outrageous but always respectful, always had time for other people, none of this, "Can you shut the door on your way out." I have always tried to remember that.

It's not just a matter of politeness; they were so solid about what they know, what they were. They didn't have to put on any airs. So solid in their talent. I was just nineteen—a kid. They were always sweet to me. It was unique. I am thankful that I was there and got to play and learn from people that I thought I would never meet. People whom I basically idolized, and then suddenly I am working with them and I'm being taken on the same level. To be accepted amongst some of the greats, that was the most amazing thing for me right then. They gave me so much confidence.

Bill Wyman: Top of the bill was the Everly Brothers. Fantastic. Second was Bo Diddley. Our idol. We'd been playing his songs every night. Then they brought in Little Richard. We spent every show in the wings watching what they did and how they did it. All over England. Bo Diddley was stunning. But kids raved over us. Our three little songs. Cheering and getting mobbed outside. It was fun. We all laughed about it. They tore my jacket. Charlie lost his buttons. He'd be furious. You had your hair pulled out in handfuls. We didn't wear scarves because the girls got the ends and we were getting strangled.

Andrew Loog Oldham: Okay, the end of '63 is "I Wanna Be Your Man," and that still didn't really open the gates for us; this is still a very provisional time for the Rolling Stones. We don't go top 5 with a single until February or March of 1964, with "Not Fade Away."

So what that means is that every time we go above Birmingham, we're in danger land, man, because that's Beatles territory. I would say our audience is still sixty percent boys going nuts. But it was still, "Are they going to make it?" I mean, the jury was still out.

Anthony Calder: Sixty-three was just sex, drugs, and rock and roll. We were in vogue. "Can you do this? Or help us with that?" "We have this record. What can you do with it?" It was nonstop. It was exciting, because the Stones broke, then Marianne Faithfull broke. We'd done the Beatles' publicity. Andrew and I had the talent—entrepreneurial. And we loved it. We could smell it. We picked up Cilla Black, and later Jimmy Page, Rod Stewart, Eric Clapton, Jeff Beck, and Peter Frampton. Andrew idolized Jeff Beck. I thought Eric was better.

Peter Frampton: The fork in the road for me was the Preachers with Bill Wyman. Bill was with the Stones but he produced and managed this band. They were offered a residency at the Flamingo every Saturday night. I was working in the music shop on a Saturday. "You want to join a band? We're all semipros." I was still thirteen. And I said, "Yeah!"

We started gigging while at school. Saturday and Sunday we'd go to Birmingham. The neighbors said to my mother, "How do you allow this?" And my mother said, "Never try to stop Niagara Falls." We were doing two gigs a night in Leicester and Birmingham. The others were older and very protective of me. The English teacher would go to the teachers' lunchroom and complain to my father how I was dozing off in English on Monday morning. He read her the riot act and said, "Don't tell me any more. I don't want to hear about it."

Then Bill gets involved and we go up to town, Decca Studios. End of '63. So much happened in such a short space of time. We've got to record a single—two tracks. This was my first big session. With Glyn Johns [*a legendary British recording engineer who has recently been inducted into the Rock and Roll Hall of Fame*]. It was starting at the top. The Stones' bass player is managing the band and Johns is producing us.

We did *Ready Steady Go* with the Stones. It was before my fourteenth birthday. I remember sitting and watching Keith Richards getting his sound check. After the show we all went to watch the playback before it was broadcast. I am thirteen and standing between Mick and Keith, and they are watching *me*. It was freaky.

I would go see Davy [Bowie] playing. He was in the Comrades, a big local band, playing sax. Davy was such a role model for me. He had the poses. He was so good.

During the summer holiday the Herd come and watch me in the Preachers and ask me to sit in with the band, as they are losing a rhythm guitarist during the summer, and if it worked out they'd offer me a place in the band. I said, "Fantastic, but I don't know what my dad would say. I'm supposed to go back to school and the music college."

My dad speaks to the manager and he does a deal. He says, "Look, I'm not thrilled about this. If you left school at fifteen and got a regular job at the post office you'd make fifteen pounds a week. Can they guarantee you fifteen pounds a week?"

The Herd agreed to it. I'd get fifteen pounds—they wanted me in the band that badly. The going rate was forty pounds for the whole band. We were on *Top of the Pops* [*a BBC television show*]. Davy Jones is watching from home, and he says, "That's Peter! What the hell is he doing on TV? He should be at school."

Jeff Lynne: In '63 there was a different feeling in the air. Things were suddenly coming okay and music was going to take over everything. I hoped it would become a profession. I knew I was good—I was learning things quicker than most. My dream was to have my own band and perform. There was nothing else I wanted to do. I dreamed about that life and not having to go to work—to get in the van and go to a gig.

I was doing all those funny jobs in offices and warehouses and playing my guitar, and then in the newspaper it said, "Lead Guitarist Wanted for Nightriders."

No. That's me!

I was so adamant it was me. That's my job. I went for the audition, and I was really scared. They were my favorite local group, and, how could I be with them? The singer Mike Sheridan had left a few months before so they needed another vocalist and a lead guitar. I auditioned in the drummer's front room. And I got the job. Who would have thunk it?

I was trying to write in '63. I had bought a Fender Esquire: 115 guineas—a lot of money—and I bought it on the drip [*installment plan*]. I had to get an amplifier. I got a Vox AV 30 on the drip. And I got into trouble. Every week there would be a letter saying how much I owed. It would be worse every week. On Wednesday I'd get up at six a.m. to get the mail so my dad wouldn't find the letter. I was in debt, but once I joined the Nightriders I could pay it off in a matter of weeks. I was earning fifteen pounds a week, which was much better than the average wage. The debt was a big worry to me. It haunted me. I'd apologize to the guy in the shop. I just used to blatantly not pay him back and then suddenly pay it all off and buy an acoustic at the same time.

Eric Stewart: By the time the Mindbenders happened I was earning more in one night than my father did in a week. It was nice to do stuff with the money eventually, but at that stage it was about getting on-stage and having a ball.

The Stones told us that when you got paid you went straight to the Mayfair fashion designer Mr. Fish and bought clothes and bought records. We did. We'd come down to London and to Carnaby Street. We'd buy just everyday clothes, and we'd just be copying the Beatles. We had blue suits with leather waistcoats.

Hilton Valentine: We were gigging. Our money went up to twenty-five pounds, then to fifty—the big time. It was the time to be in London for sure. It was the start of the drug days, I suppose. There was a gig in Manchester at a place called the Twisted Wheel. It was a club on the circuit. My first time smoking hash.

This was the beginning, in late '63 and before we are well-known. What happened was I had the toke on it and felt my mind going *wow*, and then I felt nauseous and I was going to throw up, so I went out of the dressing room, up the stairs to the blackness of the street, and right next to it was a shop doorway.

I got myself in there and heaved, and pulled myself together, and then I heard, "Oi, what's going on here?" And it was a copper. I said, "I'm playing in the band and I must have had too much to drink." So he said, "Ah, well you'd better get yourself back down there." So I went back, got plugged in, and started off on the first song, and I thought, "I've never heard anything like this in my life." The sound was incredible, and I was really flying high. I had the bad scenario spewing up and then I got back on and it was Technicolor. Just me. I was elated and blown away by it.

It became a habit. I wouldn't say I was addicted, but it sounded better when I was stoned. It wasn't like I had to have it. There were many nights when I didn't have it. But when it was available I would do it. I did lose myself down the road with LSD. Brian Jones turned me on to it.

Eric Stewart: We were traveling a lot, touring. Recording an album was done in four days. You rehearsed before hitting the London clubs—the Marquee, the Ad Lib, Dolly's, and the Flamingo.

We were in control of our own lives. We had fire in us and we had money. I could buy a four-hundred-pound car. A serious luxury. My family had never owned a car.

At sixteen I'd gone to my headmaster to get a job reference. In those days you needed a character reference from your headmaster or a professional person who could speak for you to get a job. Of course, I didn't know then that I didn't need one to be a musician. I just assumed I would and asked for it.

He said, "What do you want to be?" I said, "A musician." He said, "Be serious." I mean, nobody had ever asked him for a reference to be a rock star before—he wrote character references for sixteen-year-olds addressed to employers like banks or factory managers, but then he'd said, "Oh, for chrissakes, you write the reference and I'll sign it."

His name was Mr. Organ. He signed it and said, "Good luck, Stewart." I passed the school a few years later. I'm making good money with a band, I'm in my own car, a Ford Zephyr—it was a big thing to be a teenager with your own car in those days, a car meant you'd made it—and he was standing in the rain. And I stopped and wound down the window and said, "Hello, Mr. Organ," and he just glared at me. At eighteen. It was phenomenal.

Drugs were appearing. Keith Moon scoffing handfuls of pills—off his face. Keith would take mouthfuls of pills. He stood next to me in the bog [restroom] in the Cromwellian and he said, "Do you want some stuff, Eric? I've got blues, I've got purples and . . ."

"No thanks, I'll stick to scotch and coke." And he just whacked a whole mouthful down.

Peter Brown: They were all on amphetamines—the Beatles, and Brian, they all used to do it—but I didn't. I liked to have wine. The only time I actually did occasionally attempt it is when I was going down to London so much, and I would come back to Liverpool and I would be tired from partying, I'd have to get the early train back. I'd start to wilt, and I'd take an upper. But fortunately I never got hooked on them. I never took that many of them.

They were so young, and we'd hang out at the various clubs, the Ad Lib, Dolly's, so you'd end up with the Stones in that corner, a couple of Beatles in this corner; the atmosphere was very cool. You didn't circulate, you were just hanging out having a good time, and the records were playing and everyone is drinking and smoking. It was somewhere to go. We were all equal.

Chrissie Most: Now [that] we'd found the Animals, I said, "We have to get something in writing. Mickie was dyslexic and didn't do stuff on papers. And he said, "No. We are all friends." I said "You've got to have a contract." I had a typewriter, and I just typed out this agreement. I couldn't spell. We never thought of a lawyer. They all signed it.

This guy from Manchester drove me mad and wanted Mickie to record his band, Herman & the Hermits. He kept phoning me, and I was at home dealing with the baby. "Mickie, for chrissake do something with this man and get him off my back." He sent a photo of this man, Peter Noone, and Mickie said, "He looks like a young Kennedy. He will appeal to the Americans." And so they came to London and he recorded them.

He'd cottoned on that they could be a big success by then. Their first hit was a Carole King song from the Brill Building Mickie brought back from a trip to New York. Mickie always said the [hit] songs are in America. He always had this thing for America.

Eric Stewart: We hung out just talking about the music in the Ad Lib and the Cromwellian. You had to pay to go into the Ad Lib—it was classy and there were actresses and actors and film stars. The money set. The other set. You really had to have someone to let you in. That wasn't my scene. The fun places were the Flamingo and the Marquee.

The pill. That was the other link to freedom, for the girls. The posh birds were after a bit of rough trade. They wanted the working-class lads—they were glamorous then. I was never the front man, not even in 10cc. I never wanted to be. I was the moody guy in the back just getting off on that. It was a very enviable profession. Adoring fans and people were throwing money at you. My mum was astounded by it.

Cilla Black: My first trip to London to promote the single I stayed at the Russell Hotel on Russell Square. I was just so excited because there was a phone by my bed. Most people didn't have phones in Britain in those days because they were expensive, and I remember picking the phone up to call someone, but everybody that I knew or that I wanted to talk to didn't have a phone.

I mean, how I heard I was number one was in Liverpool. Brian said, "I'll call you to tell you whether you're gonna be number one," because the amount of records you're selling per day was a hundred thousand. It was a cover version of Dionne Warwick's "Anyone Who Had a Heart" by Bacharach and Hal Davis.

So I said to Brian, "I know the number of the phone box outside the post office. What time do you want to call? I'll be there at one o'clock." I was hoping and praying that nobody would be on the phone at one o'clock. There wasn't, and that's how I heard.

Jeff Lynne: My mum used to love thumping up the stairs. "Get up you lazy bugger, go to work!" Then I found out I got the Nightriders job. And me mum bounded up the stairs, and I remember her face. I said, "Hold it—before you start, I never have to get up ever again because I'm now a professional musician." And I went back to bed. Her face! She couldn't do anything about it. The band was earning, and I was earning fifteen and then twenty pounds a week within a few months.

All I ever wanted was that chance to be professional, and we played all 'round Birmingham. You could play all 'round there for a month and never play the same place twice. That was the best feeling and the happiest you could be: having just gone professional, and getting confident and getting good on the guitar and singing good. I had a tape recorder. I made demos, and that was how I recorded music. The tape recorder was what made me—made my life, really.

Eric Clapton: I had no aspirations for the future. I never thought I'd live past thirty, for a start. We were doing a lot of drink and drugs. My ambition was to do this for as long as I could get away with it. I didn't see a profession or a career as a musician. I was always going from one band to another. I liked being a sideman; there was more freedom. I bummed around or slept on girls' couches. A career didn't matter. It was the last thing I wanted. Of course, it's what we've ended up with.

We thought it might last a couple of years and let's enjoy it while we can. That was exciting to me. I loved being able to go into a club, say Soho or somewhere, and see who was playing and just disappearing into the wallpaper. And someone would say, "Do you want to play?" And I'd go onstage and play and then get off and stand in the corner, and no one would even bat an eyelid. There wouldn't be any palaver [*commotion*] about it. It was, in the pure sense, about the music.

In October 1963, I knew these guys from the pubs I was playing with —the Roosters and Casey Jones. One of my local haunts was in Kingston. The songs I was learning as an individual musician were folk and old blues. And these guys would be around that circuit, so they asked me to join the Yardbirds. My understanding is that we would be creating a nucleus to play serious music—jazz, R&B, or whatever—but serious. There was a guy, their manager, Giorgio Gomelski, and he had the Stones before Andrew Loog Oldham, and lost them, and I think with the Yardbirds he decided he would never let that happen again.

So when the opportunity came he started to steer us in a commercial way. We were part of a very strong underground, and the singer had a pretty astute understanding of R&B and blues, but he wanted to be popular. So we met that fork in the road.

Eric Stewart: I think people like Keith or Eric or myself were really into this whole thing for the music, not the fame or adoration. Jeff Lynne's the same. I mean, success and money are great, but exploring music and what you are capable of working with others drives us.

Serious musicians love their guitars; like Jeff or Eric, they are tools to be cared for and cherished. Les Pauls had something—the way the wood was made and the way the neck was connected, there was a sustain that happened naturally. And the Les Pauls had this fabulous quality, and that's why they sell for 450,000 pounds now. Stratocasters were great because they were designed by an airplane engineer. It was an Apple compared to a PC.

The really great guitarists are all self-taught. None of them read music. I can't. Every great musician I have ever worked with can't read music. Clapton can't. McCartney can't. Lennon couldn't. Paul might have learnt to read since, but he couldn't read dots then, and I couldn't read dots. We played from the soul rather than through the eyes.

Eric Clapton: For me, to be in a band was to make it sound right in the space we were in. Everyone to be in tune, in time, and if possible, to create something different every night. That was the ideal. It had nothing to do with popularity.

I still sometimes prefer rehearsals to the show. The audience introduces that dynamic— "Oh, do they like it?" All musicians who I have ever respected have done it for very selfish reasons. We do it to express the way we feel and to do it in harmony with other musicians.

If I consciously figure out how to engage or touch that guy over there with the glasses on, I will go crazy. I don't know what he's in tune to, so it's better if I follow my intuition and express what I'm feeling. It may be coincidental that he experiences something he likes and it resonates, but I can't control that.

I didn't have the confidence to do it on my own. I was very shy. Even if I played in a club, I was always facing a wall. I had no stagecraft. I've never tried to work or understand what makes an audience tick. So I don't think I could even do it now. A lot of my contemporaries, Neil Young and Elton, went on the road on their own, but I had no idea how they pulled that off. It takes an awful lot of courage. I'm always with the lads. You'll never see me alone.

Bill Wyman: I miss the naïveté and the newness—this magic thing was happening and you didn't know where it was going. No one expected it to go on and on and on. It just got bigger and bigger. It took over our lives.

Sir Alan Parker: The revolution of the times allowed us to have other aspirations, and I don't think I thought much about it—there were explosions of opportunity going on all around you, so you just marched on.

I lapped up anything that was American. In advertising our heroes were Bill Bernbach, George Lois, and Howard Zieff. We couldn't wait to get the new copy of *The New Yorker,* not for the essays or cartoons, but the new Volkswagen ads. [*The ad campaigns were innovative, humorous, and irreverent.*]

Peter Brown: The Beatles did this gig at Hammersmith that was a big deal. The girls were going crazy at that point, they were top of the bill and then, you know, they didn't do more than thirty-five minutes in those days, so you'd have about five other acts, and that was the show.

I don't think that a lot changed the Beatles in 1963; they were still a band of brothers. They hadn't got wives or children or distractions in that way, and of course, they had to be on the road, and in between make a record. It was back to back, very hard work. They were working all the time.

The mood was very excited. But there was always anxiety because as an artist, you're always only as good as the last thing you did. That was successful, but what about the next one? Will we be able to keep up?

Norman Jopling: I got to see the Beatles perform in the final month of their first big year—saw them but hardly heard them. The Southern Area Fan Club get-together was held on a cold Saturday at Wimbledon, and for three shillings and sixpence the fan club members—90 percent female—could queue up and shuffle past the Fab Four, shake their hands, get their autographs, exchange a few words. I wrote it up: "Oh! What a Day It Was for the Beatle Fan." There were faintings galore, and even the burly attendants couldn't stop a few determined fans from leaping over the tables and caressing their particular fave.

You had to hand it to the Beatles, who were the souls of good humor and patience throughout what must have been, for them, an ordeal that went on for hours and hours. They smoked a lot of cigarettes. And when every fan was satisfied, they got up and played for nearly three-quarters of an hour, longer than for any gig, serenaded by continuous screaming, rising and falling.

Phenomenal was the only word to describe it. And troopers that they were, they played the Wimbledon Palais that same evening. This was also the first year the Beatles sent out a specially recorded Christmas record to their fans, a thoughtful tradition that would be kept up to the end of their career. Epstein certainly knew about building fan loyalty, I guess because, really, he was the biggest fan of all.

Cilla Black: They could have sang the national anthem, the kids wouldn't have known because of all the screaming and the hysteria, and that's what the Beatles didn't like. I could tell that, 'cause I did three weeks with them at the Astoria Finsbury Park in London, where we were all together, all the Liverpool acts on one bill.

We all wanted to go home to Liverpool for Christmas Day, and Brian had hired a private plane for us. It was great for us just to have Christmas at home, a Christmas Day at home with our family. We were back on the following day doing two shows a night, and that's when we all realized that's probably the last time we're all going to be here together on one bill. It was the end of an era, 'cause the rest is history.

Peter Brown: When the Beatles came back from Stockholm [for the Christmas shows], Ed Sullivan saw them. The story is that he was in London Airport going back to New York. In those days you didn't have jetways, you went up and down the stairs. And the airport was brought to a standstill because the Beatles were coming back from a gig in Sweden. [*An estimated fifteen hundred girls were on the roof of the terminal.*] And Sullivan said, "Who are these people? What is this all about?"

Cilla Black: Brian had said to the producer of *The Ed Sullivan Show*, "Well, you can't have the Beatles unless you have Cilla." I went in to record Burt Bacharach's "Anyone Who Had a Heart" in early '64. Dionne Warwick recorded it in the States. I went to number one in the UK in February while the Beatles were doing *Ed Sullivan*. They paved the way.

Peter Brown: Now of course, everyone in America of a certain age says they saw that show. It changed everything.

PART FOUR

It's been a hard day's night
And I've been working like a dog
It's been a hard day's night
I should be sleeping like a log

THE BEATLES

By the end of 1963, the Beatles had completed an exhausting marathon of six tours, more than 250 live shows, numerous television appearances, three number one songs, and three albums, and they were making their first movie.

As 1964 opened, New York City's Idlewild Airport had been renamed for the recently slain John F. Kennedy, and the Warren Commission began its closed-session investigations into his assassination. Kennedy's successor, Lyndon B. Johnson, declared war on poverty while preparing to increase military aid to South Vietnam. The U.S. Surgeon General announced that smoking is hazardous to your health.

Italy, meanwhile, asked the world for technical expertise to help prevent the collapse of the Leaning Tower of Pisa, and Richard Burton proposed to his Cleopatra costar, Elizabeth Taylor. A fishing trawler anchored off British waters to begin broadcasting "the new music," while Indiana Governor Matthew Walsh declared the Kingsmen's single "Louie Louie" pornographic and requested that DJs ban it from the airwaves.

The BBC launched Top of the Pops *in Britain to compete with* Ready Steady Go. *The Beatles released their first U.S. single, "I Wanna Hold Your Hand," and vaulted to number one on February 1. Six days later they landed at JFK on Pan Am flight 101 and were greeted by five thousand screaming girls in the upper balcony of the arrivals lounge. Ringo Starr would later comment, "It was so exciting. On the plane, flying into the airport, I felt as though there was a big octopus with tentacles that were grabbing the plane and dragging us down into New York."*

Among their many photo ops, the Beatles meet a young Cassius Clay in training for his heavyweight championship bout with Sonny Liston in Miami. They also record their first appearance on The Ed Sullivan Show; *in February, an estimated seventy-three million viewers tuned in. By April, the Beatles' songs hold the top five spots in the U.S. Billboard charts and account for sixty percent of all U.S. record sales. And the Rolling Stones and a host of British bands are feted by U.S. record labels and broadcasters.*

The British Invasion has begun.

8

ACCESSION

"There are three versions of the sixties: from '57 to
'62, then the Beatles, [then] '63 to '67. And then there
is the [version] that the people actually think is the
sixties: roughly '67 to '73—Woodstock. You know, they
concertina the time together, and they go, 'Oh yeah,
man, the Beatles, peace and love.' Bollocks!"

ANDREW LOOG OLDHAM

*Beginning on November 22, 1963, America marked time to mourn a pres-
ident. For a few months, the revolution paused, but in February 1964, at
least one-quarter of the population was ready to revitalize it. More than sev-
enty million Americans tuned in to* The Ed Sullivan Show *to watch the
new British band, the Beatles, perform on three consecutive Sundays. Their
music was infectious, their appearance beguiling. After the trauma of JFK's
assassination, America was ready to celebrate again. The revolution would
go forward.*

Henry Diltz: We were doing this folk and jazz caravan for weeks and
weeks and months. We were just bubbling under, and close to suc-

cess. We'd done a couple of albums. We weren't producing hits. So here's what happens. Life was really good. We had this wonderful young president and his wife. The world was our oyster. One of these tours we were up in New England, and Kennedy got shot.

We spent three days in a hotel watching the funeral. Wow. Such a horrible feeling. What huge disillusionment. The government killed him, Johnson killed him—everyone had a theory. Then the Beatles came, and we were ready for some change and some entertainment. We heard about the Beatles playing on *Ed Sullivan*. Everybody watched *Ed Sullivan*, and we were on the road, and we got a hotel room early enough to watch, and—holy shit!

"Look at those guys. 'I Wanna Hold Your Hand'?"

They have electric instruments. We had a stand-up bass and we were playing acoustic guitars and banjos. They were having so much fun and singing about love. We wanted to have fun like that. That's what I wanted. I don't want to sing the stodgy old folk music anymore.

Bob Gruen: When the Beatles came out in '64 I remember being with friends. We went to dinner at a hotel, and it was our first night, and we walked in and heard screaming in the lobby, and I saw the TV. I wondered what was going on. I had never seen people screaming on the TV. I thought it was pretty cool. I liked it a lot.

A few years ago I saw that *Ed Sullivan Show* again, and all the acts that were on. Looking back at it, Doris Day was dancing with giant stuffed animals. The level of the show and the humor was so lame that the Beatles looked wilder than the Sex Pistols. If you see just the clip of the Beatles, they look tame, but if you see them in the context of where they were coming from, it was wild. "What the fuck is this?" It was chaos and screaming. Loud rock and roll. It was live on national TV. It was a big deal.

Carly Simon: Everybody was into the Beatles. I loved the Beatles. I adored them. Boy, was that an exciting time. When [my sister] Lucy and I were in Toronto playing at the Purple Onion and we went to the Beatles concert in 1964—the first they played in Canada—it was amazing. I'd never had the experience that you couldn't hear anyone sing because everyone was screaming.

Henry Diltz: The Beatles changed it all. It was the end of folk music. We went right out and got electric bass and guitars and started singing a couple of songs with Stephen Stills [*of Crosby, Stills & Nash*]. We were always going to New York, back and forth across the country. We always played the Troubadour in LA. On this one trip back from New York after we'd heard the Beatles, we are electric and doing a sound test and the owner comes roaring out of his office: "We don't have electric music in this club. I hired a folk group."

We made a deal: we'll play our pure folk music and then play our new kind of music. The second show of the night—our music—broke the mold and the rule there. We changed it. James Taylor and Joni Mitchell played electric, and the Byrds after that point. It was joyfulness that the Beatles brought with them. Something of the magic of those guys.

Bob Gruen: What I didn't like was that the girls loved John, Paul, George, and Ringo. And we'd think, "What about me?" They were fascinated with them and we wanted them to think more about us, not these floppy-haired guys from England. I was bugged that all the girls liked the Beatles.

Eric Stewart: The whole Beatlemania thing changed it all. Trying to get through the crowd at the stage door, the girls were ripping at our clothes and our hair. One time someone in the band opened up the fire hose and sprayed the police with water. He shouted at the police.

"You didn't protect me. Fuck you." They came and arrested him then. He got back [from custody] in time to go onstage.

There was a program about the Beatles. They said they'd stop touring in 1966. They were just sick of the lack of privacy. The Mindbenders were getting that, too. Everywhere you went there were people there. You became an inconvenience to the hotel even if you were booking fourteen rooms with your road crew.

But the Beatles turned us all on to writing our own stuff. I hadn't written anything until I thought, "We've got a hit record, we hope, but what are we going to do on the B-side?" So I started writing. I thought, if the Beatles could do it, then so could I. This thought kept going through all our minds in 1963: you could do anything you wanted. You didn't have to conform to the market; once you've got your name, you could experiment.

Peter Noone: Our first record, "I'm into Something Good," Mickie Most had got us from Goffin and King [*the songwriting team of Gerry Goffin and Carole King*] at the Brill [Building] in New York. [In] 1964 . . . we went straight to America because I was an "America-phile." Our first show was in Allentown, Pennsylvania, in a high school, and the band starts to play and everyone in the audience came onstage with us. Every girl—there were no men in those days—joined me onstage. We never got to play a note; they had to clear the place and the police wouldn't let the show go on. They'd heard us on the radio. We did *Ed Sullivan*, and we got an agent in America, and he signs us for the Dick Clark *Caravan of Stars*, and he pays us five hundred dollars a night for eighty days, and now we've got a deal—for forty thousand dollars!

By about the third week we had three records in the top 20. That's how you did it then. We'd show up at a radio show and be funny. I'd be up for twenty-four hours a day doing interviews and stuff.

Chrissie Most: "I'm into Something Good" was the first Hermits song. We had murders over that song. I thought it was wonderful, but

Mickie said the production was crap and he wasn't going to release it. We went on holiday to Majorca, and I said, "Unless you put that record out as it is, I'm divorcing you." I forced him to put it out, and it went to number one.

Peter Noone: We broke in America before Britain. We did loads of tours. In one year we did 365 concerts. We were unstoppable. The Beatles thought we were fluff. I had no feelings about that. I just wanted to be me. The Stones were happening in America and were these bad guys of rock and roll. We were the good guys. We didn't do drugs or anything. We didn't really care about being respected by the other bands. We knew we were good at what we did. We weren't in the same league. We were not competitive. We were happy to be given what we could get.

Our experience on *The Ed Sullivan Show*—he really liked me and I liked him—we did it because I wanted to meet the Four Seasons. People wanted to meet everyone. The Four Seasons were having a fistfight over which color jackets they are going to wear on the show. Frankie Valli won it cause he was the lead singer. I go back and tell the guys "We are lucky—we only have the stage suit and the clothes we wear every day." When we went on *The Danny Kaye Show*, he was wearing a Hermits fan club T-shirt.

I miss the camaraderie between the bands. The Beatles came to our dressing room—"Good to have you on the show." We'd go to theirs. We all got it from Roy Orbison. A Southern gentleman.

Terry O'Neill: America just pulled us in and hugged us. After '63 I went to Los Angeles to do a shoot and met Fred Astaire. He quizzed me repeatedly about the Beatles: Did I know them? What were they like? And that's when it hit me: my god, if a huge film star like Fred Astaire has heard about them and is fascinated by them then something big must be happening. Perhaps what we'd been experiencing in London wasn't just a flash in the pan.

Allen Jones: If you went to a party, people would say, "This is an English artist." The Beatles were so huge at the time that they would qualify you by saying you were. It was sort of embarrassing. "Do you know the Beatles?" and all that stuff. The British thing really—the music and the Beatles—was overwhelming.

I remember Vidal Sassoon and I got interviewed and photographed; it was the first satellite transmission of a color photograph from America to Britain. They wanted a photograph of British people in New York who were successful.

Eric Stewart: People from my background didn't believe that these things could happen to young working-class people. And then suddenly it happened. We were famous, we were successful, we were on television. It couldn't have happened at another time. We were on tour a lot. Hotels, gigs, airplanes.

Nineteen sixty-three was when it all came to the boil. We put in the work, touring, recording, doing publicity, and getting better, and by 1964 the world was waking up to everything that had been happening in England in '63. We were being exported—music, clothes, and our attitude. We had taken over.

By late '64, like the Stones, the Animals, and just after the Beatles, we were already booked to go to the United States. We had "Game of Love," and we were headlining.

Terry O'Neill: Nineteen sixty-three was one big party for us all in London, but there was always this issue of, what next? At first we'd assumed it would all end after a short burst of fun and then we'd have to settle down. But America started to wake up to us, it wanted what we were having, so by the end of 1963 we had our answer. What next? America!

Only two or three years earlier I'd wanted to go there to play drums in jazz clubs. The Stones, the Beatles, for all of us, it was a mecca—and after 1963, it wanted *us*!

Andrew Loog Oldham: At the end of '63 is "I Wanna Be Your Man," and we go to top 10, but that still didn't really open the gates for us. This is still a very provisional time for the Rolling Stones. Nineteen sixty-three it was still, are they going to make it? Are they not going to make it?

One of the big differences with the Beatles and the Rolling Stones is the Beatles made it in America. The Rolling Stones were *made* by America. Once we got to America we went, oh, wow, this is magic. We, the Rolling Stones, were home in the mecca of everything the band lived for.

Anthony Calder: Andrew [Loog Oldham], the Stones—we started to do quite well. Early '64, I think, we were moving offices, and Andrew took a two-bedroom hotel suite because the office wasn't ready yet.

Marianne Faithfull arrives: "Can I use the bedroom? I have Brian [Jones] coming." Brian leaves. "Oh, Keith is coming in a minute." Keith comes up, takes his boots off and his socks, and goes in the room with a bottle of vodka.

At nine o'clock the next morning, when I come in, Keith comes out and asks me to get a cab. After he leaves, Marianne says, "Can we get the maid to change the sheets? Mick's coming over." We didn't think anything of it. There was no judgment.

Eric Stewart: The Mindbenders went to Andrew's office. He said, "Come over to my office. I want to play you something." We hadn't had a big hit by then. He picked us up from the hotel in a great big American car with tailfins, and in the back he's playing a huge voice track. And I sat in the back, and the driver's hurtling down Oxford Street, and the police stop him. The driver says, "Very sorry, he's had a heart attack and I need to get him to the hospital." And Andrew has by now slipped down in his seat and is groaning. We got away with it.

Anthony Calder: I miss nothing about this time. I don't romanticize. I am just a simple boy. The drugs were great. The girls were great. Whatever you wanted to do, you could do it. It was great. It makes me realize that everyone you have to deal with today are arseholes, cunts, and overpaid idiots. We were young kids and it was a time where I learned the tools of the trade. And you learned what we could do and couldn't do.

Terry O'Neill: When I think back to 1963, I think, I didn't know what the hell I was doing with a camera, but now I realize that's what made it special, I was doing what felt right and natural rather than what I was being taught to do, like the pop artists or the musicians. I was doing my thing.

Suddenly the mainstream newspapers and magazines wanted my photographs, everyone was trying to copy what the *Sunday Times Magazine* was doing, defying convention in journalism and design.

That was happening in America, too. My photographs of the people who populated the London scene were suddenly being printed abroad. Bailey was the toast of *American Vogue*. We were hot. And American journalism was changing, too, the writers, like the photographers, were becoming important; their views, opinions, were part of the narrative of profiles and interviews, less respectful or servile to stardom, and more opinionated.

Robert Christgau: I read a striking observation: the Beatles did not lead their generation. The great thing was that they *went along* with their generation.

At this point I wanted to be a novelist, not a journalist. But because of my pop epiphany I didn't look down on journalism as a form. I read it avidly. I got cub reporter kind of jobs. I loved Tom Wolfe. So I wrote a feature for *New York* magazine and it earned awards, and then the calls start. Then the pop column.

But in '64, what was different about things was *me*. I decided to become a journalist then.

Gay Talese: I was breaking boundaries in journalism. I always felt journalism could be an art form. I knew it. Tom Wolfe thought up the term [*"new journalism"*]. I didn't put a label on it. I wanted to be a literary figure in nonfiction. So we were the beginning of a group who were rising to be literary figures and we weren't having to make it up. You don't have to make it up. Learn something about other people—get out there.

I still live that time. It hasn't changed at all. I didn't know that time was *that* time. Only in retrospect did I know it. I was getting a lot of letters, especially for the *Esquire* stuff, and getting on television. I was getting full-page ads for my pieces. When a piece came out for *Esquire* they would take a full-page ad in the *New York Times*—$5,000, $6,000 maybe. That piece on "Looking for Hemingway," it got a lot of reaction. You don't get that anymore.

I was spending my money on clothes and going out. I never went to a restaurant because it had four stars. I went to see people. I was traveling first class. I always travel first class. I put money in travel, cars. I had sports cars. What I did was I bought things I liked and thought I wanted to keep. I'm not like most people. I keep things for a long time.

I have a wardrobe with a hundred suits. I have more clothes than anybody. Some are fifty years old. I'll spend $2,500 dollars on hand-made shoes because I like them. I like things. But there are things I wouldn't spend money on, like a boat. I wouldn't do that. I don't event swim. I like entertaining people and taking people to dinner. I can pick up the check. I like going to restaurants because it's personal. I like relationships. I will know the waiter and I will know the table number. I know the key quiet tables. I started going in '63, '64—that was the beginning of it all for me.

Terry O'Neill: It was the beginning for all of us—clothes, money, it was just mind-blowing how suddenly everything took off. I'd started 1963 taking pictures of unknown bands, and at the start of 1964 they were making movies, for god sake. First the Beatles— they were already working on *A Hard Day's Night* when they went to America.

Pattie Boyd: My agent phoned me. I'd been to an audition. I thought it was for a commercial. Then he said I had got a part in some Beatles film and I wasn't to tell anyone. I panicked because I thought, "I can't act." He said, "Don't worry, you won't have to say anything, just walk on as a schoolgirl."

I must have told Bailey, because he lent me his Beatles record. I think that was in February '64; I wasn't twenty yet. [The Beatles] must have just got back from America. That was exciting because I was with two other girls who were also dressed as schoolgirls, too. We got on the train at Paddington, and we were sitting in this carriage [*train car*], and I was thinking, "This is weird." Then way out of London the train stopped at this deserted station, there were four figures there. I thought, "God, it must be the Beatles." They all leapt onto the train, bouncing into our carriage. They were so sweet. That's the first time I met George.

Edina Ronay: I had a small part in it. There were two versions of *A Hard Day's Night*. I've seen both. In one of them I had a part dancing and talking to John Lennon, and in the other I was the model that George Harrison falls in love with.

I just remember John. I always thought he was the most fanciable of them. So when we danced together he sort of said, "Well, what's your name?" I said "Edina," and he started doing this rhyming thing— "Edina, medina . . . ." And you know what I thought to myself? "This guy is really uncool."

Then I was going to be in the film with Dave Clark; it was me and another girl who were going for the lead part in the Dave Clark Five film *Catch Us if You Can*.

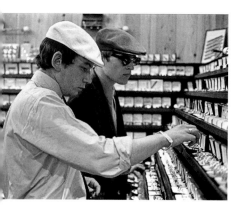

"I heard about this band the Animals coming into London from Newcastle. I took them shopping first, then to a studio, because they didn't look the business. They looked like laborers."

Terry O'Neill

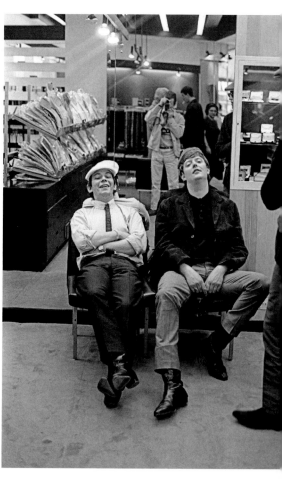

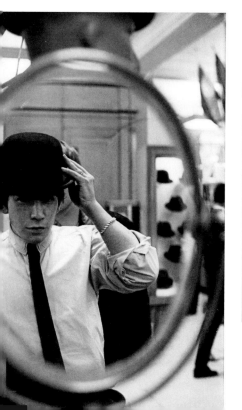

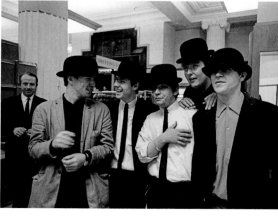

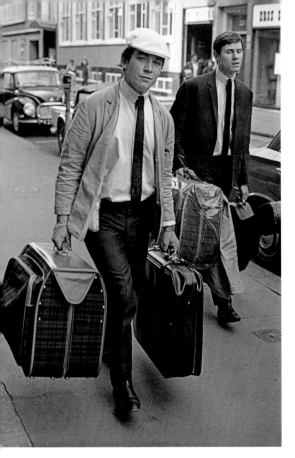

Eric Burden (left) and lead guitarist Hilton Valentine. "I don't know when we changed our name to the Animals but I think it was our first trip down to London."

Hilton Valentine

"The Animals were very tough cookies. Very suspicious. Alan Price *(below)* was very smart, and Chas Chandler was physically hard."

Georgie Fame

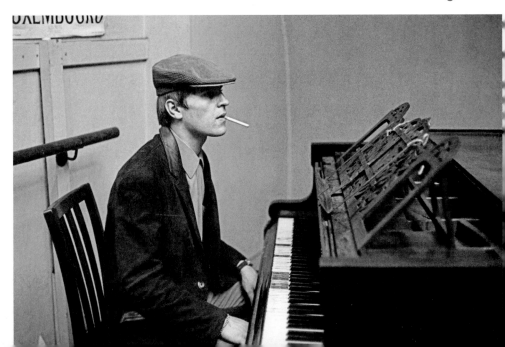

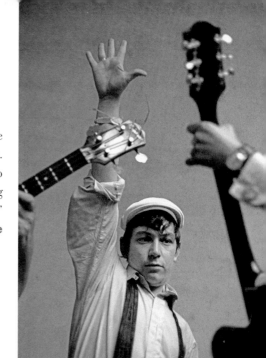

"The studio was a rehearsal place where violinists went. We didn't last long there. They told us to leave because we were so loud. It was unusual in the beginning being photographed. And it *was* the beginning."
Hilton Valentine

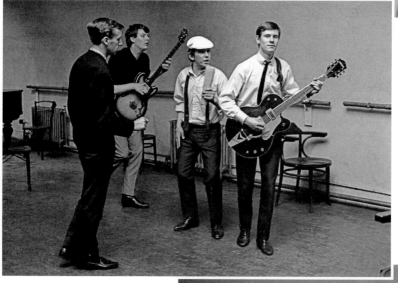

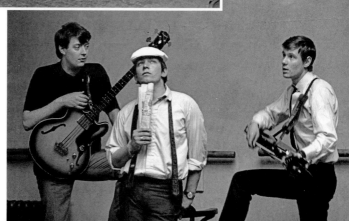

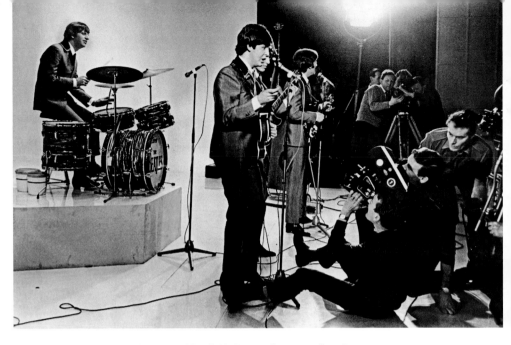

The Beatles film a scene for *A Hard Day's Night* at a theater in London.

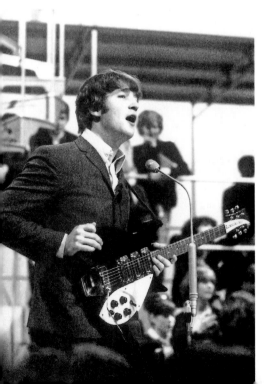

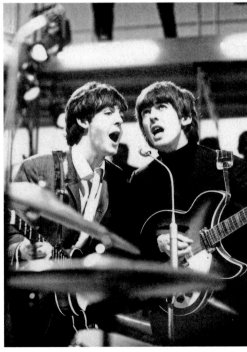

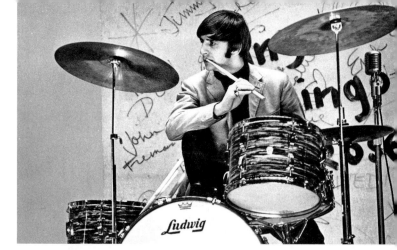

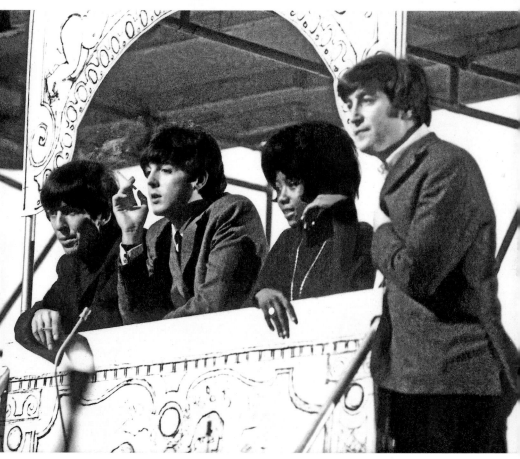

Within a year of the release of "Please Please Me," the Beatles had performed before 75 million Americans on *The Ed Sullivan Show* and flown home to film *A Hard Day's Night* and record *Around the Beatles*.

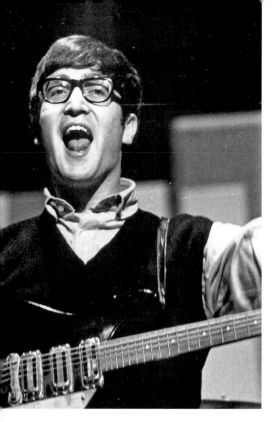

During the filming of *Around the Beatles*, McCartney and Lennon spoofed Pyramus and Thisbe (from Shakespeare's *A Midsummer Night's Dream*), seen here in rehearsals, and Ringo Starr donned a Tudor costume for his part.

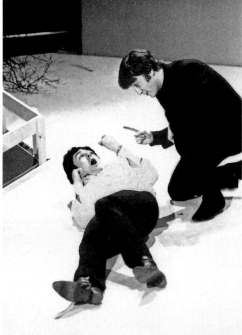

ALL PHOTOGRAPHS BY TERRY O'NEILL

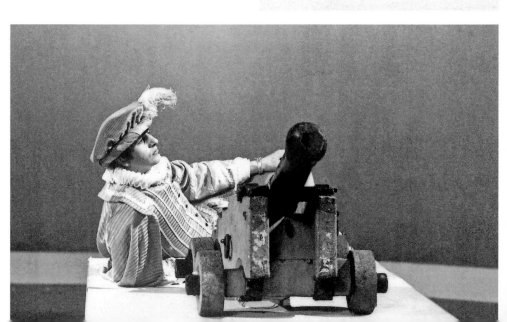

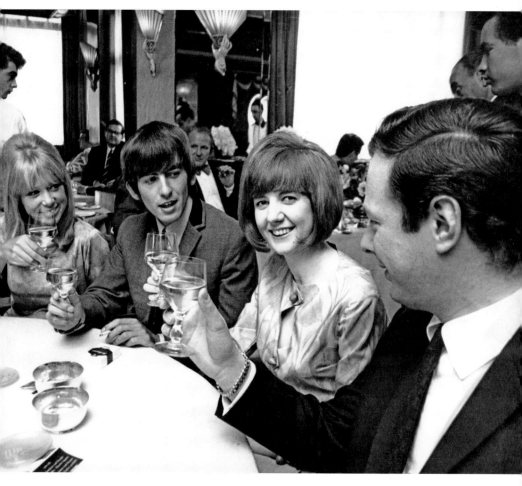

Pattie Boyd, her future husband George Harrison, Cilla Black, and Brian Epstein dine out in London during filming of *A Hard Day's Night*.   CREDIT: GETTY IMAGES

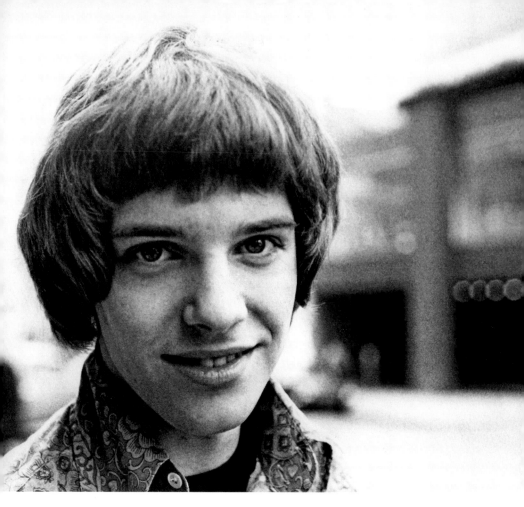

"Davy Jones [David Bowie] and I would bring our guitars to school and sit on the stairs and play during the lunch break. I was thirteen. He was sixteen."

Peter Frampton   CREDIT: GETTY IMAGES

Terry O'Neill: The Stones, Dave Clark, and Herman's Hermits were all knocking out movies. The kids' appetite for the bands was insatiable. Not just records—films, TV specials, dedicated magazines, picture books, merchandise, plastic Beatles wigs, Beatles boots—every radio was tuned to Radio Caroline.

Ronan O'Rahilly: Radio Caroline started broadcasting in March '64, all the music the BBC wouldn't play that I liked. The British government tried to close us down.

Chrissie Most: Mickie came home one day and said, "I've bought a boat." What did we need a boat for? I asked. He had this idea we'd sail out to the pirate radio station to give them our records to play. We didn't sail—we didn't know how to work it or navigate. But off we went and sailed around and eventually we found it, and we pulled up alongside the radio ship, and Mickie began throwing the discs up onto the deck, but the wind kept catching them and blowing them overboard.

Carly Simon: Everybody was into the Beatles. It wasn't until the Stones were on the *Sullivan Show* that I became more of a Stones fan. You were either a Stones fan or a Beatles fan. I didn't meet the Beatles or the Stones. I didn't meet Mick till 1970. I was more influenced and mesmerized by Mick than any of the Beatles. I loved the Beatles, I adored them, but I was more excited by the Stones. "Little Red Rooster" and "Walking in the Cotton Fields." Boy, was that an exciting time.

Mary Wilson: In '64 we did the TAMI show. [*The* Teenage Awards Music International *show was filmed in Santa Monica, California, and featured British and American rock-and-roll acts.*] Everyone who was anybody was on it—Marvin Gaye, Beach Boys—and we are all beginning to be on top as a name. We thought, "How are all these people going to be placed on the bill?" [*Others on the bill included Chuck Berry and Gerry & the Pacemakers.*] And then there were the Rolling Stones, and we said, "Who the hell are they?"

We'd never heard of them. We heard them rehearsing and then we were told they were going on over James Brown. No one goes on over James Brown. But there must have been some politics backstage because the Stones agreed to go on after James. [*Keith Richards has said it was the "biggest mistake of the Stones' career" because "no matter how well we performed, we could not top Brown's performance."*]

Linda Geiser: The Rolling Stones? I didn't know what rock and roll was. I knew the Beatles. I saw them on Ed Sullivan's show. I saw these screaming girls. I thought they were nicely dressed and they had nice haircuts. Smart and lovely. They sang lovely songs. And Leonard Bernstein said they were the new Schubert.

The Rolling Stones? I never heard of them until I went on a tour and we ended up in Boston in '64 for ten months, and their first concert was in Boston.

In our hotel was the British ballet, on our floor were the ballerinas. And when they moved out we saw a bus park in front of the hotel. A big silver thing. It was written all over with lipsticks. What is this? I went inside the hotel and said, "What is this?"

"Don't you know? It's the Rolling Stones?"

"What is that?"

We go up to our floor. There are police everywhere. Where are those Rolling Stones? The police crawled under the beds and behind the curtains looking for girls. In the morning, there was a heavy smell of marijuana in the hallway, and there was a knock on my door, and there is a young man—Keith Richards. "Got an umbrella, luv?" Not a hello or nothing. "Yes I have, but it's raining and I need it myself."

They had a concert the next day. And then the bus was gone. So I never really met them.

Eric Stewart: Everywhere you went there were people there. Somebody would let somebody know. We did a concert to support the Stones, and Brian Jones came off with his fingers bleeding from the tambourine, and he came up, "Eric, have you got anything on you?"

"What do you mean?"

"I'm a bit mashed up and a bit rough. You are always smiling, so what are you on?"

"I'm not on anything. I'm just enjoying myself." I said, "Honestly, Brian I don't." This poor character. He was really doing bad drugs by then. It was *his* band but there was the Jagger thing with him, there was always this angst. Brian was much more musically educated and he was a great blues aficionado, too. But he was very fragile.

Hilton Valentine: It's about the emergence of LSD in music rather than weed and speed.

It was the start of the drug days I suppose. I did lose myself down the road with LSD. Brian Jones actually turned me on to it. I was in New York and we found out that the Stones were in town, and they came over to our hotel and said to us, "Let's go down to this club."

Brian comes in, "Ah, have you tried LSD yet?" and he said it's the same as hash but better. Well, OK, cheers. I popped it. It was a sugar cube. So we go off to this club. We are sitting there in special booths set up for the visiting bands. So we are getting high, and Keith is there, and Eric [Burdon], and I start to really freak out in a nice way. With a lot of colors. *Wow, this is fantastic.*

Eric is sitting next to me and he says, "I want to get up and jam." You know—he hadn't taken LSD, just hash. And Chas [Chandler] is sitting opposite me and he says, "No. We are big stars now. We can't just get up and jam in clubs." Eric picks up his knife and fork and goes, "I want to jam. I want to jam." And Chas says, "Settle down, Eric."

But he keeps going "I want to jam. I want to jam." In the end we get up and we jam with the resident band, and it was great. Fantastic. I go back to the hotel, and now I know I'm tripping. The walk down to the elevator is lined with bellboys. I had pulled [*hooked up with*] this girl with a low-cut dress, all foxy. In the room the telephone rings. "We understand, Mr. Valentine, you have a lady in your room. This is Immigration."

I don't know what the hell is going on. What is real or what isn't real. Was it someone playing a trick? I don't remember much. But I had a very good time.

Peter Noone: We started out as a band and then it turns against you. It happened to us all. I was the leader and the spokesperson. I became the person everyone wanted to talk to. Bit by bit it started to piss off the Hermits more and more. I was so young, and I didn't even notice that was happening. I didn't see it coming.

One of the guys says to me, "How come I don't get interviews? How come I don't get to talk to the press?" I say I'll fix the problem, [but] then nobody wants to talk to him. It became more and more obvious. There were videos, and it would be them at the pool splashing all day. And I would say, "Why am I not in those home videos?" And they'd say, "Because you are always doing the interviews."

"You think I wouldn't prefer to be in the pool with all the babes?"

It came to a head. The Royal Command Performance [*a once-a-year variety show for charity with the Royal Family in attendance*]. The Queen Mother, she only meets one person in each band, and in my band it was me, lined up with Andy Williams and Tom Jones. We had our own dressing room but they put all the Hermits upstairs with the dancers, and that broke their hearts.

I didn't realize how hurtful that was. I didn't know. I was too young and too busy. I was naïve. I had no idea any of this stuff, the brooding, was going on.

Bill Wyman: I really do miss the naïveté of it. Not thinking further than what you were doing at the time. The amateur way we did things.

There were no pressures, like from record companies—well, there were, but we took no notice. As we became famous we had to make a better single, a better album, do better interviews. There was none of that back then.

Naïveté and the newness and this magic thing happening slowly, and you didn't know where it was going. I have press articles where Mick says, "When I am twenty-five I wont be doing this anymore." It just got bigger and bigger. It took over our lives. That's why I left in 1990—that was thirty fucking years of my life.

Hilton Valentine: There was a time in New York in Central Park. The Animals were fighting to try and get time off. There was one tour after another tour after another tour. We were in this catch-22. It came to a head in Central Park when we did this gig. We were so successful and the promoters booked another gig, one after the other. But we said no, this is our time off, and the promoter was on his hands and knees begging us with this story about this and that, about hardship, and we ended up playing the gig. We were all going to go and scream and down guitars [quit]. Even the workers in the shipyards have a holiday.

Bill Wyman: We had all these people doing stuff around us and we'd see things changing, like the miniskirt and tights instead of stockings, but you were in the midst of it and you couldn't see it from outside.

We were all entering into something that we didn't know what it was, how long it would last, or how special it was. We just took it day by day. It wasn't intentional. We didn't plan to be rebels, and neither did the fashion people or photographers. They were just doing their normal job with new ideas. It wasn't preplanned or organized—it just happened. Everyone tries to make things happen now. We weren't trying to make things happen. That's why it will never happen again. We just wanted to play the music.

Keith Richards: Fame wasn't a problem at all. It's something you grew into. I have been a star since the sixties. You are talking to a mad man. . . . Now there is no normal life for me. I have lived a life that is so extreme. Luckily, I have always managed to retain good friends and to keep at least one foot on the ground.

Before the money and the pressure there was just the enjoyment, just being there and part of the movement. I still feel the same way. Can't really rationalize about it but it was an amazing period. Thank God I was there.

Bob Gruen: I saw no future for myself. I didn't see the possibility of wearing a suit and tie. I couldn't see the kind of danger I enjoyed— driving fast, drinking, climbing trees was what I was drawn to. I don't know why but I remember not thinking I would have much of a life. I didn't plan for the future because I didn't think I had one.

But there was an innocence that we don't have now. I remember discovering some reels of films in a friend's garage of scantily clad women, and we thought that was very risqué. Today's porn leaves nothing to the imagination. Way beyond *my* imagination. Everyone knows everything, and if they don't, it takes eight seconds to google it. It's a good thing, but on the other hand it's very relaxing not to have to know everything. You have wonder and discover. Not everything is known and given. The kids seem very bored that they know everything.

Vicki Wickham: I miss the camaraderie. And the feeling we were changing things with new music. We were booking music acts from the U.S. The first ones we booked were Stevie Wonder and Dionne Warwick. I thought we'd died and gone to heaven.

Mary Wilson: We still weren't big at the start of '64. We did a tour over there. We go over there and we do this show, and no one came to see us. We called it the ghost tour. Stevie Wonder was on. No one came to see us, even with a lineup like that. Then Dusty Springfield—she did a lot of shows with us in New York—somehow she got us on *Ready Steady Go*. Once the TV show aired, Motown blew up. "Where Did Our Love Go" went to number three in the UK and number one in America.

Robert Christgau: I went back to Berkeley in '64 and had no radio. A friend who was a GI got me a seven-dollar transistor radio and I started walking around with a little earphone. You heard the Beatles all the time. They had the top songs. Then I bought my first car and drove back to New York, and my recollection was hearing the Beatles and the Supremes and "It's All Over Now," the first Stones hit.

One of the things that's great about the Stones is they were the realists, while the Beatles were the utopians. The Stones were sardonic and it was very welcome—it's the classic thing that blues does, it takes pain and translates it into joy. But it begins with "I'm not going to be miserable. I'm going to be happy."

You could hear it in the tone of Jagger that he always sounds a little sarcastic. That record meant a lot to me. I was a copyboy at the *New York Times*. I drove my '50 Plymouth and I'd be amazed that I could park in Times Square! And I remember hearing "It's All Over Now" and thinking what a great song it was.

If I write my book, if it will be about anything, it will be about the Beatles and the Stones and the Supremes in '64.

Henry Diltz: So we did one more tour across the country in a motor home, and we would smoke grass every day. A few tokes and you would start reading or writing or playing. Colors were becoming so important to me. We pulled in to a little secondhand store in Michigan and ran in a little high to spend money on junk, and there was a table with secondhand cameras. We all bought a camera. We were always a little high, and it made life fun.

The first picture I took was a toilet with a flower growing out of it. A field of cows. A friend got a new bass case and he wanted to blow up the old one with firecrackers, like junior dynamite. We are in the Arizona desert and he lights it and runs like hell, and "bang!" it flies up in the air, and I caught a picture of that. I still have that picture. It was in the moment.

I said, "I must take more of these damn things." I started doing album covers. [*Diltz photographed the Doors'* Morrison Hotel, *among others.*] We need publicity photos and they were always black-and-white for the newspaper. So I started doing black-and-white. It was like playing another instrument. Is it music or photography? In my heart I am a musician but in my head and eyes I am a photographer.

Bob Gruen: At one point I got a job in a photo store and that helped me a lot. I could steal film, and it came with prepaid processing. That was the film I used to take my first pictures at Newport Folk Festival. I took a bunch of pictures, some of which came out okay. I took a picture of Dylan, and that's been used forever. He's got the guitar and he looks rock-and-roll. I only have a couple of pictures that survive from that time.

I met a daughter I never knew about a while back. She'd remembered my name. I met her mother at the Newport festival. And that was [on] my first day as a music photographer.

I knew the mother for about an hour. She told me a few months later she was pregnant, but since she waited four months I didn't believe it was mine and thought she wanted me to support her financially. We spent a couple of hours in my apartment, and suddenly she was pregnant? I thought it could be true but [that] she [probably] put the baby up for adoption. Neither of us had a life to take care of a child. I had no money. There was nothing for me to do. Once the child is adopted the records are sealed.

Every couple of years I would wonder, "Do I have a kid? Have I ever walked past her?" One day I got a letter. The weird thing is that it was registered. I thought, "I wonder if this is the letter I thought I might get?" The first thing I saw was *biological father.* Oh shit. Then I saw, "I don't want anything from you but to know you."

We have become pretty good friends, and she and my son are closer to each other than to me. They spend weekends together. She grew up in Brooklyn. She is a doctor. She was adopted by a family in Brooklyn.

Barbara Hulanicki: At that age you didn't plan your life. Back then, it was evolving. No, we never had any plans. Everyone was on the same page. I remember that *Time* magazine article coming out—in 1966—about swinging London. Swinging London was 1963 and 1964. Richard Avedon came in [to my shop]. Can you imagine? He came in to see what it was all about. Everyone came to experience the music, the culture, the fashion, and took [it] away to Paris, Milan, and America.

Today it's all so commercial, calculated, about industry, money, marketing, branding. Back then it was so pure.

Vidal Sassoon: There was something so lovely about it, and being such a part of it was very special and very different from saying, "I am a big success." Once you say that to yourself you are on the way down. What it's all about is what comes next! What can I do next? Your mind is flowing like crazy. We didn't stop to think we were a success, we just kept going on and thinking of what comes next.

Everyone was judged by their talent, not where they were born. We were very naughty boys. What I'm getting at is that we pushed one another and sparred with one another. You can't make a change by yourself. It was a whole team of people with ideas, creativity, and excitement that changed the London scene. The U.S. was four years behind, and in '65 they were still four years behind. Those times were so insane. I'm eighty-four and I've had a great life, a wonderful time. I wouldn't mind the sixties being here again. I miss London, I miss the theater and Chelsea [football club]. Instead of seeing a psychiatrist, I went to see Chelsea play.

Mary Quant: We worked and worked and worked but loved it so it didn't matter. I went through all of Vidal's haircuts. I think I tried most of them. Vidal is an enchanting man. There's always new things and new ways to be provocative. I find Lady Gaga rather amusing but not shocking.

I was made aware that I was doing something different by the attention I received in the magazine and color sections. I was caught up in it day and night. It was terrifying to keep up with it, and the pressure. One day in came a young man who said, "I want you to turn a collection for J. C. Penney. For 165 stores in America." So I started to design for J. C. Penney for ten to twelve years. They wanted things for young people.

Everyone came to London. Brigitte Bardot and Leslie Caron. Americans and musicians and their girlfriends would come to buy clothes. And John and the Beatles came.

The first time I went to America I was flown in by *Life* magazine. We were photographed running down Fifth Avenue with a sheepdog. I loved New York. We went over there and took the top models with us and put on shows across America. A city a day. They went mad with excitement.

There was a sense of camaraderie more than competition. It was quite a crusade. It was tough, so the people who were doing it hung together and fought together. Everything was possible for a bit—that was lovely.

Justin de Villeneuve: It was easy come and easy go. It was a lark. There's this quite acrimonious thing between me and Twiggs. She thinks I squandered money. I had five Rolls Royces and two Lamborghinis and an E-Type Jag. But we never thought years ahead. I didn't think I was going to grow old. The time was a big influence. Life wasn't hard then. It was easy. You could do anything you wanted to do—really! We weren't driven to make money. Never. It came along and it was useful. I'd have my suits made, then my shoes. Never thought about buying property. Wish I had. It was all a good time. I never got into drugs. Twiggs and I kept away from it. There weren't hard drugs. Mostly cannabis. You couldn't get heroin.

Mandy Rice-Davies: I can't say I ever sat back and said, "What a life I am leading!" I just took it for granted. The attempt by the establishment to surround me with shame didn't work. I didn't feel ashamed. I came through that very quickly. I remembered the phrase from my childhood—"Don't be afraid in front of horses because they will attack you."

There is residual anger but it didn't defeat me. I began singing and acting almost immediately.

Norma Kamali: I think periods like that come rarely. It wasn't just fashion, it was music and film. It was such a *future* time, and it defined everything up to now. The newness was exciting. A pioneering time where there was a surprise and then another idea and another surprise. I am so fortunate to have been there. Whatever the happening was that got me there, I know I was given a big gift—to be liberated. I wish this generation could have an experience that would liberate. It would be very empowering, especially for women. It would be extraordinary, for the economy, people's minds, personal freedom and expression. That was the best thing of that period.

We've had all these years and we just kept rehashing it. The new has come through technology, not through music this time. Original things last and become timeless. The young outnumbered everyone. We weren't a minority group. It wouldn't have worked as well if we were.

It took time for everything I saw in London to get here. That seed had been planted there at that time. If I hadn't experienced London I would have done something completely different.

Neil Sedaka: An old friend of mine said that since the Beatles came here and the British have such a great respect for your original recordings, you should move to the UK. So I picked up my wife and two kids and we moved to London. I worked in small workingmen's clubs, trying to sing over the slot machines and the drunks. I was an outsider and a ghost from the fifties. I went to concerts and there I met Elton John, and he said, "I am a great fan of your earlier records. Can I come to your flat and hear what you are writing?"

He said I was a great influence. He had all my songs. "Happy Birthday Sweet Sixteen," "Calendar Girl"—he had them all.

Elton said, "I am starting a company called Rocket. I can make you a recording star again." We released the first single, "Laughter in the Rain," and lo and behold, I was number one again. Only now there was a face—I was just a voice on the radio in the fifties. Now I was a face. They saw what Neil Sedaka looked like.

[Nonetheless,] these days that blank page still frightens me. It's a scary thing, that blank paper.

Eric Clapton: I have tremendous self-doubt. I have wandered off and on my path my whole life and, I come back to it. That's the beauty of it for me. I will always come back to my roots and remember, "This is why you like to play the guitar."

It's not because of money or to be famous. Not even just to express something, or to be special or the best, but because I love music. I love listening. I'd still do it if no one responded. It's a relationship I have with the music. I miss the idea of going out on my own. That doesn't happen anymore for me. It's all much bigger stuff. [Nineteen sixty-three] was freedom. The absolute freedom to be a musician.

Jeff Lynne: I wasn't interested to be the big man or the front man or in the fame. I wanted control. I had a clear idea of the sounds I wanted to make. In '63 I'd listen to the music not just as a punter [*fan, customer*], I would listen to how it was made, even when I knew nothing. How did they make that happen? Who made that? I used to think like that. I analyzed sounds. I am a terrible engineer, but a good producer. It was more how sounds work, not gadgets, that got me.

Eric Stewart: I'd jam with Brian Auger & the Trinity. Jeff Beck would get up and play. Jimmy Page was a session musician then. When we were in the studio recording "The Game of Love," Jimmy was in doing a solo for P.J. Proby in the next studio. He had this beautiful black custom guitar, and he said, "What are you doing. . . . That's not a hit, so why don't you use my guitar?" You can hear it [on "Game of Love"].

The next time I saw him he was with Led Zeppelin and had soared to something phenomenal. None of us read music. That was the great luxury for us all. We played from the soul rather than through the eyes. That was why string players were so frustrating when you brought orchestras into the studio. They were always behind the beat because they were looking at the dots and the conductor, and they were always behind us. It was so frustrating.

Georgie Fame: I worked with icons—I hate that word—with sensational players. I was playing with Count Basie and all the greatest jazz musicians. I was from another generation, learning from them when they were in their fifties and sixties. I was still a young lion but they were just cruising then. I thought that day would come for me a few years ago, but it hasn't.

We all still get butterflies before we get on and play. I learn something different every night when I play live. Someone said keep the mistakes—it's part of the jazz. If you listen to all the greats live, there's always a mistake, something out of tune. But no matter.

I now live part of the year in Sweden and away from everybody else. Everyone went down south—France and Spain—and I went in the opposite direction. I'm still practicing. You never stop learning. That's what's unique about art or music; there's no retirement age. I play now with my two sons.

So long as there are people wanting to listen to you and share the experience, that's all there is. There's no reason to quit.

AFTERWORD

Was 1963 a year of revolution? Before we render a verdict, let's adjourn for a moment and hear the counterrevolutionary establishment voices that were raised against the rebels.

When the Beatles landed at Idlewild Airport on Pan Am flight 101 on February 7, 1964, they were greeted by thousands of fans and a bemused and sneering press corps two hundred strong. While girls screamed adoringly and dismissed Frank Sinatra ("a fossil in a tux") and a twenty-nine-year-old Elvis ("He's old and ugly," spat one female Beatles fan), the gentlemen of the press scoffed at four working-class lads from Liverpool.

"Are you gonna get a haircut while you are here?" asked one reporter.

"I had one yesterday," responded George Harrison in all seriousness.

"Which do you consider the greatest danger to your careers: nuclear bombs or dandruff?" asked another.

"Bombs," responded Ringo. "We've already got dandruff."

As *Time* magazine would later report, "Olympian disdain masked simple ignorance." The revolution had already been fought and won. The battle for hearts and minds was over. *Time* went on: "In the next ten days, the Beatles came, were seen, and conquered. If they could make it here, they could make it everywhere, and what they made was history."

By August 1964, President Lyndon B. Johnson's press office was requesting an audience with the Beatles at the White House. The Beatles politely declined. So the administration was forced to turn to the next biggest act among the British invaders and invited the Dave Clark Five aboard Air Force One so the president could get their autographs for his daughter, Luci Baines. Lennon and McCartney had given one of their songs to another struggling young band called the Rolling Stones and helped foster a brand that has spanned six decades.

The new heroes of art, film, literature, and music were working-class boys and girls—the British had defeated Napoleon "on the playing fields of Eton" [*the elite college that schooled the nobility, patricians and officer classes*], and now its cultural conquest of the world was being directed by those who, only a generation earlier, would have been the old Etonians' valets and chauffeurs.

Within two years of 1963, the four mop-tops from Liverpool were meeting Her Majesty Queen Elizabeth II to receive awards normally reserved for military exemplars and civic leaders, and John Lennon would state, with some conviction, "We're more popular than Jesus now."

Attitudes about sex had been transformed. The pill liberated both women *and* men in an age when sex didn't kill. The combination of the Beatles and freely available contraception was immortalized in literature when the English poet Philip Larkin wrote his enduring homage, "Annus Mirabilis."

> *Sexual intercourse began*
> *In nineteen sixty-three*
> *(which was rather late for me)—*
> *Between the end of the Chatterley ban*
> *And the Beatles' first LP*

"Up to then" penned Larkin, "there'd only been / a sort of bargaining, / a wrangle for the ring. . . ." For this generation's parents, sex and shame had been uncomfortable bedfellows. Sex was to be furtive, preferably performed with the lights out and the curtains drawn, any guilty afterglow absolved by a prayer for forgiveness offered up before sleep. But their children embraced it, paraded it, and celebrated it. Feminism exhorted women that sex should be pleasurable for them, too.

The established order recognized the political, cultural—and commercial—power of youth and tried to harness and absorb it. But young people were indifferent. They were relishing their clout and flaunting their sexuality, their opinions, and their freedom to the accompaniment of new kinds of music, fashion, and the arts. They flouted social and spiritual mores and vocally opposed elected leaders. Protest sprang from the music festivals and from new, samizdat magazines and newspapers founded by would-be revolutionaries who created a heady mix of politics, art, and music in innovative and explicit cover stories.

Before 1963, youth was largely acquiescent and acquisitive. After 1963, they were impossible to ignore. They were catered to. They were marketed to. They were listened to. They were *heard*.

Young people marched on capitols, asserting their own standards of allegiance. Students boycotted classes and picketed federal buildings. Musicians composed the battle hymns of the counterculture; rallied troops, poets, artists, writers, and filmmakers; and questioned and subverted authority and statutes. Some died by the bullets of their own "protectors" by order of their own elected leaders.

Vietnam, the nuclear arms race, feminism, civil rights, colonialism, capitalism, and the suppression and censorship of speech, art, and literature were all causes engaged by the emancipated youth of 1963. Issues that had been minority casus belli before 1963 were grounds for large-scale social warfare fought on streets and campuses around the world.

The aftershocks of 1963 have continued for decades. The pioneering revolutionaries of that year blazed a trail trod all the way to the White House and Wall Street. In politics and commerce, youth was an asset. Bill Clinton was a child of that revolution, blowing on a saxophone—and shaking hands with JFK at just sixteen years of age. Another sixteen-year-old called Richard Branson started his own company called Virgin, selling records and undercutting the Main Street music shops.

This was the generation that made youth ascendant. *Vogue* models were mere teenagers; Wall Street traders barely out of grade school called the shots. The DNA of 1963 endures in the Gateses and Zuckerbergs of the digital age, when a teenager can become a billionaire overnight. Age is no longer a barrier. Wisdom, experience and gravitas play second fiddle to ambition and talent.

In 1963, the voices of young people were not only viable, they were vital. Some were followers, some were leaders, but all were united by a transformative energy. Fueled by curiosity or outrage or a desire to expand and explore their minds, young men and women were liberated from a proscribed path and eager to search for individual purpose and truth.

The generation that emerged from 1963 with power and motive is best described in the earlier writings of George Bernard Shaw: "Revolutionary moments attract those who are not good enough for established institutions—as well as those who are too good for them."

Nineteen sixty-three anointed a multitude of new prophets and conjured wizards with guitars, brushes, and scissors. The alchemy of that year produced a generation of freethinkers. It *was* a year of revolution—when youth changed the world with music, fashion, and art.

> *And life was never better than*
> *In nineteen sixty-three*
> *Between the end of the Chatterley ban*
> *And the Beatles' first LP*

ACKNOWLEDGMENTS

These people deserve our gratitude and thanks for their enthusiastic support and unwavering confidence.

Carrie Kania, the former editorial director of It Books, fanned the spark of an idea into a consuming passion.

Her successor, Cal Morgan, carried the torch for us.

The skill, diligence, and perspicacity of our editor, Denise Oswald, enabled us to assemble a narrative that wedded the voices of fifty years ago into a coherent celebration of youth's ascendance.

Behind the scenes, our agent, Rob Weisbach, deployed his wisdom and charm.

Many, many hours of taped interviews were diligently transcribed by Lisa Ter Haar, Alice and Grace Ter Haar, and Robert Morgan.

And finally, we owe a special debt of thanks to the gracious and generous Vidal Sassoon, who invited us into his home, his body wracked by illness, knowing he was only weeks from death, and allowed us to sift through his memories.

Robin Morgan and Ariel Leve

INDEX